HOW CLASS WORKS

HOW CLASS WORKS

POWER AND SOCIAL MOVEMENT

STANLEY ARONOWITZ

YALE UNIVERSITY PRESS/NEW HAVEN AND LONDON

Published with assistance from the foundation established in memory of Amasa Stone Mather of the Class of 1907, Yale College.

Designed by Mary Valencia
Set in Stone Serif and Sans type by The Composing Room of Michigan, Inc., Grand Rapids, Michigan.
Printed in the United States of America by Vail-Ballou Press, Binghamton, New York.

The Library of Congress has cataloged the hardcover edition as follows:

Aronowitz, Stanley.
How class works : power and social movement / Stanley Aronowitz.
p. cm.
Includes bibliographical references and index.
ISBN 0-300-09859-6 (cloth : alk. paper)
1. Social classes—United States. 2. Social movements—United States. 3. Power (Social sciences)—United States. I. Title.
HN90.S6 A75 2003
305.5—dc21

2002151179

A catalogue record for this book is available from the British Library.

The paper in this book meets the guidelines for permanence and durability of the Committee on Production Guidelines for Book Longevity of the Council on Library Resources.

ISBN 0-300-10504-5 (pbk. : alk. paper)
10 9 8 7 6 5 4 3 2

CONTENTS

ACKNOWLEDGMENTS

A book of this scope inevitably accumulates considerable debts. I was fortunate to have friends and colleagues who read all or part of the manuscript and provided salient comments and suggestions: Bill DiFazio, Jeff Lustig, Randy Martin, and Ellen Willis. Ellen Willis gave me detailed editorial suggestions on almost the entire manuscript and often sent me back to square one. My readers, George Lipsitz and Howard Kimmeldorf, were as unsparing in their critique as they were helpful in their proposals to improve the book. Micah Kleit and Tony O'Brien read several chapters and provided helpful feedback. As always my agent Neeti Madan was a source of constant encouragement. And Lara Heimert shepherded the manuscript through the hurdles. Last but not least, I thank students attending my course and several lectures at CUNY Graduate Center on social class who read and criticized chapter 2.

INTRODUCTION

When I tell friends that I have written a book on class, especially class in the United States, the news is received with either incredulity or cheerleading. The "posts"—liberals and postmodernists—question whether the concept is still useful and often suggest I use another term. If they acknowledge the salience of class at all in these times, most relegate it to a narrative—one of the stories Americans tell about history—or a figure of vernacular speech. The other response is gratitude that someone is (finally) going to blast the myth of American classlessness and its contemporary displacement, stratification. Stratification designates distinction without conflict. Those who replace class with strata deny that society is propelled by social struggles; for the stratification theorists, people are arranged along a social grid by occupation or income. The category is merely descriptive of status and differential opportunities for jobs and goods. Enthusiasts are frequently outraged that any intelligent social thinker can fail to observe the obvious signs of class difference, especially the ample evidence that at the political level the U.S. democratic system retains considerable deference to money and its bearers in the determination of social and economic policy. Plainly there is no longer agreement that the concept of class tells us anything about how social structure or history is constituted.

Unfortunately this book may give little comfort to those who defend the received wisdom about class and class struggles. For the unreconstructed marxist, class is a relation of social groups to ownership and control of the means of material production, and political and social power derives from ownership of productive property. They remain convinced that the fundamental relations within capitalist society are, with slight variations, as they were two hundred years ago at the dawn of the industrial revolution. The adherents of this doctrine never tire of quoting scripture and proclaiming their faith. For them people like me are apostates. To this state of being I plead guilty. I remain loyal to the questions posed by the founders of historical materialism and to their reliance on history to provide the solutions to vexing problems of power. But it cannot be true that the answers are immutable. On this claim we end up in an infinite outpouring of blame and vituperation. Life is too short for constant fulmination.

The marginalization of class in contemporary political and theoretical conversation is rooted in real changes in the shape of world politics. First, the collapse of East European communism, African socialism, and the drift of China toward the world capitalist market leave precious few countries that proclaim themselves revolutionary societies. Observers have interpreted these dramatic events as solid evidence that marxism is wrong in its prediction that socialism will succeed capitalism, even though most of the leaders of these once-revolutionary societies had an increasingly remote relationship to marxism's philosophical basis, the precepts of historical materialism. Certainly none of them adhered, even rhetorically, to Marx's libertarian political beliefs which held that workers themselves, not the state, would control the key institutions of the economy and of political life. Marx admitted only that a state might be necessary for a short period after revolutionary power was established. The twentieth-century regimes that established themselves in the name of marxian socialism were (and are) staffed by a near-permanent bureaucracy and one-party political leadership that has no intention of relinquishing power, except if forced by circumstances. Although I reject the idea that on these grounds marxism "failed," as I have already indicated there are good reasons for believing that we need new concepts that are adequate to the conditions of historical transformations.

The traditional definition proposed by Marx and Engels in the 1840s—that, in general, relations of ownership and control of the means of material production cleaved society into two main antagonistic classes—is challenged from a number of quarters. They expected capital's domination of society to consign all intermediate classes to near oblivion. Indeed some of these predictions have proven prescient. For example, despite the persistence of myth the independent farmer has become a rarity in the United States. Agriculture is no longer marked by individual ownership, but rather by corporate or small capitalist farms on which wage laborers perform most of the tasks; since the turn of the twentieth century individual artisans who at the dawn of the nineteenth century accounted for most manufacturing have gradually been reduced to skilled wage workers by large industrial enterprises; in most regions of the United States the small grocery store has yielded to supermarket chains, just as department stores have progressively displaced the independent retail merchant. In recent years even the medium-sized department store has fallen on tough times. Huge chains such as Walmart—now at the top of the Fortune 500 largest corporations—have relentlessly captured ever-larger market shares. These developments seemed to confirm Marx's underlying two-class theorem. But even though they fail at a 90 percent rate in the first year, small businesses constantly try to reproduce themselves. Transnational capitalism notwithstanding, the ideology of entrepreneurship is interwoven with the dreams and aspirations of wide sections of the American people.

And if the old middle class of small proprietors has suffered economic and political marginalization, the formation of a new middle class introduced complexity into the class map. As the introduction of rationalized methods of production and scientifically based technologies at the turn of the twentieth century transformed industrial production, much of the craft knowledge accumulated by skilled labor was transferred to machines, a process directed by managers and implemented by the design efficiency of engineers and technicians, perhaps the most important new social formation of advanced capitalism. The twentieth century witnessed the emergence of a new class of salaried managers and trained scientific and technical intellectuals, none of whom can credibly be described as either traditional proletarians or capitalists. At least on the surface the two-class model of developed capitalism seemed to have been severely attenuated if not entirely refuted. But those who perform what I shall call immaterial labor do not, in the main, enjoy the autonomy of traditional self-employed professionals. In fact their subordination under management in large-scale enterprises has become one of the most explosive social questions of our time.

On the side of capital things have changed as well. Beginning in the mid–nineteenth century the family-owned company yielded to a legal and organizational entity, the corporation, in which, some claim, shareholders retain only a very limited voice. Many writers have observed that although they are not owners of substantial productive capital the managers and professional employees now effectively control the corporate enterprise, not only on the shop floor but in all aspects of business: machine design, sales, distribution, and finance. The so-called managerial revolution announced by such writers as Thorstein Veblen, A. A. Berle, and James Burnham spurred a veritable cottage industry of writers and consultants who survive today. The concept of the managerial revolution has gone out of fashion, but its implications for class thinking remain important. Whether or not capitalism has changed its composition so that owners of capital have become bystanders, the enhanced role of very high priced employees in its operation is undeniable, although the extent of their ultimate power is contested. As the twenty-first century began, the professional-managerial class—that is, employees who, owing to credentials or to bureaucratic office, are presumed to enjoy considerable autonomy in the performance of what Marx called "the labor of management"—had become a visible, often powerful sector of American and other advanced industrial societies.[1]

In recent years, however, we have seen how vulnerable top executives are, as boards of directors dismiss them after a few quarters of low profitability. That many chief executive officers (CEOs) and division heads are given a "golden parachute" (substantial severance packages including stock options) does not obviate the fact that they are routinely fired for presiding over poor profit performance; or that they may be discharged for any reason by representatives of major stockholders. The resurgent role of boards of directors, holders of large business loans, and other investors since the 1970s has undermined the force of the thesis of the separation of capital and management, but not entirely refuted it. There are historically wrought hierarchies within capital as well. What Marx called the "social division of labor" has shifted several times since the dawn of the industrial revolution. The capitalist "class" is not identical to the ruling class. The social division concerns the various domains of production and distribution, in the first place between agriculture and industry and commerce, then, within each, the relation of various industries. Once America consisted mainly of owners of relatively small productive property: farmers, artisans, and manufacturers who employed few workers; and merchants: store owners, owners of banks of modest capitalization, and wholesalers. From colonial times to the mid–nineteenth century, while there were struggles for political and economic supremacy among these groups, the main battle was against the plantation aristocracy whose slaveholding mode of production threatened agricultural and industrial expansion on the basis of free labor. To call these smallholders a ruling class would be excessive and even absurd.[2]

The term *ruling class* begins to have relevance during the industrial revolution of the latter half of the nineteenth century, when the family-owned business is supplanted by large corporations, in the first place the railroad companies and then the expanding banking sector. Within the emergence and development of industrial capitalism once-dominant sectors are relegated to subordinate positions by newer formations. In 1850, America was overwhelmingly agrarian, and agricultural interests not only dominated political life at the state level but also were major forces in national politics. At the turn of the twentieth century half the country was engaged in agricultural production and in businesses and occupations related to it. Owing to the rapid pace of mechanization of farm production—a phenomenon that turned farms into industrial enterprises and drove out small producers—by the year 2000 only 5 percent of the working population was engaged in agriculture on farms and in food processing, distribution, and transportation. If so-called farm states still exercised considerable political influence it was owing more to constitutional safeguards of the power of small states (for example, equal representation in the Senate, the electoral college) than to the numerical influence of farmers. In the 1870s and 1880s the blatant, undisguised power of these corporations was not confined to the economy but also dominated politics and culture.

As always, absolute power did not remain uncontested. By the 1880s two major mass movements emerged to challenge the hegemony of the powerful private corporations: a national labor movement that took the form of several distinct and competing organizations, mainly in the old crafts, and a movement of small farmers, north and south, that formed state and national political parties to challenge the two major parties, generally understood to be representatives of big capital. Radical laborism took two primary forms: the incipient efforts to form mass labor unions, that is, unskilled as well as skilled industrial unions in the new industries like steel and garments; and the development of socialist and anarchist organizations that were relatively small but steadily grew until the outbreak of World War I. The radical agrarians, having determined that both major parties were hopelessly in the thrall of the large rail and processing corporations, formed the Peoples or Populist Party and ran a third-party candidate for president in the elections of 1888 and 1892. The new party quickly became a dominant force in several midwestern and southwestern state governments and legislatures, among them Texas, Oklahoma, Arkansas, and Nebraska.[3]

The efforts to unite the two wings of American radicalism stumbled on the rock of faction and sect. But they had an enduring effect on American politics. The Democratic Party and progressive Republicans joined to place limits on the freedom of big capital to dominate markets; corrupt state and local governments were ejected from office. And during this era social legislation was enacted to protect workers from onerous factory and living conditions. That regulation was sought by some of the large corporations to rationalize their cannibalistic tendencies is undeniable, and there is no doubt that progressivism was a cautious response to the fury of popular dissent. Yet it was class movements that made possible the reforms enacted between 1900 and the New Deal. History was, in these cases, made by class struggles, even if the outcomes were incommensurable with many of the demands of the powerless.

The years 1900–40 marked a sharp turn in the relative weight of manufacturing sectors within capital: once-dominant textiles, which are closely linked to cotton and wool farming, and coal and metal mining were relegated to middle levels of economic power. These were replaced by four rising industries: steel, automobiles, electrical manufacturing, and chemicals, the most important sectors of which were oil refining and organic chemicals. With the growing role of "capital goods" in industrial production—raw materials, rails, machinery, and huge industrial plants—the role of banks and the stock market became more important because few industrial corporations were able to finance their own expansion. In the last three decades of the twentieth century another major power shift occurred: new forces, notably electronics and information/communications, appeared to challenge the economic and social weight of the industries such as steel, autos, and appliances that were once bellwethers of the economy. That technological change played a huge role in each of these shifts often masks the power struggles that go on within the capitalist class itself. Students of American power have debated whether the introduction of the new information and communications sector has shifted the locus of economic and political power in the new globalism from industrial corporations to financial institutions.

The third major challenge to the classical marxist formula is the claim that the advent of consumer society has tended to flatten class differences or, in another register, has placed social differences on a new terrain. Industrial and service workers are themselves stratified according to their access to the means of consumption, and the relation of their consumption level to their position in the occupational hierarchy may be mediated by a number of factors: for example, whether they are unionized, the position of their employer in the economy, credit policies of banks and other lending agencies. On this idea some industrial workers are better off than some professionals, such as teachers and nurses, whose incomes often do not match those of the skilled trades. Fourth—perhaps the greatest challenge to the concept of class—is the effects of the advent of deskilling, work rationalization, technological change, and opportunities for mobility on the putative working class to the course of history. In this respect the changes in the social position of workers have contradictory effects. On the one hand even well-paid unskilled and semiskilled industrial and service workers are placed in insecure positions by their loss of recognized skill. On the other hand trade union organization has significantly mitigated deskilling. At the same time, given the rapid changes in capitalist work regimes, workers and their unions turn increasingly to the state for amelioration. Jobless insurance, social security, public education, and, in Europe and most other advanced industrial countries, national health care are cushions against market fluctuations that once rendered many destitute within weeks of unemployment or sickness.

Marx and Engels insisted that classes and class struggles constitute what they meant by history. Many writers have noted that even though trade unions and labor and socialist parties are players in the economic and political systems of advanced capitalist societies, neither the wars nor the economic crises that punctuated the twentieth century—two world wars, a major economic crisis (and many small economic ruptures that economists call recessions), countless military interventions and civil wars, and structural as well as cyclical unemployment—stirred the workers to revolt, except episodically. In fact it may be argued that the power of workers and their organizations to achieve reforms within, and not against, capitalist formations amounts to an indefinite postponement of the chances for more fundamental changes. Meanwhile even as economic inequality stalks the century and beyond, all boats have been lifted. Simply stated, even if stark poverty still afflicts a substantial portion of the population—in the United States estimates range from 10 to 20 percent—most of the population has benefited from the growth of capitalism despite the persistence of great inequalities of wealth and power.

Some even argue that workers, at least in the leading economic sectors, have, literally as well as figuratively, become stakeholders in the system even while simultaneously they are exploited under it. Union pension plans invest workers' funds in the stock and bond markets and, in some cases, distribute the fruits of these investments to employees in the form of annuities or savings accounts that supplement and frequently exceed the benefits of Social Security. Some industrial and service workers have enough money to play the market individually, and their numbers have steadily expanded since the end of World War II. Many have been able to purchase homes and own late model cars, boats, and even second homes that they maintain for investment or income. That these amenities entail working huge quantities of overtime or holding two or three jobs only occasionally results in manifest discontent. Stakeholders normally defend the system that has given them ownership. Whether this is true of the so-called developing societies remains an issue, the answer to which depends on how one views their industrialization over the past several decades. I shall explore this apparent paradox in chapters 3 and 4.

Conceptions of social difference that deny the salience of class adopt implicitly a static, top-down view of social structure. If they retain history as a referent, they also renounce struggles over class as a, much less the, major form of structuration.[4] Or having replaced the materiality of structure with language and text they claim narrative's materiality. But if one takes social practice rather than either social grids or stories as the point of departure for understanding how social things change there is no alternative but to adopt some concept of class and class struggle. Changes are not signified solely or even primarily by institutional expressions of social practices-cum-struggles. Class practices leave material sediments in the labor process, in institutions, in everyday life, and in vernacular speech even when the goals of the actors are not fully realized or are not manifested as overt forms of political or social conflict. And these practices often contradict actors' stated beliefs and norms. In short, we mean what we say but sometimes our actions speak in a voice different from our moral voice.

Let me briefly mention a few examples. A worker who does not believe in strikes on religious or other moral grounds finds herself on a picket line, giving full throat to grievances at a demonstration, or engages in a job action that withholds her labor. A parent opposed to abortion takes her daughter to obtain an abortion. A black nationalist joins forces with white civil rights adherents to oppose the crippling of affirmative action. In the 1950s and 1960s labor productivity in many American industrial plants lagged behind that of European factories producing the same goods. At a time of unchallenged U.S. dominance of world markets for capital, agricultural, and consumer goods some of this lag was the result of decisions of major corporations not to invest in the most up-to-date technology available, a decision that eventually reduced the viability of several major U.S. industrial sectors. In fact, American corporations engaged in extensive capital investment to rebuild European industries and expanded to developing countries as well. But equally important, wages rose faster than labor productivity, and this economic imbalance was largely due to unprecedented worker militancy on the shop floor in the auto, steel, and other industries linked to them.

This was the era of frequent strikes and spontaneous walkouts, notably the 116-day steel strike of 1959 and an extensive series of unauthorized walkouts in the auto plants between 1954 and 1960. Between 1969 and 1972, workers, black and white, resumed combat against their employers but also against an entrenched union leadership that had become committed to labor peace and higher productivity norms. The early 1970s was also a time of worker resistance to the speedup of assembly lines in many sectors: periodic breakdowns; de facto sabotage that resulted in defective product, which necessitated repairs after the product had been assembled; widespread lateness and absenteeism; and determined struggles to preserve and extend restrictive work rules that limited the power of management to direct the workforce. Freed from the fear of unemployment that had afflicted an older, depression-scarred generation, young workers, many of them war veterans, were prone to lead these struggles, switch jobs when they were dissatisfied, and spend as much time as they could during working hours smoking dope or drinking.

The well-known student protests of the 1960s were by no means confined to antiwar demonstrations. The student movement began as resentment against the industrialization of university and college life. Far from offering an education, their universities were training them to take professional and technical places in the late capitalist machine. In the 1960s, students and some workers throughout the world reinvented a political counterculture but also a social counterculture that echoed the bohemian revolt against commercialism of the nineteenth century. What some writers have called "the refusal to work" spread throughout both the capitalist and state socialist world. Although the general student and workers' strike of May 1968 in France is, perhaps, emblematic of the deep dissatisfaction expressed by youth against what many intellectuals had termed postindustrial consumer society, similar movements appeared among Italian workers, German students, and, of course, American youth. In the Vietnam War era many students opted out of the draft, challenging the patriotic assumptions of their childhood. Working-class men forced to enter the armed forces became notorious for their unsoldierly conduct in and out of combat. They felt that their country had put them in harm's way for no clear reason and spent much of their military service figuring out how not to be killed. One way was to refuse orders to engage in combat or, when pressed under threat of court-martial, to kill or otherwise disable their superior officers.

Taken from the angle of practice, the revolt against late capitalist work and the culture of consumerism changed the history of the last half of the twentieth century.[5] Throughout this period the rulers of nearly every advanced industrial society were confronted with unprecedented disturbances: at the workplace, especially among industrial workers; in the universities; and among consumers, many of whom were members of the new class who, despite their relatively secure economic position, perceived that the quality of their lives had deteriorated. Perhaps freedom from want and the fear of physical annihilation led to their firm conviction that they were entitled to a healthy environment. In different registers amid the Cold War–induced economic boom of the fifties and sixties women and blacks demanded more freedom. In their view, in the wake of unparalleled prosperity they were an oppressed and exploited class because the system had failed to deliver on the promise of equal opportunity, the liberal reply to revolutionary demands for equality. Perhaps more to the point, the accelerating entrance of women into paid work prompted some to ask whether women were a "class" burdened with a double shift: to their traditional job of unpaid household labor was added a second one that was waged.[6] The color line, W. E. B. Du Bois's central problem of the twentieth century, had matured into a permanent class divide. Some blacks might rise to managerial or professional employment, but, in the main, blacks were—and are—consigned to the lower rungs of production and service labor, a situation that has been exacerbated by massive deindustrialization since the 1970s; further, black rates of unemployment, poverty, and infant mortality are twice the national average.[7]

This book differs from most treatments of class and stratification in several respects. First, it proposes to define the class divide according to the line of power, which includes but is not limited to questions of ownership and control of the key means of material and immaterial production. In general, social rule is wielded by a power bloc in which the political directorate at the national level plays an important role in addition to the decisive groups of owners of capital. Depending on the specific features of any social formation the composition of the power bloc varies. For example, whether the military is part of the ruling class or which sectors of capital are included is a matter of historical specificity. Second, if power becomes the fault line of class division, the divide between workers and other social movements is a historical occurrence not rooted in bio-identities. In capitalist societies such as the United States the practice of class power is to create a huge rift between a multiplicity of social formations—on one side, wage workers, elements of the "new class" who have been the main activists in the environmental and anti-AIDS movements, women, blacks, and other racially oppressed groups; and on the other a diverse ruling class that generally consists of the most decisive sectors of capital, the national and international political directorate, and other, more variable formations. On neither side of the power divide can one observe a single economic class formation, but rather an alliance of a multiplicity of formations, some of which are coded as social or cultural. But, as we shall see, the women's movement, for example, is also a labor movement in several meanings of the term, and the interpenetration of economic and social issues is ineluctable in the workers' ranks. Social formations struggle over class when their demands result in a fissure in society. Having succeeded—or failed—to force new arrangements, classes may mutate or disappear.

Thus, as opposed to writers for whom capitalist social relations are relatively stable over large expanses of time, I claim that classes and their struggles for power within a system of social relations have historicity. By "historicity" I mean that they come into existence under specific conditions that, almost inevitably, are superseded by new conditions and new social formations. Yet within the history of capitalism these social formations are often cleaved into antagonistic blocs; consensus rather than cleavage is the exception rather than the rule and is usually achieved, as are major technological innovations that turn the lives of many workers upside down, in war situations. Enter nationalism and patriotism. These are the tools of suppression and displacement of class antagonisms. But even as the nation as a cultural imaginary persists, it is constantly challenged both from within by social cleavages and, increasingly, from without by autonomous transnational capital, with which it is obliged to make alliances against the common enemy, the people. Third, following the insight of Adam Pzeworski, I argue that most struggles are about class formation rather than class struggles that are forever imbedded in the capitalist relations of production. I do not conclude that class formation and class struggle no longer constitute history if the outcome is not revolution and the appearance of a new mode of production. Instead, as I argue in chapters 2 and 3, class occurs when insurgent social formation(s) make demands that cleave society and engender new social and cultural relations. Needless to say, rulers may, with varying success, incorporate or integrate elements of these demands in order to thwart their class-producing consequences.[8]

Others have insisted on one or another of these propositions. I argue that class is constituted by the totality of these conditions.

1
CLASS MATTERS

PREAMBLE

One of the more visible human preoccupations is the effort to understand social relationships. In every historical period writers have speculated, theorized, and told stories about the ways we live together, why and how we fight each other, and how we survive (when we do not conquer) the perceived assaults of the external physical world. These inquiries constitute the substance of philosophy, history, literary study, the social sciences, and the arts. The myriad observations that result are typically organized through the use of concepts.

Perhaps the most commonplace of these concepts is the social or society. In their quest to meet the challenges of their environment, animals, including humans, live in groups and enter into relationships with their own and other species, associations that, as one major social thinker, Karl Marx, says, are ultimately "independent of their will." They enter into antagonistic as well as cooperative relations, even if they tend to disguise the antagonisms with a rhetoric of cooperation.[1]

Western civilization is the rubric used to describe those who are descended from the intellectual and moral traditions generated by Athens and Greco-Roman city-states of the six centuries before the birth of Christ and from the religious traditions of Jews and Christians. It also demarcates European-centered societies from those of Africa and Asia. But there are serious problems with the conflation of the two traditions. Democracy and citizenship, so powerful in the European Enlightenment, do not derive from the so-called Judeo-Christian legacy or from any monotheistic religion, since its core is to surrender human agency to a deity. In fact, religious leaders frequently deny that democracy applies to the internal organization of the church, and none of the major Western religions was in the forefront of the struggle for democracy in the Age of Revolution, which defined much of the eighteenth and nineteenth centuries. Like the corporation, which reserves power for those who own its shares, most religions distinguish between the flock, which provides financial support and social legitimacy, and the priests, whose professional training and certification confer power to rule the institution. Democracy and its concomitant concept citizenship are the product of the polytheistic Athenian society, which insisted that all citizens participate in every aspect of community life (though it also denied citizenship to slaves, artisans, and women; indeed Aristotle's concept of citizenship explicitly excludes all but those who possess the leisure to participate in the affairs of state).

The conflation of Western civilization with the Judeo-Christian tradition is the doing of conservative philosophers—almost all of those who arose in the wake of the scientific enlightenment of the seventeenth and eighteenth centuries—for whom a moral order is the primary value of any social arrangement properly termed civilized. Christians have followed Jews in emphasizing the power of the moral code, popularly termed the Ten Commandments, which according to the Old Testament God handed down to Moses after humans proved unable to govern themselves without engaging in riotous and self-destructive behavior. Henceforth people would learn to live together without killing each other on a whim or in a fit of anger; would not covet another's wife or dissolve the family bond, thereby inviting personal violence; and, perhaps most significant for economic life, would not steal another's personal property or, indeed, community property for private gain.

For many writers associated with the tradition of Western liberalism, whose key idea is the connection between freedom and the market, the chief characteristic of Western civilization, at least since the Protestant Reformation, is that it is a society of individuals. The object of human association is to achieve harmony by overcoming our differences. Accordingly, liberalism rejects the idea that hidden forces of any kind, let alone such abstractions as cooperation and class antagonism, structure our modes of life. People inevitably engage each other for the purposes of trade, friendship, and the fulfillment of household responsibilities, but, according to John Locke, the basis of social interaction is the Self, always conceived as an integral whole. As Adam Smith noted, individuals act on the basis of self-interest; the hidden hand of God will ensure order. For Thomas Hobbes, the presence of individuals who disrupt social relations in their pursuit of pecuniary gain requires the imposition of common rules of conduct. Society survives its internal fissures by imposing sanctions and restrictions that individuals obey in their self-interest.[2] In the society of individuals, Great Men (or Women) are the true makers of history: advances in human knowledge occur because some individual has an idea and the means of realizing it; and when those who own property vigorously pursue their own interests they promote the general welfare by employing labor, encouraging invention and cultural development, and advancing overall prosperity. That a small number of property owners is motivated by moral suasion to take responsibility for the poor and the sick is salutary but does not obviate the fact that the good is best realized when the wealthy do what they do best, accumulate wealth.[3]

The conceit of this book is that what has been said and done in the name of class and class struggles is not only worth knowing but still relevant for making sense of our own times, not only in the global south and east but in the United States and the developed societies of Europe. This claim contradicts the prevailing American wisdom and a growing body of European opinion as well. The story of the American exception to the European rule that classes constitute the bone and marrow of society is deeply embedded in our national identity. At the turn of the century the historian Frederick Jackson Turner and the German sociologist Werner Sombart, among others, argued that class politics had little impact on the nineteenth century and would continue to be marginal in the twentieth century.[4] According to the conventional story, the United States had three main advantages over Europe: ample raw materials within its borders, which enabled its industries to produce and transport products more cheaply and pay relatively less for production labor; a frontier of plentiful agricultural land that acted as a safety valve against frequent economic blows to the working population, preventing the formation of working-class political parties and the development of class ideologies; and perhaps most important, the absence of a feudal tradition, which according to most historians made for a rigid class structure in England and other European countries. Never mind that many historians found that by the Civil War the frontier was largely ended and that many workers endured employment conditions that resembled feudal indenture: the belief in American exceptionalism has had great staying power in the popular mind well beyond the years that it had some material basis.

Exceptionalism is not merely an intellectual construct; class denial is woven into the fabric of American life. American culture rests on the proposition that, in the words of the singer Jimmy Cliff, "You can make it if you really want, but you must try, try and try, try and try / You'll succeed at last." While Cliff's words drip with irony that undercuts their celebration of unlimited opportunity, many Americans take "equality of opportunity" literally. They believe that being born poor or working class is not economic destiny, that with a combination of luck and hard work—whether that means earning educational credentials, starting a small business, or hitting the lottery—they can get rich or at least achieve economic security. Even the ample evidence that fewer than a third of Americans move beyond their social origins, and then only to become professional or technical salaried employees rather than entrepreneurs, fails to dampen the dreams of many. After all, one in three is not bad odds.

Denial is also endemic among historians. While land deprivation and abject poverty were widespread in American cities at the time of the Revolution and throughout the nineteenth century, most historians portray America at the inception of the Republic as a nation of independent property owners.[5] Few—notably the chroniclers of the Anti-Federalists Joshua Miller and Jackson Main and the historians of the nineteenth-century working class Eric Foner, David Montgomery, and Herbert Gutman—have recognized the existence of a substantial class of propertyless wage workers and marginal small owners. The nineteenth-century American story is inevitably seen through the eyes of skilled craftspeople or immigrants who were able to step through the "Golden Door."[6]

According to the main narrative, Americans are indelibly a middle-class people, a status engraved not only in their national culture but in the hearts and minds of even the most humble citizens. Although males without property gained suffrage during the administration of Andrew Jackson, and workingmen formed their own political parties in several states, it was the great middle-class parties, for which productive property was the main criterion of active citizenship, that dominated American politics throughout the nineteenth and twentieth centuries.[7] Although workingmen could vote, they were distant from actual participation in governance, except in their own labor unions, fraternal organizations, and veterans groups. By the turn of the twentieth century organized labor had achieved some rights at the workplace, but with the rise of labor unions there also emerged a permanent officialdom that increasingly dominated these organizations and whose income and lifestyles resembled those of the middle class rather than those of their constituents. The fraternal organizations that cropped up in the wake of the second great immigration of southern and eastern Europeans were led by the tiny fraction of small business people such as undertakers, independent professionals, and grocery store owners.

Even as large industrial and financial corporations emerged in the late nineteenth century and many smallholders were driven into the ranks of wage workers, the term *middle class* remained as both description and aspiration. In the twentieth century, as private productive property became highly concentrated and the number of farmers and small businesspeople shrank relative to waged and salaried employees, the concept lost its original connection to owners of productive property and became a category of consumption. The "middle-class standard of living" now designates a mode of life that many believe cuts across property relations and occupational hierarchies. In fact the term *property* has been expanded to mean ownership of any kind: a house, patents, savings accounts, small stock and bond holdings.

Because economic expansion has allowed some to advance from the ranks of manual and clerical labor to professional occupations, many Americans are firmly convinced there are no stable class boundaries. As implied by the example of Abraham Lincoln, whose mythic stature owes much to his diligence in pursuing an education, the challenge for individuals who want to make it is to put their noses to the grindstone. Most who fail to rise have themselves to blame. The visible and highly publicized stories of people who did rise sustain our national ideology. This deeply ingrained ideology, with its half-truths and blithe hope, dovetails with another tenacious American myth: that schools are democratizing institutions that blur class differences. In reality, schooling has the opposite effect. Credentials provide an alleged objective basis for social hierarchy and for selection into the higher and lower ranks. But all credentials are not equal. A diploma from public elementary and high schools, even those coded as academically excellent, does not confer status and opportunity equivalent to one from elite private boarding schools like Andover and Choate or leading private day schools.

A baccalaureate from state colleges and universities (except for preeminent research institutions like the University of California and some of the Big Ten) is not the equivalent of a degree from an Ivy League institution or a leading private university like Stanford or Chicago. In my experience as a member of a graduate faculty that recruits nationally, there are huge holes in the educational preparation of those who have graduated from schools like Oberlin, Brown, and Princeton. Yet most students who have attended the handful of elite colleges have accumulated considerable cultural capital:

they are self-confident, know the names if not necessarily the ideas of writers of high theory, have seen major works of visual art, and generally write adequately. These students rarely sweat their job prospects but assume they will land on their feet. Equally bright graduates of most public colleges and nonelite privates usually lack salient intellectual references and are fatalistic about their life chances.[8]

Merit has little to do with this. Scions of Old Money and members of the high political class are routinely admitted to the Ivy Leagues and, with few exceptions, spend their undergraduate years avoiding their schools' well-endowed libraries. President George W. Bush is only the latest in a long line of poorly educated Ivy graduates who have made good. His years at Yale were marked by studied avoidance of scholarship no less than were Franklin D. Roosevelt's at Harvard. Within the limits established by the elite schools, admissions policies for the hundred of thousands who vie for a few thousand seats are scandalously arbitrary. As Paul Attewell has demonstrated, a graduate of an elite New York City public high school in which most students achieve grade point averages of A or B+ has less chance of being accepted at Harvard or Yale than an A student from a rural district in Missouri in which curricular demands may be far less rigorous. While many of the leading universities have adopted income- and race-blind policies of admission and disdain quotas based on race, religion, and ethnic identity, they are able to get around these moral strictures by maintaining fairly harsh, informal regional distributions.[9]

"CORPORATE GREED" OR CLASS RULE?

That evidence of class and class struggle should come up against a wall of denial reflects America's general penchant for social amnesia. Perhaps no other people have a fainter sense of their own history, for the condition of their well-known practice of perpetual self-reinvention is that they not be burdened by the past. Americans pride themselves on being a nation of immigrants, but few know their family histories or their ancestral languages. It is a uniquely American characteristic that some whites are tied neither to their name, family histories, and ethnicity nor to their class origins and can simply shed inconvenient or despised identities. In the face of anti-Semitism, for example, Jews have often changed their last names. Blacks, on the other hand, have had their histories erased by slavery, yet they cannot be born anew because, despite emancipation, skin color remains a stigma.

When not considered downright un-American, those who insist on the salience of class are dismissed as dogmatic, ideological, or deluded. During the recession of the early 1990s, when millions were laid off from well-paying factory jobs, middle management positions, and even some professions, the senior George Bush announced that America was a classless society. This elevation of American classlessness to semiofficial doctrine was the mirror image of the frequent charge, uttered by conservatives and liberals alike during election campaigns and legislative battles, that the other side is fomenting class warfare, as if this were a deliberate act rather than a social condition.[10]

Americans often admit that some large corporations, like oil and tobacco companies, are bad citizens; and that many politicians and elected officials do the bidding of the corporate interests that fund them, particularly on issues like the environment and social welfare. But such betrayals of the public trust are usually ascribed to corruption, greed, or ethical lapses rather than to a structural relation between large capital concentrations and the institutions of government. Each case, each corporation is treated as a moral issue. Corporate officials who disregard or deceive the public are cast as individual noxious villains, as in Michael Moore's docucritique, *Roger and Me,* which accuses General Motors CEO Roger Smith of heartlessly abandoning the city of Flint and his erstwhile workers. The model is that of the Western, with its cowboys and rustlers. And the remedy, citizens are asked to believe, is a change of corporate ethic from plunder to public responsibility, encouraged by mild legal and moral sanctions. The power of shame or exposure to the glare of public opinion is supposed to persuade corporations to do the right thing. This is the thinking behind the progressive version of the Reagan/Clinton-era policy of voluntary compliance rather than regulatory sanctions and of material incentives for corporations to limit their profligate antienvironment behavior.

Indeed, Americans are inclined to let the evildoers off the hook as long as they put something back into society. So even as he and Microsoft are slapped with a massive antitrust suit by the government, CEO Bill Gates has claimed the mantle of a modern Robin Hood. Sure, he's made a lot of money, but he has reinvented himself as a philanthropist. While he has made billions on computer software he is donating millions to solve some of the most intractable social problems on the planet, such as the AIDS epidemic in Africa, and has recently discovered poverty and urban educational deprivation. Even when the entire tobacco industry is generally understood to be guilty of lying to the public about the pathological effects of tobacco, the largest tobacco corporation, Phillip Morris, is a major sponsor of the arts.

Even as major oil corporations visit environmental havoc on U.S. waters and air, *ExxonMobil Masterpiece Theatre* offers video versions of literary classics on the Public Broadcasting System. Auto corporations are regularly required to recall hundreds of thousands of unsafe vehicles, but the names Ford, Carnegie, Mellon, and Rockefeller adorn university buildings and fellowships, still dominate the philanthropic world, and are a permanent billboard advertising capitalist compassion. Their intervention in the cultural, educational, and policy spheres constitutes an ongoing legitimation of the role of corporate capitalism in public life.

In part, we Americans are soft on the robber barons because we admire them despite their transgressions. Bill Gates is a folk hero; the ubiquitous Jack Welch of General Electric is frequently featured in the fashion and gossip pages. As a country obsessed with competitive sports we love winners, whatever their moral failings, and identify with baseball manager Leo Durocher's dictum, "Nice guys finish last."

We hate the gloomy conclusions of the so-called debunking sciences, particularly sociology and political economy, which have historically portrayed perfidious behavior as the ordinary fare of corporate capitalism, evidence of the banality of evil: after all, the debunkers side with the losers. Under severe attack, the social sciences have responded by toning down their critical thrust, proclaiming the neutrality of their findings in the service of objective science, and becoming technical experts to policy makers and the media. As a result—though the United States is currently home to the largest concentration of economic wealth in history and the most dramatic income inequality in the world—there are few publicly visible social critics comparable to Thorstein Veblen, John Kenneth Galbraith, or C. Wright Mills.[11]

CLASS POLITICS OR POLITICAL PLURALISM?

The dominant concept of American democracy directly opposes a class analysis of our political institutions. Elected representatives rarely reflect the needs and opinions of a majority of their constituents, usually catering to those who pay their bills, except on occasions when they must respond to public pressure around a fairly narrow range of issues. Pluralists who defend representative democracy as the best of all possible worlds, even if not the ideal political system, refuse these criticisms (you know the slogan, "American democracy is deeply flawed, except in comparison with the rest"). In their view power derives from the efforts of a plurality of groups who form coalitions based on common interests within the great two-party system.

Power is conceived in the figure of the mathematical vector—law and public policy are the outcome of the myriad compromises between (temporarily) opposing groups who get things done by reaching compromise or consensus. Workers, professionals, consumers, and business interests form their own institutions, called pressure groups, that participate in this pluralist politics. Since they are not understood as being irreconcilably opposed, pressure groups can decide to work together or reach consensus. When political scientists discuss these arrangements, unions and corporations are factored into the mix. Even American unions deny they are class organizations that engage in class struggles (although they sometimes accuse the large corporations of fomenting such struggles). In the current trade union vernacular they are defenders of the interests of working families (what happened to single people?) but never of the working class. By invoking the phrase *working families,* the labor movement not only elides class, but places itself on the side of one of the icons of conservative culture, the nuclear family, with all of its religious, homophobic, and exclusionary connotations.[12]

For politicians and most commentators on American social mobility, the new frontier is technology. The electronic revolutions in computers, fiber optics, and lasers have inspired an outburst of utopian thinking: in a generation nearly everyone will be what Robert Reich terms a "symbolic analyst," manipulating ideas, not things; no social problem is exempt from the technological fix; it is just a matter of time before educational and income inequality will be a memory, although nobody goes so far as to claim that we will all be rich; even if there are ongoing layoffs in the high tech firms, there is more entrepreneurship among engineers and other qualified workers, especially in the information and communications sectors.[13]

Nothing has done more in the recent period to support this view than the explosion of the number of millionaires who have made their fortune in the information industries. Many of these people worked in relatively modest professional and technical occupations of engineering and computer programing. The iconic status enjoyed by this concentrated cohort in American culture is closely linked to the reproduction of the ideology of classlessness in America. They became rich because of entrepreneurial risk taking, combined with their solid technical knowledge. In their outward appearance these people do not correspond to the ruthless banker in Frank Capra's *It's a Wonderful Life.* Presenting himself in the image of a self-made man, Bill Gates meets none of the traditional criteria of a blue meanie. He's like the rest of us but just a little smarter and more aggressive. Against the formal dress of most CEOs he dresses casually in open collars and loosely fit sweaters, presumably to emphasize that he is a working executive. Moreover, he constantly reminds us that he and his fellow parvenus have created hundreds of thousands of new jobs, many of them well paying, and have made incalculable contributions to a once-booming economy.

The United States is the center of garage capitalism. But for every instant millionaire produced by startup companies, thousands of programers and technicians are still wage or salaried employees. For example, the workplace at Microsoft, the leading computer software corporation, is organized by a two-tier system: a minority of its engineers and programers have stock options that enabled a few thousand to become wealthy, but a larger proportion of its employees, including many in these occupations, are contingent workers with no benefits. Moreover, after an initial surge of startups, the rate of failure far outdistances the rate of survival. At the end of the year 2000 press reports abounded in accounts of mass layoffs in established as well as dot.com startup firms. Others who had foregone higher salaries for stock options woke to the news that their shares had sunk to near worthlessness. Perhaps the low point of this trend was the collapse of the global energy trader Enron, which, in the face of its plummeting stock price, refused to permit employees to withdraw their equity in the company, while at the same time awarding huge bonuses to its top executives. Many saw their retirement income evaporate.

Still, the neoliberal economic doctrine proclaiming the superiority of free markets over public ownership, or even public regulation of private economic activity, has become the conventional wisdom, not only among conservatives but among social progressives. Accordingly it is assumed that any attempt to regulate trade to protect the interests of workers, small businesspeople such as farmers, and those engaged in light manufacturing such as clothing will thwart economic progress. In a free market economy the outcome of competition may be that some get more than others, but if the economy grows enough everybody gets something. The American plan of open markets for labor and for capital investment seems, on the surface at least, supremely triumphant throughout Europe, including the former Communist countries. If class struggle has been replaced by competition and differential status of various occupational and consumer groups, then, as Francis Fukuyama has recently declared, we have arrived at the end of history, if by this concept we mean not merely the chronological train of events, but, through revolutionary change, the century and a half of epochal transformations of social relations from the French to the Russian Revolutions. For prophets like Fukuyama, if Communism is dead, so is history. All that is left is to fine-tune an almost perfect social system of democratic capitalism and make sure it spreads to all corners of the globe.[14]

It would be inaccurate to say we don't talk about class—we use the word all the time. But the ways we use it amount to another form of denial. *Upper middle class,* for example, is as much a cultural designation as it is economic: it goes with certain neighborhoods and styles of life, including tastes in clothing, entertainment, and choices of secondary and higher education institutions. Another evasion is the widespread use of *class* as a pejorative applying to groups—whether professional politicians or leaders of unions, civil rights groups, environmentalist and feminist organizations—that are considered to be pursuing their own interests rather than representing their constituents.

In our everyday conceptions and conversations we have an implicit map of social structure into which we classify individuals and groups. Class infuses social perception and has become another marker of distinction. Neoconservatives and sociologists refer to intellectuals as a "new class" in different ways: the conservatives use the term in an ideological sense and confine their designation to those on the Left who have entered the fields of social policy and the professoriate; a substantial body of literature, which claims to be value free, strives to place the broadest category of intellectual labor in their social maps. These maps may or may not tell us something about political activity and could have consequences for the shape of history.

In addition to the hotly debated question about whether the poor constitute an underclass—the one exception to the rule of classlessness, repeated over and over—many speak confidently of a middle class that embraces all but a narrow fraction of rich people at the top and a shrinking but still substantial group of the more than forty million poor at the bottom. Since World War II many industrial and service workers have lifted themselves from the ranks of the poor and are now generally perceived to be proud members of this vast middle class. The main criterion for middle-class membership is one's participation in the huge consumer celebration; through its propensity to spend at increasing levels, this middle class is credited with sustaining high levels of production, profits, and employment.

I argue that in actual historical struggles the pure case as described in the *Communist Manifesto,* in which two great historical actors confront each other on the battlefield of history, never exists. Struggles about class are always constituted as alliances on both sides of the power divide. These alliances are related to questions of productive property but invariably address issues of culture and politics as well, in recent years focusing around questions relating to domination and freedom that have a multiplicity of referents: womens' demand to be free of the chains of family responsibilities as well as their excess exploitation as wage labor; the long battle of the black freedom movement against slavery and then against economic exploitation, political marginality, and social subordination; and the fervor of many in the new class to replace capital's rationality with an ecological rationality which, on the basis of its idea of the universal interest in the planet's survival, challenges the system-logic of capital accumulation. I reserve further discussion for chapter 2.[15]

CLASS FORMATION

Despite conventional wisdom, Americans have in fact entered a period of intense social conflict marked by struggles over class formation. To talk of such conflicts is to distinguish between class as a description of social and economic inequalities as they affect individuals and groups and the process by which class may become a force in shaping our collective destiny. I say "may" because historical class movements are not the inevitable result of a mechanical or religious principle but depend on the grasping of opportunities. In 1981, for instance, the nation's air traffic controllers went on strike for more control over their stressful working conditions. Because the strike was illegal under federal law, Ronald Reagan fired all eleven thousand controllers. At this point organized labor faced the challenge of class formation. It had to decide whether to struggle to become a class movement rather than a series of unions. This would have involved several options familiar to many labor movements around the world: a one-day general strike, such as that which took place in Italy in April 2002; or a million-worker march on Washington. Although unions were already considerably weakened, they still had power in transportation, construction, and key manufacturing sectors and, in some cities, comprised between a quarter and a third of the workforce.

The AFL-CIO executive council decided instead to send a delegation to the president to seek executive clemency. Reagan declined the opportunity and labor lost the chance to demonstrate its power and solidarity and to shift the terrain of national political life. Reagan's bold maneuver sealed the fate of labor for nearly a generation. It exposed the chronic political weakness of the largest voluntary secular organization in the United States. Of course the refusal of the trade unions to take a path of confrontation and resistance was prepared by the pattern of collaboration with "their" corporations, with the law, and with successive Democratic national administrations that dominated American politics through the 1960s. This collaboration meant that they had become dependent variables in the political economy and had renounced political independence. Indeed organized labor had staked its well-being on these arrangements for nearly forty years, and it paid off handsomely for a sizable minority of the working class. It could be argued that so accustomed were they to subordination that they were ill-prepared to confront the first openly antilabor administration since the early 1930s.[16]

The 1980s and early 1990s witnessed the most dramatic about-face in labor's fate since the 1920s. Corporate America launched a massive assault on workers and their unions with the intention of halting or even reversing rising living standards, which until then had seemed an endemic feature of the postwar era. Capital flight and technological change accelerated, and unions made concessions in contract protections, especially on issues bearing on productivity, safety, and management rights to direct the workforces. In this period real wages, which had outstripped inflation for most of the postwar era, actually declined by 25 percent over the next two decades, and union wages stagnated. When local unions in production industries resisted management demands, they were often condemned by their national unions and left to hang out to dry. The moment for class formation passed when the unions refused to struggle to become a social movement. Their refusal had dire historical consequences.

In contrast, the growing international movement by labor, environmental groups, students, and women against the effects of globalization presents the best opportunity in recent times for the emergence of a new class movement. It is about class formation whose outcome depends entirely on whether, across national boundaries, workers and their unions challenge the terms under which a new empire wants to foster a new world order. In December 1999 a meeting of the World Trade Organization (WTO) in Seattle was greeted by more than fifty thousand demonstrators from unions, environmentalists, and sweatshop opponents of WTO's efforts to lower remaining third world barriers to capital investment and trade. American unions demanded WTO's assurance that it would promote fair labor standards in order to prevent job losses at home. These include provisions that would limit child labor, require wage floors, and enforce safety and health standards in factories. Some trade unionists joined the broader demand for democratizing by including nongovernmental organizations in the negotiations and on the WTO's governing bodies and requested an end to secrecy in its operations. During the protests the West Coast Longshore union shut down ports from San Diego to Puget Sound. The marches and rallies, which virtually closed down Seattle and disrupted the meeting, were widely covered by the American and international press and set a new agenda for social struggle in the next period.

TAKING CLASS SERIOUSLY

What does it mean to take class seriously? First, it suggests an entirely different way of looking at contemporary and historical politics and culture. Although class discourse has suffered eclipse in official representations, it lives an underground existence; class has become an important component of our political and cultural unconscious. Class remains salient, not only to understanding how history was made—from ancient times to the recent past—but also as a better concept for grasping the present and the future than competing explanations. Moreover some of these explanations can be legitimately read as variants of class analysis. For example, neoliberals conceive the destruction of millions of factory jobs and their (partial) replacement by service and technical occupations over the past thirty years as enhanced opportunities for class mobility. Alternatively, we may assess these changes in technologically advanced capitalist societies in terms of horizontal social space—as changes in skills and education but not as a movement upward. In the years of the greatest displacements of industrial labor, 1978 to 1994, more than nine million industrial workers lost their jobs to labor-displacing technologies, capital flight to low-wage areas in both the United States, mainly in the South, and Latin America and Asia. Most of the displaced workers were not retrained for jobs as computer programers or for other occupations in the so-called new economy. Most eventually found other jobs, but they were in lower-paid factory work, often without benefits, retail services, and nonunion construction that paid wages that hovered around the minimum wage. Many middle-aged men and women discovered they had become redundant and were obliged to compete with teenagers for so-called McJobs. Others were forced into early retirement before they were eligible for government or union pension benefits.[17]

Since class mobility is a recurring theme in American ideology, the new high-tech economy may be understood as stunning evidence that, in this dynamic country of unlimited opportunity, the new information sectors open up new vistas. There is no doubt that a growing portion of wage and salary labor is now technically qualified. Workers engage in immaterial labor, which requires formal education and training. They manipulate signs, work with concepts rather than being subordinate to routinized directions, and, in theory, retain some autonomy in the performance of their immediate tasks. Their responsibilities often overlap with work that was once associated with that of management, a historical development that has rendered much of line and middle management redundant. The question is, Have these workers moved out of the working class? Even if they do not own productive property and are required to work for salaries, do they enjoy a greater measure of control over their labor? have they achieved self-management? In spring 2000, sixteen thousand Boeing engineers—characteristic immaterial workers, immaterial because what they produce is ideas, concepts, and images—walked off the job to protest speedup and arbitary managerial authority over them. As fervent believers in one of the cornerstones of professional ideology—that as educated and qualified workers they themselves rather than managers should determine the pace and the strategies of job performance—they were outraged that the company was treating them without respect. Similarly, computer programers and systems analysts, managers, and physicians—three bedrock occupations suffused with the ideology of individualism—are seeking to form unions, a tacit recognition that their social position resembles wage labor more than it does independent professionals or entrepreneurs.

Unlike the prevailing commonsense and that of many social scientists as well, I do not evaluate class according to income criteria. While it is true that many highly paid blue-collar workers have been able to buy homes and appliances and send their kids to college, in the past twenty years of deindustrialization and deterritorialized production they have become aware how precarious their position in the work world really is. What distinguishes the working class is its lack of relative power over the terms and conditions of employment, relative power because unions do make a difference. Collective bargaining agreements fix a definite wage and series of benefits and, equally important, by specifying certain practices and the right to grieve their violation, grant employees a degree of control over their working conditions. But even the strongest unions have not been able to address adequately the effects of technological change, economic recession, and capital flight which have devastated dozens of industrial communities.

There is no more vivid illustration of the claim for the salience of class perspectives than in the long debate about globalization which today dominates political debate and action. Thinking about the present economic and political situation on a global scale, I draw radically different conclusions from the mainstream consensus that class is a concept best left to the historians. What is at stake in my insistence upon class discourse and class analysis is nothing less than how to interpret the truly climactic changes in the shape of global societies since the early 1970s. Perhaps the most widely acknowledged change in the nature of capitalism is that national economies are becoming interlinked into a global system of trade, finance, and labor exchange. National borders, including those of the United States, are becoming porous. And national political and industrial cultures are disappearing. The question is, How do we interpret the origin and significance of this shift from sovereign nation-states to a world system in which governments must answer to financial markets and to such institutions as the International Monetary Fund (IMF) and the World Bank (WB), which virtually dictate their economic and social policies? One way to understand the deterritorialization of production and investment is to recall the experience of class combat from the end of World War II to the early 1970s.

This was a period in the United States as well as Western Europe of mass strikes, among which was the virtual general strike of U.S. industrial workers in 1946. All leading monopolistic industries were affected. This strike established what became known as the American standard of living. It was followed by steady gains for a substantial minority of American workers, in and out of the trade unions, not only in money wages and in private consumption, but in the social wage as well. By 1953, 35 percent of the nonagricultural labor force was in unions, almost none in the public sector. Although union density—the proportion of union members to the labor force—diminished somewhat over the next twenty years, by 1973 every major production industry except textiles and other southern-based plants was overwhelmingly unionized. Labor's power was not confined to securing higher wages and benefits: among its most important effects was its job control, manifested mainly in its ability to regulate production norms on the shop floor and, at a time when the United States was the only industrial superpower, to contain the pace and applications of new technologies. The struggle to set the pace of production was starkly evident in the long series of wildcat walkouts from 1955 to 1971 in the auto industry, so called because they were in violation of a provision of the collective bargaining agreement which prohibited work stoppages during the life of the contract.

Globalization may be read as capital's counterattack against the constraints on its power won by labor movements throughout the world, including the United States. Workers and their unions throttled employers' ability to fire workers; to introduce new technologies without bargaining; to unilaterally set wages and benefits. In addition, the social wage, whether negotiated at the bargaining table or in legislatures, afford a measure of income security and tended to keep wages from plummeting during recessions. The last quarter of the twentieth century introduces a new phase in the internationalization of labor as well as of capital. After 1973 capital went on strike against the welfare state and in the 1980s against union bargaining power. And, despite immigration laws, U.S. borders were thrown open for reasons of foreign policy but also to break the power of labor by reducing wages.

Perhaps the most serious glitch in the mood of the American celebration has been the decade-long disagreement over trade issues between the labor movement and the large, transnational corporations, whose sway over the economic ideas and policies of government agencies and officials of nearly all types seems fairly complete. If class has any public representation in America, the question of protectionism once consigned by the free traders to history's archive has risen from the dead. In the 1970s the ideas and policies of Keynesian economics—according to which government must intervene in the operations of the economy in order to maintain high levels of employment, investment, and consumption—were renounced by capital and its bipartisan allies at the highest levels of government. Since then, the United States and nearly all advanced industrial countries have adopted an alternative doctrine to Keynesianism with its advocacy of progressive taxation to finance programs to increase the social wage (social security in its broadest significance), job creation to alleviate unemployment, and regulation of transportation, banking, and international trade as the key to economic growth, stability, and general prosperity. Neo-Smithian or neoliberal economics has a major objective: to lower all barriers to the free flow of capital as well as goods. Neoliberal economics should not be confused with what might be termed modern liberalism, the commonly used term for interventionist economic policies and social welfare. Neoliberal economic policy derives from the theories of Adam Smith, who argued for the reign of the market as opposed to high tariffs and other regulations that tend to distort the free relationship between buyers and sellers of commodities. He theorized that the relentless pursuit of self-interest by owners of productive property would benefit workers as well as capitalists.[18]

Neoliberalism advocates a sharp reduction of the role of government in economic life, especially income security programs that might discourage workers from accepting lower-waged labor. Under the banner of free trade and open markets the neoliberals want to confine the government to its policing functions, with one major exception: they favor aggressive monetary policies to replace fiscal policies. Keynesian fiscal policy employs public spending to boost investment and employment and favors such legislation as minimum wages, pension, and public support for education, housing, and health to supply a floor under income. On the theory that these policies discourage workers from accepting jobs at minimum wages, and that union-sponsored social benefits and job monopolies lead to wage rises that cause inflation when labor productivity is low, the neoliberal monetarists want to regulate interest to moderate or depress investment, accelerate layoffs, and thereby scare workers from seeking higher wages. But in testimony to Congress in July 2000, Federal Reserve Chair Alan Greenspan said that technological change, which displaced labor and made it more productive, was equally effective in that fear of redundancy discouraged workers from exerting wage pressure. At the same time economists and policy makers urge labor discipline by encouraging investors to seek areas which offer plentiful supplies of low-wage workers, a strict regime of suppressing labor unions, and subsidies such as tax breaks, government-built production facilities, and cheap power. Meanwhile corporations can deduct these investments from their tax returns.

Global capitalism continues, largely through the power of its leading financial institutions, to reproduce the subordination of the overwhelming majority of the earth's people. Under pressure from protest and resistance, the power of the WB and the IMF over the policies and practices of developing countries has become more visible. Answering the call of their own leaders and of the WB, the Chinese state, for example, has effected the most massive enclosure in world history. Tens of millions of Chinese peasants have been driven off their land into the great cities, where they have been pressed into factories owned by private, largely foreign capital and into construction projects to build industrial plants and the infrastructure needed to accommodate them. Indian economic growth is fueled almost entirely by an extraordinary military sector, among whose side benefits is the creation of a scientific-technical elite that has sold much of its talent to United States–based multinational corporations.

Latin America is a textbook example of economic development that has produced severe class differences but is also punctuated by sustained and militant class struggles. In the 1960s Mexico and Brazil became leading targets of capital investment because their governments were willing and able to offer foreign corporations such concessions as long-term tax abatements, free industrial plants, and plentiful supplies of low-wage labor. Mexico's border region with the United States occupies a special place in the intensity and extent of its U.S. foreign investment. American auto, parts, and light manufacturing firms have employed tens of thousands of workers in the maquiladores near Ciudad Juárez and other border towns. But Argentina, whose historic Peronismo was an essentially working-class movement, is, in the wake of intracontinental economic competition for capital, losing its relatively broad industrial base to Brazil. Brazil's neoliberal government gave permission to foreign capital to develop the country's precious rain forests for lumber and paper mills and, replicating the English experience of three hundred years earlier, recruit millions of former peasants to work in the development process. In Brazil and Korea, which are creating a highly sophisticated industrial capitalism, class and class strife have punctuated this era. The 1980s and 1990s were marked by the emergence of a popular workers' party that captured Brazil's presidency in 2002, and mass strikes were a regular occurrence in Korea's auto industry.

Globalization was forged on a widened wage and employment gap. Living standards in the vast developing world have actually declined for many since the new phase of accelerated global capital investment began in the 1980s. The International Labor Organization (ILO) has estimated that one-third of the world's labor force—more than a billion people—are unemployed or underemployed.[19] In the United States and the United Kingdom the concept of the family wage—an idea signifying that a single income can support a household at the customary material level—has been increasingly consigned to a small fraction of the upper middle classes. Workers' living conditions have been maintained only because millions of women have entered the paid labor force on a part- or full-time basis. But the growing number of working women has also put traditional male domination in the home on trial. Rebelling against the double shift, many women wage earners have lost patience with their husbands' expectations that the old privileges will be maintained. Divorce rates are climbing in every industrialized country, leaving both partners materially worse off than they were during the period of marital misery. In the United States, where the social safety net has all but disappeared for the working poor, two million children suffer from malnutrition, and hunger is more widespread at a time when the official jobless rate hovered around 4 percent, unprecedented since the first half of the 1950s.[20]

THE CLASS UNCONSCIOUS

Having been forced underground, class is deeply embedded in the recesses of our cultural and political unconscious. In every crevice of everyday life we find signs of class difference; we are acutely aware that class plays a decisive role in social relations. Professionals and managers do not mingle much with service or industrial workers, immaterial workers of all sorts are rarely in the company of blue-collar workers, and none of the above socialize with the poor, working or not. In sum, black or white, there is little blending of people from sharply disparate economic backgrounds. They inhabit different neighborhoods, even in the suburbs, where once social scientists purported to discover class blending. Different socioeconomic groups attend different churches, increasingly send their kids to different schools, and have different forms of leisure-time activity. Professionals and businesspeople attend classical music concerts, go to the theater, and until recently were the core of voluntarism, that peculiarly American form of religiously grounded philanthropy. Working-class people and the professional/managerial groups do not share the same cultural tastes, even in popular music, which in the past two decades has lost its universal appeal (the exception seems to be teenagers, for whom hiphop has become *the* popular genre).

For the most part the upper crusts eat different foods: their taste is conditioned by their reading about nutrition and by their financial ability to frequent restaurants that offer exotic dishes. In the last decades they have successively discerned the difference between Northern and Southern Italian cooking, discovered sushi and Thai cuisine, and have experienced, on health criteria, a renewed enthusiasm for vegetarian eating. Many have eschewed red meat because of concerns over cholesterol, and they have learned that commercial farm companies add growth hormones and use pesticides to grow the feed for steers. In short, the professional/managerial class and entrepreneurial groups cultivate new tastes, which is a cultural posit and is made possible by higher disposable income. While some in the lower orders may discover the virtues of these departures from heavy ethnic cooking which features a lot of red meat or the equally fatty, cholesterol-laden classic American fare of hamburger, pork specialties, meatloaf, and chicken, the cost of eating a notch or two higher acts as a prohibition for some, and plain ignorance is the reason others do not venture forth.

Males of all classes frequent drinking holes, but the ambience and location of these venues is class determined. The tavern or the gin mill are the habitats of traditional workers, while professionals and managers often drink in upscale bars or clubs reserved for members only. In the local tavern the television is firmly ensconced in the center even though, except in sports bars and on special occasions when the TV broadcasts championship events, it is a visual background for conversation, pool, dart games, or shuffleboard.

Upscale bars are places to meet women and men; the bar is a roar of conversation, and there are usually no games in the facility. If sports is, to some extent, the main class leveler in America, the style differs between social categories. For example, some workers play golf and, if no public course is available, join the local club, where they may encounter managers and businessmen on the course. But if they have conversations, they are short, and the subject matter is trivial because they simply do not inhabit the same worlds. Moreover, you do not see too many women from families of high corporate officials or professionals and managers spending their Monday nights playing bingo in the local Catholic church.

Magazines devoted to the seamy as well as glorious side of the lives of the rich and famous adorn supermarket shelves. The reader, usually a homemaker or a blue- or white-collar worker, enjoys such tales with a mixture of voyeuristic pleasure, envy, and inchoate anger. Professionals and managers may browse these 'zines on the checkout line, but their periodical reading is generally directed to financial newspapers, where they check out their stocks and get the latest merger and acquisition news, or to professional and trade journals, where they keep track of technical developments in their field. The audience for newspapers like the *New York Times* is on the economic upper end of the population. A cursory examination of its real estate section or classified ads—especially employment and autos sales—demonstrates that unless the reader from a lower economic niche is slumming, there is no practical address to her. There are regular major ads from New York's leading European car dealers, and many of the job offerings are for professional and managerial groups. Since Manhattan rental and coop apartments, let alone townhouses, are out of reach for many who earn in the low six figures, the intended reader for vacancies is beyond the reach of the middle consumer. Similarly, the food and health sections are directed to those who can drop a hundred dollars for dinner or who have geographic and financial access to gourmet and health food stores. The *Times* underlines its orientation by full-page ads from stores like Bergdorf Goodman, Lord and Taylor, and Brooks Brothers, who never make a secret of their profiled clientele.

The million and a half readers of the *Times*'s local competitors, the *Daily News* and the *New York Post,* are treated to a steady diet of comics, gossip, stories of murder and mayhem, a relatively narrow spectrum of regular columnists who supply much of the political news and commentary, and extensive sports sections that make up a quarter of the noncommercial content of the papers. Whatever hard news there is in these pages is crammed into five-hundred-word pieces. As you would expect, the ads are those of mass market department stores like Macy's—which is the most elegant of them—and Kmart; automobile ads are for American-made brands. One can find out where to obtain such services as electrolysis, astrology-based counseling, car and appliance repair. Unlike the *Times,* the *Daily News* and the *Post* carry no bridge columns, but the food and restaurant columns are beginning to broaden their horizon to include health and gourmet information. One reason for this visionary innovation may be that, given the superiority of their sports coverage, the tabloids attract a sliver of upper-middle-class men who might peruse the rest of the paper. Since the *Times* disdains the gossip columnists and the latter-day purveyors of advice to the lovelorn, some women undoubtedly pick up the papers to read "Dear Abby" and the late Ann Landers and to devour page 6 of the *Post* for the latest tidbits about their favorite celebrities. Yet these concessions to elite interests are few, and the extent of coverage is slight.

An executive of a leading investment banking house ran in the New Jersey Democratic senatorial primary in spring 2000. Financing his campaign almost exclusively with his own money to the tune of $34.5 million, he was accused by his opponent of buying the election. At times the campaign was fought in the surprising rhetoric of class because the banker's Democratic primary opponent, a longtime politician from one of the state's poorest areas, accused him of using his fortune to buy the election. The banker's decisive victory elicited some concern that perhaps class unconsciousness has gone too far. Not to be outclassed, a relatively independent player in the financial information industry, Michael Bloomberg, propelled himself from virtual obscurity to become mayor of New York City, with the help of $65 million of his own money.

While not powerful enough to replace the prevailing doctrine of classlessness, the current health crisis shows the class unconscious burbling to the surface. In recent years more Americans have become aware of the emergence of a three-class health care system: one for the rich and upper middle class;, another for the self-insured, most of whom have won this benefit through union agreements or, as a union deterrent, by the strategic acumen of large- and medium-sized corporations; and a third for the poor, who are forced to use the public hospitals, places which have become chronically underfunded and therefore understaffed. But in the past decade the value of self-insured health care has eroded because of more deductibles and the advent of managed care. Many who once enjoyed full hospital, surgical, medical, and drug coverage are obliged to make copayments and are at the mercy of for-profit Health Maintenance Organizations (HMOs), which ruthlessly reduce services in the interests of cutting costs. Increasingly the physicians who attend the first tier do not accept payment from prepaid health plans because the reimbursement is based on a formula they feel grossly undervalues their services. As a consequence many people who once were treated by a primary care physician are forced into medical groups, which, because of the practices of cost containment, do not necessarily provide what the patient needs or expects. The old belief that a self-insured middle-class patient can receive first-class medical care has been severely shaken as more physicians refuse to join HMOs, and, in turn, these managed care groups announce they will no longer accept Medicaid patients.

In this, the second coming of the Gilded Age, the ubiquity of the corporate war on low- and middle-income workers, more Americans are becoming aware that income disparity between the top and the bottom is growing, and as the government surrenders more of its social functions, the gap has enormous consequences for health, education, housing, and almost every amenity. The salaries and the perquisites of top management of the largest corporations have ballooned far beyond the limits of conventional reason. While Japanese and European corporate CEOs may earn ten to fifteen times the average wage of employees in their companies, their American counterparts draw forty or fifty times the income of shop floor or clerical employees.

Almost nobody really believes anymore that public education is the Great Leveler. In recent years we have witnessed the most dramatic reversals of this egalitarian ethos. As never before a tiering system has developed at every level of schooling. Although there have always been private schools, many of them traditionally sites of privilege (except perhaps the extensive parochial school systems that attracted many children of working-class families for a variety of reasons, including the desire for religious instruction), the ferocious devaluation of public education in large cities promulgated by organized conservative ideologues and think tanks has reopened the question of whether there really is a class system in education. Believing that their children's economic future is at stake, most urban middle-class parents have responded to this attack by rushing to the private schools, often at the cost of draining their savings and depleting their disposable income. The exodus from public schools resembles the panic in the wake of the stock market crash of 1929 or the stampede of an audience fleeing fire in a theater. Although well-heeled suburbs have not yet been infected—largely because parents have been willing to furnish financial assistance where the public coffers are chronically empty—there is much evidence that the virus of privatization is spreading, leaving many destroyed illusions in its wake, most strikingly the idea that through universal public education every individual has an equal opportunity to move up the social and economic ladder. Public schooling is increasingly viewed as second-class education, and, as a result, working-class kids—white, black, Asian, and Latino—who are not eventually chosen by private schools and colleges have been, in effect, consigned to the bottom of the economic ladder.

Some, on the Right, tacitly admit of some class differences but argue that, compared to all but European societies the alleged American poor are well off. They contend that inequality in America is trumped by the fact that all social groups benefited from the country's rapid economic growth for much of the twentieth century. Consequently, the class argument has a hollow ring when the bottom rung in America lives a princely existence compared to billions of people in Africa, Asia, and Latin America. Norman Podhoretz, for example, reminds us that 72 percent of the poor own their own homes and that a much larger percentage own automobiles and television sets. If access to consumer goods is the measure of contentment, Podhoretz and his fellow Rightists contend, the argument for closing the inequality gap is bound to fall on deaf ears. People do not care if some are doing better than others as long as most are doing well. But the condition of the poor and more stable workers resembles less serenity than anxiety. Workers in the advanced industrial societies are instructed to work harder for less remuneration on penalty of losing more of their diminishing comparative advantages to third world labor and, in Chairman Greenspan's terms, to recognize that the scarcity of good jobs is a permanent feature of the new globalized economy. For this reason the chairman predicts workers will continue to keep their mouths shut.[21]

What is wrong with the argument against the urgency of addressing inequality and its most searing manifestation, poverty, is its failure to understand that people measure their well-being not on the living standard of an Indian peasant but according to whether their own situation is equal to the historical level of material culture—the living standard needed to enjoy a decent life within a specific economic and cultural context. In terms not of the third world, but of what it takes to live decently in America and Western Europe, talk about the poor enjoying home ownership, cars, and television sets is beside the point. In America millions of dwellings are trailers, small mobile homes, and flimsy prefabricated houses. In most instances the working poor must own their own homes because they live in areas in which rental housing is either nonexistent or offered at rents beyond their means. Many who own these structures can barely afford the mortgage, taxes, and utilities they must have to keep them afloat, let alone the cost of professional maintenance and repairs. It is not a rare occurrence for a homeowner to miss meals in order to pay the bank mortgage. Which accounts for the proliferation of soup kitchens and pantries in most major cities and some rural areas. Most of the working poor live in cities, suburbs, and rural areas where automobiles are the main conveyances; failure to own one often means people cannot get to and from their jobs and cannot shop in supermarkets, which are typically located in highway malls or shopping centers. Where there is no viable public transportation system, the car is both a necessity and, for people without money, a pain in the ass. Many drive old cars with their hearts in their mouths fearing the next breakdown, an inevitable eventuality that can result in being fired and not being able to shop or to visit friends or relatives.

As the sociologist Ron Lembo has shown, the TV offers solace in an otherwise isolated existence. For single parents in households and for women with several small kids whose partners are rarely available to help with housework and raising the children, thank God for the TV. It holds the kids' attention and offers a measure of entertainment for the adult when there is no money available to go out on weekends. It provides background noise and a constant referent, for bits of news, features, and relaxation. Like the car, in households in which books, magazines, and newspapers are largely absent the working television set is an absolute necessity—it is babysitter, friend, reminder of the larger world. Only for those who have insulated themselves from this reality is inequality not a public issue. Needless to say, under these circumstances when women are engaged in paid labor out of the home, the TV may assume an even larger place in the life of the household.[22]

The pluralist idea that virtually all Americans are middle class is among the sustaining myths of American ideology and political culture. That a rising level of consumption is financed by a generous credit system detains the neoliberal optimists not at all. As long as productivity exceeds income and inflation is thereby held in check, consumer debt will endanger neither the economy nor the gainfully employed individual who can pay the bills. Translated into plain English, if technological innovation can displace high-wage workers and they and others are willing to work in the lower productivity sectors for less, wages can be restrained and the system can hum on. Of course if workers insist on higher wages and resist the invocation to work harder and longer in order to keep their jobs and sustain their consumption levels, Chairman Greenspan promises to lower the boom by raising interest rates, thereby inducing strategic joblessness as a brake on wages.

The drumbeat that we are a virtually class-free middle-class society of individual consumers conveniently ignores the workplace as a sign of class difference; it never mentions that a growing fraction of the population is employed in temporary, contingent, and part-time jobs and that millions of others are on tenterhooks, waiting for the inevitable pink slip. For the fact is, in the American workplace almost nothing is nailed down. To achieve the "flexibility" capital requires to win the global economic race, the notion of job security is rapidly being relegated to a fond memory for perhaps a majority of the workforce. If the factory can close at any time, Wall Street banking firms can shed employees in the midst of a stock market boom, and a majority of employees of "new economy" information companies lack basic health and pension benefits and are often hired as consultants, that is, contingent workers, it may be simply a matter of time before class rhetoric, if not class analysis, returns to the public stage.[23]

2
TIME AND SPACE IN CLASS THEORY

CONDITIONS FOR CLASS FORMATION

Classes are historical, and their effects are intertwined with their historicity. Saying classes are historical means that their composition changes at every level of the social structure—ruling groups as well as subordinate groups. Classes form when they make historical difference. In one period the military is integrated into the ruling circles and, for a time, may be the dominant partner; in another it is plainly subordinate to the economic and the political directorate. For the past century, as C. Wright Mills has pointed out, the onetime cultural and political heart of the American nation—the old middle class of small manufacturers and owners of retail establishments—has been relegated to the middle levels of power.[1] Their power and influence have been even further restricted in the years following Mills's discovery in the mid-1950s. Since the late nineteenth century the leading circles of power have been constituted, in the main, by large corporations—the institutional form of capital—and the national political directorate. The political directorate is the top layer, that "class" for which politics is a vocation and that seems to remain a constant in the development of the nation-state. But the ruling circles are increasingly permeable. After World War I the top layer of the state bureaucracy as well as the politicos has played musical chairs with the commanding heights of the corporate bureaucracy, and these social formations are increasingly interchangeable.

Whether a social formation or a constellation of social formations becomes a class in the historical sense depends on whether their struggles effect a cleavage in social relations and pose a significant change in these relations at a specific time and place. "A specific time and place" indicates that class formation is contingent, even among owners of capital and other components of the ruling class.[2] Whether and which fractions of a social formation form a class and with whom depends on elements of the situated social context: relations of power, degree of mobilization, and whether a group's demands can, relatively speaking, be integrated by the prevailing power bloc. Against marxist teleology I do not hold a specific form of revolutionary transformation as a standard against which to measure whether these changes constitute the class power of hitherto subordinate groups. Thus there need be no imminent transfer of power over the machinery of the state for class formation to occur. What is required is that transformation in a key aspect of social relations be entailed by the demands of a social formation or, more commonly, of an alliance of several of them.

By "social formation" I refer not only to the economic domain but to the political and cultural domains as well. As many writing in the marxist tradition have shown, economic, political, and cultural relations are inextricably intertwined so that the isolation of one from another is always a theoretical reduction, the consequence of which is to prompt some to separate class from social movements.[3] Race relations were fundamentally altered when African Americans mounted a mass movement that, in alliance with fractions of white intellectuals, students, the progressive wing of the trade unions, and liberal organizations, succeeded in breaking down segregation in public accommodations and erasing the Jim Crow laws in the South that effectively denied them suffrage, condemned their schools to chronic underfunding, and barred them from admission to state colleges and universities. More to the point, the black freedom struggle changed everyday as well as legal relations. Despite these victories of which civil rights was an important aspect, the southern power bloc was not broken. Because Americans measure progress not mainly by income but by the accretion of social power, even as many have managed to escape poverty, at least by standards established by the federal government, blacks' economic and political position has deteriorated since the early 1970s.

From the early 1930s through the late 1960s the black freedom struggle was a movement over class formation because, if driven far enough, it could have broken the power of the alliance of white agricultural and industrial capital with the permanent political class. That it did not succeed may be attributed largely to the inability—or unwillingness—of the labor movement to organize the burgeoning industrial sector of the South. Its failure has a great deal to do with the fact that, except for a small group of left-wing unions, mainstream labor refused to address the race question, except legislatively, for most of the post–World War II era. Faced with a southern white membership that was often hostile to integration on the shop floor as well as in schools—indeed, in some places union halls were opened to defiant segregated schools—most unions contented themselves with issuing convention resolutions against Jim Crow and relied on the federal government to do the job. This policy meant that the labor movement was unable to seize the moment, as it had in the early 1930s, to spread unionism throughout the region.[4]

So historical struggles are over class formation rather than automatically being class struggles. Industrial workers in the first forty years after the turn of twentieth-century America struggled over class formation and, in a wave of organizing and protest, from 1933 to 1937 changed the face of political power and labor relations for the next two generations. The labor movement, which had been on the margins of economic and social rule, displayed social power and won the support of wide sections of the population because it embodied both the rage and hope of workers and large fractions of other social formations. But by the end of World War II it was integrated into the ruling coalition even as its position became increasingly precarious. Labor retained strong ties to the social liberal element of the political leadership, and, owing to its perceived necessity to develop a private welfare state through the labor agreement rather than through the state, was closely connected to important sections of the corporate bureaucracy. This strategic decision was a response to the fact that, with the end of the New Deal era, workers and their unions were unable to sustain momentum because, even though formally independent, they had become dependent on, and integrated with, the networks which constituted the power nexus of the liberal state. As a result, most unions isolated themselves from the militant black, women's, and youth insurgencies of the 1960s.

Women as a distinct social formation became a movement about class in the 1960s and 1970s, when its radical wing proposed a program of women's liberation that went beyond legal rights and demanded the end of the traditional domination of women by men. This broad aim was crystallized in struggles over a constellation of demands: women's right to control their own bodies, which entailed sexual freedom; permissive divorce laws; shared child rearing and housekeeping; and the right to abortion on demand.[5] The effects of this agenda reverberated in every aspect of economic, political, and cultural life. Since the high point of the movement around 1973, with the Supreme Court's decision in favor of abortion rights in *Roe v. Wade,* there has been considerable backsliding, and many issues raised initially remain unresolved. However, that everyday relations of power between men and women were crucially altered is self-evident and is indicated by the violence of the counterattack by conservatives against some of feminism's signature gains, especially abortion rights. When the liberationist wing was defeated by moderates, the women's movement was largely reduced to an interest group, mainly within the Democratic party. Its concerns shifted from addressing the social question to fighting for the inclusion of women in occupational hierarchies, elite higher education institutions, and the liberal political establishment. In fact, some of the leading figures in the early feminist movement, notably Betty Friedan, whose book *The Feminine Mystique* played an important role in making women's social oppression visible, spent much of the eighties and nineties renouncing the persistence of feminist demands for new relations of social power.

Family values ideology, embodied in such organizations as the Communitarian Network of academics and centrist politicians—which in the 1990s counted among its adherents the president and vice president of the United States—was a direct response to the new power and authority acquired by women in the final decades of the twentieth century. The success of the countermovement to feminism may be measured by the degree to which the AFL-CIO has adopted the phrase "working families" to define themselves, as if single persons, the majority of gays and lesbians who do not live in coupled households, and people who do not work for wages and salaries are excluded from the working class and the labor movement. More distressing is the absence of objections against such characterizations from within labor's ranks, which now includes millions of women. For a key point of feminism is to separate women's fate from the conjugal, heterosexual household, to assert their individuality and autonomy from male domination. Family values ideology directs women back to the home; if they are obliged to enter the wage-labor force this is seen as an economic expedient rather than a badge of independence.

To argue for the historicity of class opposes views of class and class structure as always already present in the same configuration across periods, eras, and epochs. Nor is the progressivist idea of irreversibility of history tenable. On the contrary, history-making social formations may disintegrate and revert to fragmented individuals and groups that occupy differential spaces on class maps; or in their organized expression they may maintain themselves as pressure or interest groups vis-à-vis the ruling institutions but have, at least provisionally, ceased to be historical agents. I also contest the idea, which has considerable currency among some intellectuals, that if the working class does not fulfill its revolutionary destiny as assigned to it by intellectuals we may conclude that from the perspective of history there is no working class, except in the sociological sense of strata or movements that pursue narrow economic self-interests. Some in this category attribute the end of the proletariat—an indefinite term that signifies the working class in all of its strata, especially the industrial workers—to its successes, which have led to its integration into the dominant society, often on fairly favorable terms. Others have theorized the dissolution of class into the broad concept of multitudes or the people, statements that describe the emergence of *generalized* proletarianization; on this view, in the last quarter of the twentieth century the overwhelming majority of the world's population has been reduced by the emergent transnational empire to economic and political marginality. Both tendencies are locked into a telos, an a priori that judges history by the concept rather than the reverse. According to this tendency, if the working class has not fulfilled its revolutionary task to redeem humankind from exploitation and other suffering, it has disappeared.[6]

In fact, the most commonly invoked criterion for class power, held by marxists and by conservatives like Francis Fukuyama—revolutions—rarely start out with the object of seizing political power. In 1917, badly battered Russian workers and soldiers and a fraction of the peasantry demanded "peace, bread and land" and joined liberal and revolutionary intellectuals, who dominated the opposition parties, in political struggle that resulted in a new social alignment. The old regime collapsed only after the czarist government refused to leave the war even after mass military desertions to bow to popular demands for land reform and material redistribution. When the liberal regime of Alexander Kerensky maintained its loyalty to the Allied war aims, thereby committing its conscript army to mass annihilation by superior German forces, it sealed its political fate and fell before the Bolshevik-led uprising. There was no inevitability about this chain of events. Had Kerensky left the war there might have ensued a relatively prolonged period of capitalist economic development, and the Bolsheviks would have been only one tendency among the opposition.

The possibilities for class formation were greatly enhanced by a historically developed political culture that valorized the concept of social transformation in terms of new democratic forms of popular power. In opposition to both authoritarian and modern liberal concepts of strong central state authority flanked by a weak representative assembly, during the Russian revolution of 1905 workers organized councils, the new form of social rule that it intended to bring into being. In contrast to the vertical structure of the liberal state, these were horizontal institutions of delegates elected by workers in factories. They functioned as institutions of both revolutionary action and administration, thereby abrogating the vertical model of the separation of state and civil society. Again in 1917 the reorganization of the councils, now consciously organized by the left political parties, prompted the Bolsheviks, who had achieved hegemony in the soviets (councils) in the key cities, to raise the slogans first of "Dual power" with the liberal government and, finally, "All Power to the Soviets" against the prevailing government that had been formed in the immediate aftermath of the February revolution.[7]

The events of May 1968 in France began as a protest against the Ministry of Education's refusal to grant a popular student request at the University of Paris-Nanterre for more authority over their own affairs, and the conflict was joined over the administration's rejection of coed dormitories. When in March demonstrations were staged the students were confronted by riot police, who used force to break up the protest. Within two months students had erected barricades in the streets of Paris and workers staged a general strike, paralyzing the country's economy and sending a fleeing President Charles DeGaulle abroad. In fact, the drift of the struggle toward revolutionary power may have been halted not by the state's force but, instead, within the ranks of the insurgency, chiefly by the Communists. The party and its trade union cadres hesitated on the precipice and, in an amazing failure of nerve, just when the effectiveness of the state's repressive apparatuses, whose early overreaching had helped widen the struggle, had been reduced, offered to settle the general strike for wage gains.

The May events may have been the first postscarcity uprising in modern history. The initial impetus for the protest—the spiritual poverty of contemporary life—presupposed that material want had been overcome and relegated to the margins, at least in France. If the historical task of capitalism was to deliver the (material) goods, its job was done. The May movement challenged the system's capacity to fulfill its promise of freedom. Students, traditional intellectuals, and a significant segment of the technical workers in large computer- and automation-producing enterprises joined industrial workers in a multilevel struggle against established authority. They fought under banners that varied from those of the older workers' movement—economic and social justice—to the newer cries for cultural freedom, and they made demands that recalled the programs for workers' control of the Paris Commune and the Russian Revolution. That the revolt never reached the point where the question of achieving state power was seriously entertained, even if it was posed, does not disqualify its character as a class movement. The impulse of the struggle was to bring about new relations of authority and power, a new way of life that would liberate its subjects from the thrall of an advancing consumer society and, like its American student counterparts, from the technocratic machine. At the same time in its embrace of the older sectors of society, industrial workers, it held the promise of a more generalized freedom. Students and intellectuals occupied the streets, constructed barricades made of overturned cars and debris, and used cobblestones as artillery, a weapon employed later by another movement, the Palestinian Intifada. The fervor of the movement finally extended to some industrial workplaces, where workers seized the factories, held managers captive or expelled them from the plants, and lived-in for weeks. In a few cases, they engaged in production.[8]

Whether rulers are able to integrate the opposition into the dominant power system is never determined in advance. Integration depends on the size of the social surplus available for redistribution, on acumen of the powers-that-be to undertake deficit financing of social benefits when resources are relatively scarce, but also on the capacity of the opposition to raise the ante rather than willingly settle for smaller potatoes, thereby exceeding the limits of system flexibility. These choices often go to psychological as well as political influences: do the subordinate groups fear the freedom entailed by taking responsibility for the whole society? are people prepared to resist and try to win over the armed forces and the police during demonstrations and strikes? does cynicism outweigh hope? are there alternative forms of rule in process to replace the hierarchical structures of the liberal or authoritarian state? and are the various fractions of the movement prepared to consult with each other before dealing separately with the established powers? Conversely, so-called revolutionary consciousness is almost never fully blown before the fact and may develop only in the course of struggles to achieve important but limited objectives.[9]

Perhaps the American feminist movement was an exception. Its early leadership forged a compelling theory of women as a class, although it, too, arose in the context of a multitude of struggles against the prevailing political and social powers, including the male-dominated 1960s New Left, which constituted a battlefield for the radical feminists.[10] Often the revolution is a consequence of the stubborn refusal of those in power to yield critical ground in the wake of the demands made by a determined mass movement for a measure of justice. The skirmishes within the ranks of the opposition are often dress rehearsals for larger struggles. From the relatively small field of the student, civil rights, and antiwar movements, in which women were excluded from leadership and habitually consigned to clerical, culinary, and housekeeping tasks, the radicals soon turned their attention to corporations and educational, cultural, and political institutions. While the movement was broadly inclusive of the reform-minded who wished for greater opportunities to enter the middle and upper reaches of the corporations and the professions, of politicos who wanted greater representation of women in elective office, and of trade union women fighting sexual harassment on the job, male domination of union leadership, and the gendered wage gap, it was the radical activists who gave the movement its early visibility and ideological edge. Their commitment to direct action and theoretical clarity enabled the more moderate forces to negotiate with the established powers.

Gathering strength, they were soon embroiled in a national struggle for abortion rights and confronted the liberal state with its own values: privacy, self-determination, individual autonomy. In the late 1960s feminists engaged in direct action, disrupting beauty contests, legislative hearings, and the solemnity of the streets. Even as they were excoriated by the media, feminists managed to make abortion rights a national issue. But finding the U.S. Congress obdurate in its refusal to enact legislation, some turned to the courts, a move that, in retrospect, entailed grave dangers as well as possibilities. For many who fought for abortion on demand in the early 1970s the Supreme Court decision in *Roe v. Wade* came as a shock; they had not fully estimated their own power to create divisions within the Court. At the same time the Supreme Court became a powerful tool for the integration and routinization of many sections of the movement. Would it have been better to greet *Roe v. Wade* and immediately launch a multileveled campaign for federal abortion rights legislation? Absent such a struggle, feminist groups, like many others in the 1970s and 1980s, on pragmatic grounds tended to bypass the legislative process, let alone direct action, to widen the purview of the movement's gains. The mainstream feminist leadership was fairly rapidly coopted into the Democratic Party via the formation of a Women's Political Caucus. By the end of the 1970s the primacy of struggles to transform social relations by means of education and confrontation gave way to attempts to gain political representation. Still, insofar as feminism changed the everyday lives of men as well as women it signaled a victory for class power.

NARRATIVES OF CLASS

Class formation is usually not a consequence of decisions of the main actors. Often actors think they are doing something other than vying for power. Grounded in an adversarial political culture revolutionary awareness typically arises after the fact, a retrospective summing up by the ideologists and by the activists of what actually occurred during the insurgency. In turn, once the mass action has been proclaimed to have been a proletarian or democratic revolution, these interpretations tend to become a social force if they are incorporated into ritual and public education and are mythologized in the stories that participants tell to others, especially the young. For this reason the importance of who controls historical narratives cannot be underestimated. They are the main components of political culture, which conditions the character and scope of subsequent struggles. In this respect it may be argued that the virtual absence of a story about the struggle for class formation of the workers' movements of the twentieth century in popular culture as well as in institutional knowledge was a major factor in the decline of organized labor after the 1960s, when unions and their gains came under fierce attack and were unable to mount an effective counterforce.

The prevailing political culture also conditions the main narratives about the formation of the American nation, which also have historicity. Among the most famous stories in American history are the Revolution against British colonial rule and the Civil War. Who tells the story often has great influence on contemporary politics as well as on how tradition is assimilated. One can trace the transformation of these nation-building narratives in different historical moments. In the midst of conservative political hegemony in recent years the American Revolution has been recoded as the War of Independence, a formulation that revises the meaning of the event. The radicalism of the revolution is denied in favor of an account that portrays it as many of those on the Right of the revolution saw it. Even some historians who proclaim its radicalism obscure or obliterate the social struggles that occurred within the ranks of the revolutionists.[11] Almost never do the historians, even those who emphasize the revolution and its democratic character, discuss the Anti-Federalists, who, on democratic grounds, opposed the separation of powers, especially the sovereignty of the courts as a third branch of government. This important opposition also objected to the bicameral system and a national bank. Nor is the social composition of the two main antagonists at the Constitutional Convention delineated. In sum, the story is told from the standpoint of the victors. Similarly, the main achievement of the Civil War, the abolition of slavery, is sometimes narrated as The War between the States and the abrogation of states' rights by the federal government. In this respect the South's appropriation of the principle of local autonomy enunciated by the Federalists was used to deny blacks civil rights but was also seized upon by its champions to strengthen centralization.

Conversely, historians of the Progressive Era, notably Charles Beard, narrated the Civil War as the second, unfinished democratic revolution, placing the struggle against slavery and other aspects of the "labor question" at the center of the conflict.[12] Another example: during the Progressive Era historians like Beard and Parker Moon—whose textbook was widely used until World War II—treated the Spanish-American War of 1898 as the inaugural conflict of American imperialism. Beard was a founder of the Anti-Imperialist League, which fought U.S. economic, military, and political intervention abroad. A recent American history high school textbook mandated in New York State substitutes the term *empire* for *imperialism* and provides a detailed account of the differing motivations for the war and its aftermath. But another tells the story as an episode in America's historic neoreligious mission to save heathens and otherwise oppressed people—in this case Latin America—from the tyrannical colonial rule of Spain.[13]

In the popular press and magazines as well as in schools the effect of the way the story is told is to marginalize, if not entirely discount, struggles over class. Labor's story rates barely a few pages in American history textbooks. A major school text of the 1990s, *America Past and Present,* devotes exactly 12 of its 1,081 pages to work, "labor unrest," and labor unions. Only 2 pages cover the rise of the industrial union movement of the 1930s and then credits labor leaders, particularly John L. Lewis, Phillip Murray, a Lewis lieutenant and chair of the Steelworkers' Organizing Committee, and Walter Reuther of the United Auto Workers rather than the New Deal—or the workers themselves—with having achieved the remarkable result of enrolling five million new union members. The remaining 10 pages are devoted to labor struggles in the nineteenth century. That the authors give labor itself some recognition for these gains is unusual in this genre of institutional storytelling; most attribute the rise of unions in mass production industries to Franklin Roosevelt and the New Deal. Similarly, the first and second waves of feminism are given short shrift. The struggle for abortion rights—the cutting edge of second-wave feminism—and the gay liberation movement receive dutiful notice in this text, but it includes little detail and analysis of their social and political significance. Yet in almost every other respect, after twenty-five years of an outpouring of revisionist American history—history as the story of struggles of ordinary people as well as of economic and political elites—even those accounts that are more consistent with the progressive tradition privilege history from above.[14]

Despite its exclusions and occlusions the virtue of history writing is that time and social changes or shifts are immanent to its discourse. In periods when profound economic, political, and cultural crises are not a topic of discussion and a struggle in the public sphere, social theorists typically privilege social space over social time and refer to classes as locations in the social hierarchy. In these circumstances classes are no longer taken as collective historical actors but are portrayed as aggregations of individuals and groups who are members of differentiated social strata. Social theory tends to freeze time and instead defines classes in terms of status groups or strata. In the definition of the twentieth century's leading functionalist theorist of social stratification, Talcott Parsons, "Only insofar as the differentiations inherent in our occupational structure, with its differential relations of the exchange system and to property, remuneration, etc., have become ramified out into a system of strata, which involve differentiations of family living based largely on income, standard of life and the style of life and the impact of these on the opportunities available to the younger generation."[15]

Parsons equates strata with the "class system" with almost no temporal reference. In the functionalist description catalogues of occupational structure replace relations of ownership and control over productive property; income plays a large role in situating these strata as a determinant of standard of living; and lifestyle becomes a component in the designation of class distinctions. In a grid in which income plays the decisive role in differentiating social groups the working class disappears and is replaced by the category lower class, which means the working poor and the unemployed. Since income obfuscates the profound insecurity and subordination of industrial and service labor in the labor process, stratification theory constructs a huge middle class that includes anyone above the poverty line and below those who are considered upper class or wealthy. Missing in this mode of analysis is the concept of class *power.* Many from marxist and nonmarxist persuasions stipulate the power of the ruling class over economic, political, and ideological relations, but, in the practical activity engage in the same work of social cartography—their work is making maps—even if their maps differ in details. What is often supposedly marxist or radical about these maps is that, unlike mainstream sociology, interlocking networks between the political and economic directorates are revealed, which explicitly or tacitly constitute a critique of the traditional liberal separation of corporate power and the state. But both become wedded to classification and draw up charts that show where social groups are placed in atemporal social grids.[16]

Curiously the scientific marxists—those that want to reconcile marxist concepts with social scientific empirical methodologies—tend to converge with the functionalists in two respects: they draw no correlations of class membership with social and political activity; and have accepted the notion that the subject of class studies is methodological individuals. Consistent with positivism, this school abjures concepts that are not subject to measurement. Eric Olin Wright, a leading marxist sociologist of the scientific functionalist bent, has gone so far as to attempt to measure class consciousness by generating categories that may be held as a standard: whether individuals fit these categories and share certain views and patterns of behavior. His social statics employs traditional sociological procedures such as surveys, interviews, and regression charts. Like Parsons, Wright takes class and class consciousness as facts that, while subject to alteration by external influences, have a thinglike existence.[17]

Some recent social theory tries to break the traditional separation of economic and cultural relations and insists that social space is structured by both. Refusing marxist teleology and its subordination of superstructure to economic infrastructure, Pierre Bourdieu conceives of class as proceeding from two principal forms of capital, material and cultural, although he names two others that have subordinate significance, social capital and symbolic capital.[18] While privileging economic capital, he insists that each is an objective determinant of status, class affiliation, and class struggles. For him the primary qualification of class membership, and the determinant of "social powers," is that social groups share conditions of social existence, which presupposes that they have roughly equal amounts of economic and cultural capital.[19] Faulting marxism for ignoring the cultural and symbolic dimensions of everyday practice, Bourdieu insists on the objectivity of the map of "multidimensional social space." He also opposes the onesidedness of functionalists. Bourdieu argues,

> If most of those who carry out empirical research are often led to accept, implicitly or explicitly, a theory which reduces the classes to simple ranked but non-antagonistic strata, this is above all because the very logic of their practice leads them to ignore what is objectively inscribed in every distribution, what has been won in previous battles and can be invested in subsequent battles; it expresses a

> state of the power relation between the classes or, more precisely, of the power of the possession of rare goods, and for the specifically political power over the distribution or redistribution of profit.[20]

The signal virtue of Bourdieu's conception of class is his insistence on the importance of "what has been won in previous battles" for accounting for the current "distribution" and as a basis for predicting what may be won in the future. For Bourdieu, class struggles are symbolic—over signs as much as over the appropriation of economic goods; they involve struggles over value as much as quantity, over lifestyle as well as over material distribution. Social groups are engaged in playing the game to determine how such practices as speech patterns, fashion, and nutritional norms are decided, and what counts as high culture and popular, or low, culture. Tastes in art, fashion, and nutrition—the most ubiquitous signs of class—are, from the standpoint of the accumulation of symbolic capital, as important as economic capital. By broadening the concept of capital to cultural and symbolic goods, Bourdieu has partially resolved the problematic distinction between economic infrastructure and the cultural and symbolic superstructure.

Bourdieu's most widely acknowledged contribution to social theory is his articulation of cultural capital in the modern age with the attainment of educational credentials. Appropriating Louis Althusser's declaration—but only implicitly—that schools are the premier "ideological state apparatus" because they have assumed primacy in the reproduction of class relations, he goes a step further to argue that education is the path to the achievement of class distinction:

> The different forms of capital, the possession of which defines class membership and the distribution of which determines position in the power relations constituting the field of power and also determines the strategies available for use in these struggles—"birth" "fortune" and "talent" in a past age, now economic capital and educational capital—are *simultaneously instruments of power* and stakes in the struggle for power; they are unequally powerful in real terms and unequally recognized as legitimate principles of authority or signs of distinction, at different moments and, of course, by the different fractions. The definition of the hierarchy between fractions or, which amounts to the same thing, the definition of the legitimatizing hierarchical principles, i.e. the legitimate instruments and stakes of the struggle is itself a stake in struggles between the factions.[21]

This is one of the most far-reaching and original theories of class formation in contemporary social science, one that ranges between the economic and cultural spheres and is highly inventive and philosophically informed. Bourdieu recognizes that struggles over appropriation constitute and presuppose the reified fixity of class maps, even if the practice of the mapmakers elides discussion of these struggles. The system's power relies on its capacity to make space, not only for those who possess the lion's share of material and cultural capital, but also for subaltern class actors to struggle over the appropriation of material and symbolic goods. Thus social space is produced by these struggles, and Bourdieu is among the few theorists who have introduced the notion of horizontal as well as vertical social space. Space is striated so that the multiplicity of positions can be described. But unlike Henri Lefebvre, whose work, in this respect, is almost entirely ignored by Bourdieu, the question of time is raised within a fairly restricted frame: in concert with Weber the system remains an internally differentiated constant in the spatiotemporal matrix.[22]

Despite its many valuable discoveries and insights, Bourdieu's theory remains a deft determinism inherited from his mentor, the anthropologist Claude Lévi-Strauss; and from Max Weber's theory of rationalization. His concepts of habitus—"the making of virtue out of necessity"—that becomes the working class's rationale for its own relative deprivation and of the "cultural arbitrary" and "symbolic violence" in schools where students are measured—and measure themselves—against a curriculum and level of performance not of their own making effectively reproduce the system of antagonistic difference and are ways the "social powers" place system boundaries on class action. Although recognizing that movement occurs as a result of the uncertainty of these processes, Bourdieu privileges the limits over their indeterminacy. However effectively social groups play the game its rules are always already given and make sure that the outcome will not disturb the "balance sheet."[23]

Bourdieu's analysis of the everyday life dynamics of the otherwise autopoeteic system of late capitalist domination is both rich and suggestive. But its conception of temporality never segues into history, except as incremental shift and oscillation. Thus, against his own polemic against objectivism and his insistence on a "plurality of visions" of social reality, the logic of his own theoretical and empirical practice is folded into scientific objectivism; and by invoking the common denominator of capital it has reasserted the primacy of the economic, even if only in the last instance. Lacking a vision of how social formations make history, insofar as its most innovative contribution, the concept of cultural capital, allows us to observe the operation of class in various institutional sites, especially education and art, Bourdieu's class theory may be considered a sophisticated update of the hidden variables of social domination.[24]

Here I offer a class theory which presupposes that space is produced by the activity of social formations and as a function of time. Therefore it distinguishes itself from the two main tendencies in twentieth-century social mapping: those who try to squeeze historically generated social groups such as the managerial, scientific, and technical strata into an otherwise immobile social structure determined by relations of ownership and control of the means of material production; and system functionalists, who map social groups on to a hierarchically arranged grid according to status and occupation. Bourdieu's class theory is surely a partial exception to the binaries of contemporary social thought. It offers a middle ground between the traditional marxist perspective of class as a relation of social formations to the ownership of productive property and the Weberian theory of stratification, modified by Parsons and others, but is consistent with the contemporary focus on how space is organized. Although adhering to ostensibly different theoretical paradigms, these varieties of social theory have abandoned concepts of social time as a fundamental theoretical framework. When time is factored into the picture painted by all three major tendencies of the modern class theory, it appears as a function of space. In both variants of social cartography the broad contour is always already given. The difference is only how the given is portrayed.

I argue as well for sundering the traditional sociological distinction between class and social movement, a distinction that presupposes the social statics of both camps of positivist class theory. Social movements change life by transforming some fundamental aspect of social relations.[25] Thus social movements are not to be confused with the activity of many groups to make gains within the existing power situation without disturbing it. The efforts of blacks to gain access to colleges and universities, of women to enter professional and managerial ranks, of parents to improve existing schools without changing the curriculum, educational ideology, or the administrative authority within which they operate are not, by this conception, social movements. Similarly, residents' who fight to halt the construction of a mall or supermarket in their neighborhood are not forming a social movement unless their demands become part of a larger struggle to change the shape of real estate development itself and thereby alter economic relations and produce new social space. It is not that class movements presuppose social movements.[26] Genuine social movements are struggles over class formation when they pose new questions concerning the conduct of institutional and everyday life and entail new arrangements. This is not to deny the importance of justice movements; they may or may not turn into class movements, depending on the response of those in power and the networks the justice movements build. Thus New York tenants' organizations after the turn of the twentieth century engaged in struggles over class in the vital sector of housing. They forged close alliances with radical parties and trade unions and, after years of rent strikes, demonstrations, and legislative lobbying, won a fairly strong rent control law that effectively changed the living conditions of millions, changed the face of the city's real estate industry, and reduced the power of landlords over city politics for nearly a half century.[27]

This is the distinction between demands for justice, which presuppose entry has been denied an aggrieved group, or interlopers threatening to change an aspect of current social arrangements, and change that entails a new configuration of the power situation. I understand power in three principal dimensions: who constructs the rules of inclusion and exclusion in institutional and social life; who tells the story of past and present, what Antonio Gramsci calls common sense; and who has power to define the future. This conception of power incorporates the proposals of the Critical Theory of the Frankfurt School and of Michel Foucault, both of which, in different ways, insist on the power/knowledge nexus. But insofar as social relations are objectified in material production, in the practices of everyday life, and in institutions such as law, corporations, religious organizations, and labor unions, this understanding of power differs from the tendency of postmodern social theory to replace class with social movements, obliterate concepts of social structure, and displace social relations to discourse such as social narratives.[28] While the "linguistic turn" in social theory has served to remind us that power often entails specifying the mechanisms by which the narrative of the past is told, even these crucial discursive practices are often countervailed by the material practices of those who seek to alter present and future space/time. The political and cultural unconscious can be articulated only retrospectively.[29]

NEW MIDDLE CLASS, NEW WORKING CLASS?

The rise of a veritable army of the so-called new middle class of managers and professional and technical employees posed the most serious challenge to conventional class theory in the twentieth century. The designation "new middle class" signified that, unlike the old middle class of small producers, independent professionals, and merchants, they are salaried.[30] Social scientists have tried to designate the space of their location in the configuration of social maps and to assess their political and social significance, especially in relation to the modern corporate bureaucracy and to the industrial and service working class. Since the end of World War I much research about social class has revolved around these exercises in social cartography. Except for the new categories of knowledge producers, class theory is largely confined to its spatial dimension. Rarely do those within conventional social science on the theoretical side of class studies consider the classic question: how has history been affected by changes in social structure that might have been brought about by new productive forces, new patterns of culture, new political arrangements? And under what conditions do these changes influence the emergence of new social actors who, in pursuit of their own ends, may unintentionally affect the shape of the present and future and produce new perspectives on the past as well? They are content to take snapshots of social structure and, unlike Weber, who understood perfectly the historicity of class and class struggles, tend to extrapolate from these pictures a definitive statement about class and status.

Finding that the task defies marxist orthodoxy, Wright has invented the concept of "contradictory class locations" to understand the position of the new knowledge strata in the system of social production. Apart from some speculative comments, absent in his calculations is an analysis of what, as a consequence of this spatial designation, their historical practice is. In fact, Wright avoids the problem of their class membership by answering, they are both middle class insofar as they often direct the work of subordinates and working class because they work for salaries and have only limited autonomy in the performance of their work. In any case, the position of the knowledge workers cannot be determined in advance. They will engage and already are engaging in struggles over their class location, and the outcome is indeterminate from the perspective of the map.[31]

On the other hand, Parsons is refreshingly blunt: "For the functional basis of the phenomenon of stratification it is necessary to analyze the problem of integrating and ordering social relationships within a social system. Some set of norms of superiority and inferiority is an inherent need of every social system. There is immense variation but this is a constant point of reference. Such a patterning or ordering is the stratification system of society." Thus since hierarchy is inevitable the specific denotative features of the stratification system are "variations" of historically wrought shifts that will inevitably be integrated by the cultural system. Some in the marxist camp might disagree with Parsons's judgments, but since their eyes have been diverted from history as well—except in the teleological sense—their practice differs little from functionalism. They, too, have become ensnared by the calculus of order and of system integration.[32]

Unlike the British and American marxist debates, which are more in sync with mainstream social science as defined by Parsons's very deliberate mutation of classes into strata, during the 1960s and early 1970s the debate about the new class within French marxism was highly historical. It was directed to the maps but only as a prelude to what the emergence of qualified labor as a major productive force might signify for the shape of political struggles and for the way in which production relations would be construed. Nicos Poulantzas and Serge Mallet debated the social position of the new knowledge class: whether, despite their salaried status, they are members of a "new petty bourgeoisie"—Poulantzas's position—or constitute a new working class, Mallet and André Gorz's view. What was at stake in these discussions was the potential of the new knowledge producers for becoming a class in radical chains and whether they were able to enter the historical stage as political actors. According to Gorz and Mallet, in advanced technological sectors, where scientific and technical knowledge has replaced manual labor as the main productive force, they have been gradually deprived of control over their work even though they are qualified and are often called upon to run the production system. This contradiction may compel them to contest the authority of management and the power of capital to construe the workplace, where knowledge has become the main productive force.[33]

In Tony Negri's terms, the mass worker—the object of the old mass production technology—has been replaced by the socialized worker, who, having acquired schooling in the principles and operation of the new technologies of automation and cybernation, has been able to overcome the divisive effects of the Taylorist production regime. Owing to her or his qualification, the new worker "can not be ordered about in the same way as before" even though her indifference to the work itself remains "but has reached a new level."[34] While Mallet and Gorz were proponents of workers' control over production, Negri's thesis was that the new socialized worker might become the linchpin of the "refusal to work," the slogan advanced among Italian autoworkers in the Hot Autumn of 1969. Yet their theoretical conclusion was strikingly similar. The new problematic of the capitalist workplace is struggles over the question of the autonomy of qualified workers in the labor process rather than the condition of abjection shared by traditional industrial workers in rapidly shrinking factories in technologically advanced sites. It is the engineers who are the agents of this shrinkage even if they are not really in power. Theory is compelled to see the possibilities for political practice among those without whom the production machine would grind to a halt—the possessors of cultural and symbolic capital who engage in immaterial labor, but with material consequences.

THREE AXIOMS OF CLASS THEORY

The first framing axiom of the class theory proposed here is the primacy of social time over social space; spatial arrangements are sedimented outcomes of struggles over class formation and, since social time is not irreversible, are marked by contingency. Therefore while class maps are valuable tools of identification in a specific historical conjunction, if taken as the substance of theory they conceal more than they reveal. The task of theory is to render an account of social transformations as well as of social integration, but the concept of transformation should be specified in relation to shifts or oscillations—the kind Bourdieu identifies as the fruits of struggle—as well as to the ambiguous term *change*. In this connection I want to call attention to the genuine transformations that occurred in the United States in the 1960s in musical, fashion, and nutritional tastes, transformations that in the past thirty years have spread throughout the postcolonial as well as the advanced capitalist nations. Bourdieu's concept of distinction is necessary but not sufficient to understand the profundity of what has occurred. What was termed "youth" culture—in musical and fashion terms a hybrid of African American music and the generational experience of late capitalist cultural impoverishment—redefined the rules of the game of cultural capital accumulation. Traditional domains of high culture, notably classical music and painting, have all but lost their aesthetic efficacy, their audience (social capital), and much of their economic base. Although these changes do not signify the disappearance of these forms, their social position has been undermined. The loss of patronage is not confined to traditional moneyed groups. Recent generations of intellectuals, once a stalwart component of the audience for these domains, have deserted them. Young academics and independent intellectuals typically know little or nothing of these forms; artists do not train in them or gravitate to them. Without a new generation of producers, performers, and audience they may just barely survive but will have lost much of their luster.

My second framing axiom is that social integration is the result of a process of struggle and presupposes disintegration of the prior social arrangements, a process that is a theoretical as much as an empirical question. Whether integration into the prevailing system of power occurs or whether the warring parties have succeeded only in living together in an unstable truce is an empirical question and cannot be determined in advance. In almost all instances integration presupposes that the ruling formation has granted substantial concessions to the subordinate classes as the price of social peace. The question to be investigated is, Do these periods of calm constitute integration, signaled by the loyalty and complicity of the subordinated groups within dominant relations? or is the relative silence of the subalterns a product of fear and an unquiet acknowledgment of the superior force of the prevailing power? If the latter, one should expect the truce to be sundered under conditions in which capital can no longer acquiesce to labor's and other social formations' conditions for social peace and undertakes an offensive against the informal social compact, including the money wage and the social wage (the welfare state package of benefits). Here, labor may include those who are culturally coded by gender, racial, and professional identities, as well as industrial and service occupations. The labor question embraces both wage labor and household labor and has political and cultural dimensions as well as economic specification. In this respect war functions as an indefinite postponement of the reckoning, for it calls the whole nation to sacrifice, and, for a time, class combat may be suppressed by force or by consent.

I use the term "subaltern" to designate not only economically abject or exploited social groups but all those who, at different levels of occupation and income, share relative economic, political, and social powerlessness. Needless to say, those who have been deprived of the ability to control their lives are not equal in terms of their potential for exercising power in the public sphere. Some social groups may possess the social location for class formation but lack the conditions necessary to conduct struggles over class. Marx made this point about the French peasantry:

> The small peasants form a vast mass, the members of which live in similar conditions, but without entering the manifold relations with one another. Their mode of production isolates them from one another, instead of bringing them into mutual intercourse. The isolation is increased by France's bad means of communication and by the poverty of the peasants. Their field of production, the small holding, admits of no division of labor in its cultivation, an application of science and, therefore the multiplicity of development, no diversity of talents, no wealth of social relationships.[35]

Thus class formation requires that people enter into "manifold relations with one another" and that they have the means of communication to form a "unity." Marx sets forth the conditions for class formation:

> In so far as millions of families live under economic conditions of existence that divide their mode of life, their interests and their culture from those of other classes, and put them in hostile contrast to the latter, they form a class. In so far as there is merely a local interconnection among these small peasants, and the identity of their interests begets no unity, no national union and no political organization, they do not form a class. They cannot represent themselves, they must be represented. Their representative must at the same time appear as their master, as an authority over them, as an unlimited governmental power that protects them against other classes, and sends them the rain and the sunshine from above.[36]

In this conception the central criterion for class formation is the capacity of a social formation or a constellation of them for self-organization and self-representation. And they must not only share common interests but have generated a culture and community of their own. While in this connection Bourdieu is right to have criticized marxism for failing to theorize the horizontal link between culture and economic interests, this connection was already suggested by Marx, especially in his several works on historical events in the nineteenth century. Nevertheless, capacity does not signal automatically that self-formation will occur. If the ruling groups remain imprisoned in the language of their presumed sovereignty and in their perception that the demands of the subaltern have exceeded the boundaries of the tacit social contract, which presupposes that the subordinate groups are still unable to organize into a unity and cannot represent themselves, they may commit, and sometimes have committed, a historically disastrous mistake.

Elsewhere in the same text Marx declares, "The social revolution cannot draw its poetry from the past, but only from the future."[37] Not so fast. I have already argued that because history is written by the victors narratives of the past powerfully shape the common sense of the present. The cultural and political opposition is compelled to retell the stories if it hopes to discard the ideological baggage loaded on by current rulers. But there is another reason to qualify Marx's statement of revolutionary futurity. Walter Benjamin has reminded us that every current generation must redeem the unfinished tasks left by the past. And the danger of losing sight of these tasks must be recognized: "For every image of the past that is not recognized by the present as one of its own concerns threatens to disappear irretrievably."[38]

Thus I propose a shift in the concept of class from a cleavage based exclusively on relations of ownership of capital, that is, of productive property, and the correlative idea that the core classes were arrayed on the basis of productive labor—that which produces surplus value—to relations of power in all of its domains, including the power to construct historical memory. With Marx I hold that the empirical question is whether the class-in-formation can organize and represent itself and make demands on the system that arrays them in "hostile contrast" to it. And because we can never know the history "as it really was," it must convincingly and selectively appropriate images that it can place on the table of contemporary politics and culture. But we must also take our poetry from the future and not remain chained to the poetry of the nineteenth and first half of the twentieth centuries. Thus I propose to shift the basis for the cleavage from an exclusive focus on capital possession, whatever its form. The axis of power/powerlessness widens the understanding of the base of subalternity to those who may perform "unproductive" labor within the traditional marxist frame of reference and those who do not enter the wage-labor system at all.[39] This is not merely an opportunistic broadening of the concept of potential class formation. It corresponds to two somewhat contradictory phenomena. The historical emergence of a huge social surplus in industrially advanced capitalist societies, which permits a considerable fraction of the population to live outside the wage-labor system, at least for a substantial period of their adult lives. Many are marginals, hippies, freelance artists and writers, and graduate students who never enter the professional or academic workforces except as temporary, part-time workers. Rather than seeking normal, full-time employment in bureaucratic, commercial, or industrial workplaces they prefer to take jobs as office temps or find niches that do not require them to keep their nose to the grindstone, to show up to the job at an appointed hour, or to work for fifty weeks out of the year. On the other hand, the spread of the commodity form makes necessary the entrance of women into the wage-labor force, most in low-wage service and administrative occupations. But in contrast to technical distinctions between productive and unproductive labor it may be argued that the vast expansion of the tertiary sector corresponds to the commodification of everyday existence; life is increasingly about buying and selling, and those involved in the sales and distribution efforts are engaged in the reproduction of both consumption and production.

Economic and political power is wielded at many levels. At the commanding heights the base of those who wield economic, political, and social power has narrowed within the national framework. Since World War II we have witnessed a new form of global capitalism in which the partnership between transnational corporations and nation-states constitutes economic and political power. But it broadens the conception of the ruling groups to a global perspective because the organization of economic institutions in transnational corporations has enormous implications for cross-national class formation. And the traditional idea that even if economic relations are global, culture remains local is now in question. What counts as cultural power is not the same as it was before the 1960s. It may be argued that while we may stipulate that culture is capital in two senses, for individuals, and has become a major source of economic capital accumulation, the power to shape cultural goods remains in contention between the producers and their audiences and those who own the means of production of cultural capital. In this connection we are in the midst of a great transformation in international economic relations; the export of culture as commodity competes with the export of other forms of capital. The phrase "the media are American" connotes relations of dominance in this new sphere.

In the liberal democracies of the United States and Western Europe, many intellectual and manual workers, through self-organization into labor unions and professional associations, have won a voice in determining their conditions of labor as well as their housing, education, and public and private consumption. A growing minority are still consigned to a situation of complete abjectness, and their ranks swell or diminish according to the level of social struggles they and others have won or lost. These gains expressed themselves at every level of society and, for more than a quarter century, attenuated and contained what capital could achieve. But since 1970, when global capital and the political classes of the constellation of nation-states of the economically developed world fought a largely successful battle to restructure economic and political power, the once-confident assumption that gains in the postwar social wage were permanent features of the social map has been severely tested, if not refuted. The power shift was undertaken to counter the impressive gains made by labor movements since World War II in money and social wages as well as their ability, through job actions, strikes, and everyday, mostly invisible sabotage within the labor process, to limit the power of capital to determine many aspects of production in the workplace. The deterritorialization of production and the consequent steep job losses that accompanied it disciplined a once-defiant labor force; capital regained much of its control over the labor process and proceeded rapidly to increase productivity through the introduction of automation and computer-mediated technologies. A succession of conservative governments adopted policies that weakened the social wage and resulted in a decline of the labor movements and consequently of living standards for large sections of the population.

In many countries unions lost members, but, because some were affiliated to Labor, Social-Democratic, and social liberal parties, their power was undermined by their compliance with some of the policies of the Center-Left as well as the ostensible Right. They became, in effect, dependent variables in the economic and social system of power. In other words, while ownership of productive property remains one of its key elements, power relations in the state and everyday practices are outcomes of struggles that are, in turn, indeterminate from the perspective of the relations of production. Capital and other powerful forces are not fated to win. To be sure, owing to the weight of the power of owners and top managers of large-scale productive property and, in the case of men, tradition, established power enjoys the advantage. The ability of the ruling groups to impose their domination depends to a large degree on whether an alliance of differentially situated social groups emerges to oppose them. Moreover, in every era only some sectors of capital are in a position to become winners. Others may lose out, even disappear, or, in some cases, especially smallholders, join the alliance.

Capitalist power is constituted by an increasingly integrated network of transnational corporations and coordinating institutions such as the WB and IMF, among others, which, however, reproduces itself within the political and cultural contours of the nation-state. The power relations within the global network are constantly shifting, and this is a component of every national context. In turn, since the local context remains the field within which transnational powers must play, mobilized national and regional social groups mediate the extent to which these institutions prevail or are required to modify their interventions. These arrangements are not the same as the power frameworks of earlier twentieth-century capitalism, which, despite international cartelization, were constructed within the confines of the nation-state. While the composition of the leading bodies of the WB, IMF, and WTO reflects the finance ministers and financial leaders of the major industrialized nations, in which the United States plays the leading role, there are struggles within fractions of capital and within nations over their direction. The new configuration of capitalism's commanding heights has, like previous arrangements, resulted in inclusions and exclusions that change the actors and restructure the cleavages within and between them.[40]

Class theory lacks an account of the historicity of social classes and of the spatial and temporal contexts within which they emerge and change. But theory also lacks reflexivity and therefore does not acknowledge its own historicity. Theory rarely tries to account for its own predispositions in relation to the historically conditioned situations that produced them. Thus my third axiom is that when widely disseminated among intellectuals and the underlying population, class theory (and social theory generally, which becomes a force in history) must account for itself. I propose to understand class in terms of its historical specificity and try to account for the changes in the struggles over class, which may help us comprehend theory's shift in the twentieth century from diachronic to synchronic frameworks (from time to space). If we abjure the logic of monocausality, that is, the idea that we may explain *b* by reference to *a* as a single causal agent, we must trace a complex, although interlinked, series of historical developments that form the context within which many of our ideas about the social world, including class relations, have been forged in the twentieth century: the contradictory effects of World War I; revolution and counterrevolution; economic crisis and relative economic stabilization; in the United States, major shifts in both economic and political power; the emergence of what social theorists termed consumer society; the virtual collapse of the labor movement in the 1920s and the rise of labor radicalism; and the counterintuitive blossoming of an adversarial artistic and bohemian culture.

Because our ideas and thought systems are inevitably intertwined with the social and historical contexts within which they are produced, I do not invoke the notion of false consciousness to denote how theory represents class relations. Although some theorists are politically motivated in constructing their thought systems—marxists seek to find an increasingly two-class model, liberals try to see classes and power relations as a plurality of forces—these standpoints do not always determine the product. More reasonably, theorists are ensconced in their own times. What Raymond Williams terms the "structure of feeling"—which is embedded in everyday life and in the transformations of social relations—often overcomes intellectual predispositions. Therefore it is necessary to discern the salient influences on that feeling-structure in order to see how certain theories displaced others. This is, in the main, a retrospective evaluation that may yield only a schematic description. Yet without such explorations thought seems to follow thought, and theory is constructed as the history of internal, hermetically sealed ideas and their influence on each other. Ideas do not have an independent history; while intellectual influences are important, they germinate, reach maturity, and have influence only under certain social circumstances. They both describe their knowledge-objects and they can be grasped in relation to their historicity.[41]

3

HISTORY AND CLASS THEORY

Twentieth-century American history is replete with struggles over class formation: to overcome divisions between black and white, native and foreign born, men and women; to create a workers' movement independent of capital, that is, with its own ideological and political institutions as well as its own organizations at the workplace; and to form an alliance for class power among social movements in civil society. Between the 1930s and the early 1950s, the insurgent labor movement seemed to hold the key to class formation. Then as now the questions were whether struggles such as those between immigrant and native-born, black and white, men and women could be addressed within the framework of a united class movement. Why and how this unity was not achieved is one of the great narratives of this century. These struggles about class remain on the political agenda of the twenty-first century.

Propelled by insurgent socialist and populist movements, the idea that class and class struggle structured society enjoyed substantial legitimacy until World War I. But the 1920s marked a partial reversal of this concept because social relations underwent a massive shift. This was the outcome of a new set of arrangements in world politics, the emergence of "Fordism," which generated a new era of mass consumer society, and a transformation in the character of social and political rule from primary reliance on force to that of consent, of which consumerism was a major aspect. In discussing the use of force, I refer not to whether citizenship rights are extended to the majority of the adult population but to whether in the workplace and civil society citizens can exercise free speech without repression by employers, police, courts, and the criminal justice system. While both workers' speech and radical speech were severely abrogated by the state throughout the twenties and early thirties, as the labor movement grew persuasion gained an equal place with force in reproducing power relations.

Both force and consent are in constant play in struggles over class formation: witness the so-called McCarthy period in post–World War II America, the South's violent reaction to the victories of the Black Freedom movement in the first half of the 1960s, and the mass roundup of Middle Eastern immigrants after the events of September 11, 2001. In the aftermath of the terrorist destruction of the World Trade Center, with the passage of the Patriot Act, civil liberties are under increased attack. But it would be premature to argue that consent has been overwhelmed by repression. In the United States consent still plays the dominant role in securing its popular legitimacy, although popular participation in civil society as well as in the political system, the hallmark of a healthy democracy, is on the wane.

Although the United States, unlike Europe, Asia, and Latin America, was never threatened with revolutionary upheaval, nevertheless, during the first four decades of the twentieth century it underwent a shift in the economic and political temper. In the 1930s and 1940s the industrial union movement waged several monumental wars for class power. While the movement tended to locate the good life within, not outside, the prevailing capitalist system, the force of mass unionism and the rebirth of ideological radicalism were sufficient to alter the very concept of the state and to force capital to yield, to a considerable extent, to its demands for redistributive justice. In some ways the American struggle was more fierce and, at least initially, more successful than that of its contemporary West European counterparts. While no mass socialist movement emerged from the many strikes, marches, and demonstrations that attended the entry of unskilled and skilled industrial labor onto the political and economic stage after 1934, if capital had hopes that it could survive the Great Depression unchallenged by a mass workers' movement, these were dashed by the largest and most militant basic industry organizing drives in American history. If auto, steel, and electrical production were the measure of advanced capitalism, the formation of mass industrial unions was an indication of the strength and maturity of a hitherto defeated and dispirited working class. But unions and other workers' organizations mutated into staid institutions that shared in the fruits of America's emerging dominance of global economic and military relations. Why did they remain both in, and of, capitalist society rather than emerging as an independent political force in national life? And why did labor remain in the thrall of the imagined community of the nation-state?[1]

THE REVOLUTION DELAYED

The twenty years between the end of World War I and the outbreak of World War II began as an apparent vindication of the proposition that deepening economic crisis and its displacement in the form of war would result in a worldwide revolutionary surge led by the working classes of the most industrially developed capitalist countries. But by World War II, in the wake of a massive victory by the most militant forces of the Right, this classical historical prediction had largely been discredited. While the rise of fascism was the most visible expression of the counterrevolutionary trend, the centralization of state institutions in democratic capitalist countries as well as in the Soviet Union called into question the transformative role of the working class.

The unparalleled destruction visited upon Europe by the world war, which left twenty million dead, most of them civilians, led many intellectuals and socialists to conclude that capitalism was chronically incapable of resolving its own contradictions and that a new Age of Revolution had finally arrived. For the revolutionary Left the war was a powerful sign that the choice before humankind was socialism or barbarism. In 1916 Lenin suggested the "general crisis of capitalism" in the contemporary period took the form of global war as much as economic depression. He predicted revolutions would first break out in the defeated countries and soon spread everywhere. Indeed, even before the armistice was signed ending the war, the humiliating defeat of Russia by the Germans a year earlier, combined with the state's paralysis, led to a revolutionary surge that ended in the conquest of power by the most radical of the major political combatants, the Bolsheviks.[2] Following the Bolshevik seizure of power, many in the defeated countries tried to emulate the Russian example, staging uprisings aimed at driving the imperial governments from power. The German and Hungarian monarchies fell and were initially replaced by revolutionary socialist regimes. But except for Russia by 1920 the revolutions sputtered, even if, at least in Germany, moderate social-democratic governments survived.

The victorious Allied powers were largely spared armed threats to their established governments, but in 1919 nearly all underwent intensified labor unrest. The United States witnessed an unprecedented series of strikes: a one-week general strike by 100,000 workers in Seattle was accompanied by the installation of a veritable workers' government in that city. In Lawrence, Massachusetts, 40,000 textile workers struck and, since textiles were the economic lifeblood of the city, led to virtual municipal paralysis. Perhaps for the forces of order the most visible and unsettling event of that year was the 365,000-strong general strike in the steel industry. Through the industrial heartland dozens of steel mills and fabricating plants were brought to a halt by an alliance of the native- and foreign-born workers who previously had been badly split by anti-immigrant chauvinism and interethnic rivalry. Employers and many political leaders declared the strike leaders "dangerous bolsheviks," even though the walkout had the official blessing of the conservative AFL. Still, they demanded that the federal and state governments send the national guards and state militia to quell the alleged revolution. The progressive Woodrow Wilson readily complied, as did the governors of several states. In western Pennsylvania, the largest steel-producing region, the companies supplied their own armed forces, the infamous coal and iron police. Wilson's attorney general, A. Mitchell Palmer, launched a series of raids to round up radical immigrants and deported about 2,500 people. In 1920, Congress passed the first of a series of laws restricting immigration.

The wave of strikes and rebellions in the immediate postwar period signified that the United States had joined Europe in a fierce class war. But the failure of these struggles, in the words of the famous American labor anthem, to "bring to birth a new world from the ashes of the old" or even to win union recognition from unyielding steel and textile employers led to a sweeping reevaluation. By the early twenties world capitalism had regained political and ideological hegemony. In most advanced capitalist countries radicals attempted to join with moderate labor unions to resist the concerted employer assaults on labor's ranks. But the German Social-Democratic-led labor movement, the British Trades Union Congress, and the American AFL rebuffed these overtures. By 1922 most leading AFL unions enacted constitutional amendments barring Communists from holding union office and, in many cases, excluded them from membership, which, in some instances, meant that Communists could not earn a living in their trade.

As large corporations increased their power over labor and the state, American workers and their unions were hard-pressed to preserve even a remnant of their wartime organizational and wage gains. In 1922 a nationwide shopworkers' strike, in which the labor Left played a prominent role, against a unilaterally employer-imposed 12 percent wage cut was crushed largely because some of the rail crafts refused to support it and worked throughout the month-long walkout. The split was an ominous sign; it foreshadowed similar divisions in other industrial sectors. Throughout the 1920s textile workers in the South as well as the North conducted a series of defensive strikes against wage cuts and stretchout, making workers operate more machines. After the 1919 Lawrence strike, in the early 1920s workers in Paterson, New Jersey, and New England centers like Pawtucket, Rhode Island, experienced major walkouts. In 1926, under Communist leadership tens of thousands of New York garment workers struck, as did workers at the huge Botany and Forstmann worsted wool mills in Passaic; and, in the South, staged walkouts over similar issues occurred at the Harriet Henderson cotton mill in North Carolina.[3]

CARROT AND STICK

But if the stick of repression suffused the political landscape, the carrots of the American Plan and Fordism combined to transform the cultural and ideological landscape. The American Plan declared that "outside" or third party forces (euphemisms for independent labor unions) were not needed to mediate labor relations. Some employers established "employee representation" programs to hear and resolve worker grievances. Independent labor unions branded them company unions since they did not recognize the right of workers to choose their own representatives or to strike if their complaints remained unresolved by mediation and negotiation. Moreover, the American Plan provided no protection against discharge and blacklisting of activists who might vocally disagree with company policies. Nevertheless, some of these employee associations survived the early years of the industrial union rebellions during the following decade and went out of existence only in the late 1930s, when the courts upheld the National Labor Relations Act, which prohibited them.

Labor's defeats were only the necessary condition preparing the triumph of postwar capitalism. Perhaps the most effective deterrent to the development of class politics in the 1920s was the introduction of Fordism. Henry Ford, the auto pioneer, added a story onto Frederick Winslow Taylor's edifice of scientific management, which introduced rationalized, repetitive tasks into the labor process. Ford's introduction of the self-moving assembly line meant the worker not only performed repetitive operations but also lost control over the pace of work and had to adjust to the speed of an apparently sovereign line. Ford's methods soon spread to the entire car industry and by the 1930s were the accepted production regime in many sectors of American industry. But the relentless line, which later became the inspiration for Charlie Chaplin's hilarious comment *Modern Times,* did not have smooth sailing even though worker productivity increased several fold. Taylor's program of piecework was feasible chiefly for the production of parts on discrete, specialized machinery, but the Ford assembly line ran on the basis of a straight-time payment system. Ford needed an incentive to prevent workers from quitting in droves or staging short-lived shop floor rebellions.[4]

Four years after the Ford Motor Company opened its giant Highland Park, Michigan, plant in 1910, the company announced the wage rate for assembly line labor would rise to $5 a day, at least twice that of comparable work elsewhere. While a carefully cultivated public image portrayed him as a modern hero, Henry Ford was by no means an altruist. Mass production entailed reducing the operative to an adjunct of the machine, performing simple repetitive tasks for the length of the workday, often without regular rest periods. In order to prevent huge labor turnover Ford determined that a higher straight-time wage was expedient. Yet Ford's paternalism had its repressive side. Workers were expected to show up every day, to perform their duties without complaint, and to conduct their private life in a manner that enabled them to hold down steady work. In the event the wage bonanza did not succeed in inculcating rigorous self-discipline, on and off the job, the company maintained its own private police force to stamp out dissent, sabotage, and unruly behavior on the line—a likely consequence of the degrading character of the work and a symptom of covert protest against arbitrary management practices—and employed an army of social workers to check up on absentees and tardy workers. The company's Social Service Department addressed workers' family problems and personal issues such as alcoholism that might interfere with their regular attendance.[5]

Ford did not make good on its $5 promise, but the policy of raising wages to compensate for subordination to the line ushered in a new era in American life. There was clearly another effect of the unprecedented practice of paying premium wages for semiskilled work. If the company was now capable of producing many times the number of vehicles as under the older methods, it would need to find more buyers. Mass production entailed mass consumption. How to achieve it? Raising wages was a necessary but not sufficient condition for boosting purchasing power. The cost of a new car was still beyond the reach of most workers, so Ford persuaded banks and other lending institutions to introduce a remarkable innovation: extending credit to consumers.

The 1920s also witnessed the opening of the era of what some termed consumer society. The concept signifies the shift of cultural as well as economic emphasis from production to consumption; henceforth work was seen as a means to the end of buying more goods, an activity that came to fill up workers' free time. The wheels for the shift were greased by the expansion of the credit system, once reserved for business and professional people who could put up property as collateral to secure their loans. Now credit was extended to a wider selection among those who held steady jobs. By the end of the decade the slogan "Buy now, pay later" was fast becoming a way of life. With the mass automobile and the one-family home came a vastly expanded highway system that enabled millions of Americans to spend more time on the road. Although the Depression slowed down the pace of mass consumption of expensive durable consumer goods, the time-payment system continued to expand.

The twenties saw the rise of a new industrial bureaucracy of managers, engineers, and administrative and clerical employees in large and medium corporations. The growth of these occupations was directly linked to the exponential growth of rationalized production technologies and the credit system, which both swelled the ranks of bank and consumer finance corporations and resulted in the spread of wholesale and retail establishments. At the same time, the growth of the school population occasioned by migration from the South, the still-vigorous immigration from southern and eastern Europe, and the policies of many states of raising the minimum age for school leavers produced a boom in teaching and other education jobs. These developments combined to create a new class of white-collar employees tied closely to corporations and to local government. The technicians were increasingly credentialed professionals, so the presumption was that, unlike production workers, they could control the pace and the content of their own work and required only minimum supervision. Most foremen were recruited from the hourly paid labor force, and managers were still promoted from the ranks of technical and clerical employees and were expected to devote themselves to the company's interests. In return, early practices of the larger corporations often exempted salaried employees from the market's vicissitudes, offering them benefits such as health and pension plans that were extended to few hourly-paid workers. In order to maintain loyal cadres, many companies kept their salaried employees on the job even during slack times. Managerial and technical employees believed they enjoyed a degree of job security. These groups usually worked long hours without additional compensation, tended to become loyal company men and women, and sometimes regarded their relation to the firm as a family affair.

Although a minority of the labor force, the number of white-collar workers grew at a rate that significantly exceeded that of factory operatives. Barely a half century after the rise of industrial labor, by 1960 in the United States the professional, clerical, and technical groups in the public and private sectors outnumbered industrial workers. As industrial workers built strong unions and, in Europe, formed political parties that won social reforms through parliamentary action, capital, in order to stem the power of the workers' movement and to restore acceptable profit rates, was moved to find new ways of organizing production to improve productivity; mainly it accelerated its investments in labor-saving machinery and eventually expanded consumption through an intensified sales effort to absorb the production gains. Seen as a strategy, the introduction of the Fordist regime was directed toward the cultural as well as economic integration of labor while simultaneously assuring the rapid expansion of capital accumulation.[6]

Sociologists studied salaried employees as much in Europe as in the United States to establish a link between their intermediate, relatively powerless economic standing and their receptivity to right wing appeals. Among these investigators were Emil Lederer, who had studied white-collar employees as early as 1910, and the cultural critic Siegfried Kracauer. Salaried white-collar workers were memorialized in Hans Fallada's novel *Little Man What Now?* For these sociologists the concept was the salaried middle class's political and cultural alienation. They approached the problem of this anomalous new class from two perspectives: on the one hand, they located certain occupations within a conventional conception of social structure, between owners of productive property and its propertyless wage workers. Lederer was among those who first mapped the intermediate social location of the vastly expanded category of salaried employee. On the other hand, sociologists and psychologists studied the ideological appeals of fascism and their effects on intermediate classes or strata. Perhaps the most celebrated exemplar of this approach was *The Authoritarian Personality* by Theodor Adorno and his associates, the product of research conducted in the mid-1940s.[7]

Imprisoned by its workerist ideology, according to which only industrial workers could make significant social change, the mainstream German Left disdained and feared the new middle class of salaried employees. As a result of the Left's failure to address the specificity of their problems and lacking their own trade union organizations or, indeed, influence in the main political parties, they were literally the prey of right wing demagogues who exhorted them to rise from their situation of anonymity and victimization and enter history by joining the fascist revolt. In retrospect many commentators have tended to reduce fascism to its program of world conquest and to the Holocaust. Yet Hitler and Mussolini presented to contemporary angry constituents of otherwise despairing petty bureaucrats, professionals, clerks, and others lacking institutional vehicles of social and political expression hope for dignity through the components of fascist ideology: populism, racial purity, and national pride. The fascists eagerly seized upon Georges Sorel and Oswald Spengler's exaltation of Myth—proposed in very different contexts—to replace bourgeois reason as the guiding precept of the new order. To which they added the purifying and cathartic function of violence, especially against a multitude of sinful groups headed by Communists, gays, Gypsies, and Jews, who, together, became the convenient scapegoats for the multiple problems of declining living standards and status loss.[8]

The conquest by the Right of many European countries found the main currents of marxist and liberal thought stuck within their conventional paradigms and without fresh ideas with which to account for the sweeping rightist victories. Both agreed that fascism could not be identified with intrinsic tendencies within the capitalist system, an evaluation that was conditioned by the faith social democracy had placed in representative government. For more than forty years before the Nazi assumption of state power, parliamentary democracy had served the workers' movement well. Prodded by socialist legislators under Bismarck, Germany had witnessed a significant development of the welfare state. For the Social Democrats it was inconceivable that the triumph of fascism could have grown out of the organs of liberal democratic capitalism, since they had played such a crucial role in shaping its central European variant. The Communists advanced the thesis that Hitler's victory was the result of the Nazi alliance with "the most reactionary, terroristic wing" of big business in the conjunction of the economic crisis and the mass support of the petty bourgeoisie.[9]

The Critical Theory of the Frankfurt School advanced a radically different viewpoint. In the first place it had a different reading of the nature of postwar capitalism. For Max Horkheimer, for example, "those who would not speak of capitalism should keep silent about fascism," a reference to the reluctance of the traditional workers' parties to link the two. Moreover, they were painfully aware of the collective experience of the working class in the wake of the rise of fascism. They proposed the highly unorthodox thesis that, far from constituting the practical agents of resistance to fascist power, the working class, as much as the middle class, had been integrated by the advent of mass society, whose two essential elements were consumerism and the triumph of irrationalism in forms such as mass hysteria, anti-Semitism, and patriotism. To which they added the triumph of authoritarianism not only in fascist nations but also in the countries of liberal democracy.[10]

As a result, the critical theorists drew divergent conclusions from the social-democratically inspired positivism of Lederer at the conjunction of the emergence of a mass public of employees with the abjection of large sections of the industrial working class that had been reduced by the economic crisis to a state of near penury and pessimism. Horkheimer and Adorno insisted that studies which focused on fixing the social location of intermediate strata within the established social structure had missed the forest for the trees: the problem was whether the traditional paradigm of a society arranged by a class grid was adequate to understand the contemporary transformation of capitalism. To be sure, the Frankfurt Institute for Social Research saw capitalism as still the chief barrier to human emancipation and understood fascism as rooted in authoritarian tendencies that were immanent to capitalism. But they questioned whether an economistic class analysis was adequate to comprehend the rise of fascism.

Critical Theory "presupposed Marx's critique of political economy," but it was opposed to orthodox marxism which relegated culture and the state to secondary importance. Chances for class formation and class politics could not be confined to the conventional marxist formula that revolution is possible in the conjunction of the inevitable capitalist crisis, the degree of working-class organization, and the efficacy of the strategies and tactics of mobilization. It insisted on the salience of the so-called private sphere of the family, of the cultural sphere, and of the new role of the state as an ideological as well as a political force. Based on the judgment that the family is a central institution of social life with historical as well as structural consequences, Erich Fromm, Frederick Pollock, Horkheimer, and others conducted extensive theoretically imbued empirical studies of authority and the family and of the fundamental shift of the capitalist state from Adam Smith's "Night Watchman" to an organizer of capital accumulation and the chief purveyor of the fascist mass appeal. Basing their work on Freud, they advanced cultural influences to the forefront of social theory. In his summary of their studies of authority and the family Horkheimer presents the core argument:

> To understand why a society functions in a certain way, why it is stable or dissolves demands therefore a knowledge of the contemporary psychic makeup of men in various social groups. This is turn requires a knowledge of how their char-

> acter has been formed in interaction with all the shaping cultural forces of the time. To regard the economic process as a determining ground of events means that one considers all other spheres of social life in their changing relationships to it and that one conceives this process itself not in its isolated mechanical form but in connection with the specific capabilities and dispositions of men, which have, of course, been developed in the economic process itself. The whole culture, therefore, is caught up in the dynamism of history, and the cultural spheres—customs, morality, art, religion and philosophy—form, in their interconnection, dynamic influences on the maintenance or breakdown of a particular form of society.[11]

In terms of authority relations the objects of investigation were framed on the basis of the homology between family and workplace. Rather than condemning such psychoanalytic concepts as the Oedipal triangle between the male child and its parents they adapted this theory to their conceptions as well as the Freudian claim that even as the child rebels against the father's authority, the stability of the existing system of social relations ("civilization" in Freud's terms) depended on his introjection of domination. Children's subordination to the father's authority prepared them for the industrial labor and for the social factory and made them susceptible to such figures of real and symbolic authority as the Nazi leaders.

They discovered that, far from constituting the heart of the political opposition and resistance to the new order, the working class had, along with the middle strata, become integrated into the system of domination. Against Communist orthodoxy that identified the middle class as the exclusive mass base of fascism but that viewed the workers as victims, the psychoanalyst Wilhelm Reich showed that a considerable number of workers had voted for the Nazis. He attributed this apostasy to their fatal attraction to Nazi racial ideology, to its invocation of the authoritarian symbolic Father, their adroit use of scapegoating to explain the plight of the German lower orders, and the Nazis' effective use of violence against Jews and other minorities. Reich argued that the fatal flaw of the Left was its refusal to develop a program that took the family and private life and its influence on popular character structure as a serious political question. While hesitating to bring the full force of their criticism to the surface, as Reich had, it was plain that the hallmark of Critical Theory's political critique was that the complex cultural sphere, which had been taken as an efflux of economic relations by orthodox marxism, was a crucial, independent moment in the accounting for the catastrophe.[12]

Far from remaining at the cusp of social transformation the proletariat had lost its autonomy and all but disappeared into mass society. This judgment was proposed in the wake of fascism's rise to power but became a theory of general applicability after World War II, when, contrary to revolutionary hope, the Soviet Union and the United States redrew the political map of the globe into new spheres of influence, a deal to which the most powerful working-class movements of the West either adhered or remained sullenly silent. Writing in 1947, Herbert Marcuse found no postwar working-class revolutionary movement. In agreement with other social theorists of this period, particularly the British sociologists John Goldthorpe and David Lockwood, he discovered a pervasive "bourgeoisification" and integration of the working class into late capitalism: "One of theory's most urgent tasks is to investigate bourgeoisification in all its manifestations. To say it again: bourgeoisification must be seen as an objective class phenomenon, not as the Social Democrats' insufficient will to revolution or their bourgeois consciousness, but rather as the economic and political integration of a large part of the working class into the system of capital, as a change in the structure of exploitation."[13]

Marcuse's concept of domination, elaborated in his later work *One-Dimensional Man* (1964), grasps the significance of what we have found in Fordism: that in societies in which consent rather than force is the characteristic mode of rule ideologies like patriotism, the doctrine of equal opportunity for social mobility, free markets, and religious appeals are not sufficient for system maintenance. Consent requires the underlying population to literally buy in to the system. In the environment of the postwar recovery and expansion workers gained material rewards while, at the same time, their labor became one of the conditions of the system's ability to provide these rewards. Technology is both the means and the end of consumerism. On the one hand, labor-saving technological innovations have relieved many of arduous labor and vastly expanded the quantity of consumer goods; technology, together with the credit system, makes these goods available to almost everyone in advanced industrial societies. Technology as electronic home entertainment, cars, and chemical drugs is a major consumer product. The pleasures of consumption have produced an addiction to commodified technology that permeates every corner of the social world. On the other hand, we can no longer think the unthinkable, there is no plausible radical futurity: if capitalism can deliver the goods to the immense majority, what is is what will be.

Marcuse's most compelling—and grim—argument is that, parallel to the development of technological society, collectively we are all in the grip of reductive, technological thought; we evaluate all of our relationships and objects according to instrumental criteria—how they might benefit our own private interests. Under the regime of technological rationality means become ends. If there is no chance that a particular concept, political position, or framework can succeed it should be abandoned to the dreamwork. Our capacity for critical thinking has shriveled, a process Marcuse likens to the metaphor of a somatic change that results in a genetic mutation. The notions truth and falsehood now have no intrinsic meaning; they are construed entirely within instrumental frames. We judge the truth of a proposition neither by its correspondence to a real or constructed object, nor with reference to its intrinsic, logical structure, but by its consequences for our private interests. Ethical considerations, political choices, and courses of action in everyday life and public sphere are viewed as contingent on particular situations and measured by their utility in achieving subjective goals.[14]

We privilege as superior alternatives what we deem to be practical to those that are considered too utopian. If utopia was identified with the end of material want, technological capitalism has accomplished this goal. For this reason we cannot even have a public conversation that exceeds the boundaries of the feasible. Thus revolutionary futurity, the best moment of utopian thought, is turned into its opposite: communism is no longer identified with freedom, but with scarcity and even slavery, economic and social equality with totalitarianism. What many critics attribute to the conspiracy of both powerful media corporations and political leaders to sharply restrict the scope of public debate and to marginalize criticism of the existing order may have as much to do with deeply embedded habits of thought as to policy. We are prone to suppress information and ideas that disturb the credo according to which we can only have knowledge that is consonant with prescribed possibilities. The advent of "the totally administered" society in which organization becomes the technology that unifies production and consumption, political thought and established political power and, in the manner of an Orwellian dystopia, real surveillance supplements and validates what we have already introjected—the feeling that even our thoughts are not private. Under these conditions, art is the sole survivor. In the midst of the immense transformations of the 1920s progress encountered a powerful reversal toward horrific forms of bondage, and what remained of civil society after its ubiquitous invasion by commodification was in the process of being swallowed by the state, a trend that was to accelerate in subsequent decades.

LABOR AND THE NEW DEAL

The theory of mass society might have provided a more adequate account of the rise of fascism in Europe but, at least in the 1930s, the United States seemed to be a counterexample. At the turn of the decade, the state of the opposition offered few grounds for hope that corporate capital's domination of the workplace and the political culture could be effectively challenged. Unions were on the defensive, and many had been reduced to shells. In response to increased pressure from southern employers to increase productivity in order to buttress sagging profits, textile strikes in 1929 at the large Loray mill in Gastonia, North Carolina, in Marion, North Carolina, and in Elizabethton, Tennessee, displayed a high degree of courage and militancy by southern textile workers, whom both experts and many union officials had believed to be docile and antiunion. The Marion and Gastonia strikes were assisted by Socialist and Communist organizers, respectively, and this gave employers, as they sought government assistance to defeat the strikes, the excuse to brand the walkouts a red conspiracy. Plagued by an avalanche of court injunctions, jailings of strike leaders, ruthless firings of union activists, the deployment of local and state police, and lack of support from the official labor movement, the resistance was overwhelmed.[15]

In the tumult of the interwar period the American New Deal and France's Popular Front were anomalies but not so much in their global policies; indeed, neither government evinced a strong antifascist passion. But in the wake of the rise of the global Right, the United States and France were distinguished by their observance of internal liberal democracy and, in the mid-1930s, by their respective programs of domestic reform. Early Left perceptions of the New Deal were less than complimentary. In 1932 Roosevelt ran on a program of a balanced budget, and he interpreted his overwhelming victory as a mandate to strengthen the institutions such as the Reconstruction Finance Corporation that his predecessor, Herbert Hoover, had established to stimulate capital investment and to constrain ruinous economic competition. Although upon taking office he provided temporary relief to the growing population of the unemployed, Roosevelt was reluctant to institutionalize income guarantees and the relatively modest public works program the administration had introduced to alleviate the disastrous impact of the crisis on millions of people.[16]

Nevertheless, both Hoover and Roosevelt faced visible mass movements of the unemployed and of ruined farmers. The jobless had staged several large demonstrations during the previous two years: in March 1930 in some two dozen cities, under radical leadership more than a million unemployed rallied and marched for unemployment insurance, immediate relief, and public funds for job creation; and in 1932 the Ex-Servicemen's League marched on Washington demanding the federal government make good on its pledge to pay a veteran's bonus that had been deferred since 1918. As they streamed into Washington by bus, old cars, and on foot, the veterans were met by U.S. army troops under the command of Gen. Douglas McArthur, who fired on the marchers. The demonstrators had set up a tent colony near the capitol, a virtual sit-in to force Congress and President Hoover to act. They went away empty-handed, but the incident did little to enhance Hoover's popular standing.

Labor's resistance to bearing the brunt of the Depression was also on the rise. And the activists in the rapidly growing Communist Party (CP) were making important inroads in the incipient electrical, transportation, auto, and retail unions. It even fostered the organization of unions of bookkeepers, architects, engineers, and chemists. In Toledo the American Workers' Party, an independent group of labor radicals, organized an impressive unemployed movement that became the base for some of the most dramatic labor struggles of the early 1930s. Organized under the aegis of a socialist-led Arkansas Farm union—rightly regarded as the precursor of the United Farmworkers of the 1960s and 1970s—thousands of farmers battled eviction, the effect of a combination of falling cotton prices and price gouging for food and other staples and for processed cotton by merchants, many of whom owned the cotton gins that prepared the raw cotton for sale. In both the ruling circles and in the Left there was a widespread perception that the long period of defeats for the workers' movement may have come to an end.[17]

The failure of the Hoover administration to respond to suffering except by making repeated paeans to the self-regenerating powers of the market and, contrarily, by introducing measures to restore capital investment through government loans was surely the necessary condition for the Democrats' return to political power. The sufficient condition for the creation of a so-called second New Deal, the expansion of the social wage, was the industrial rebellions of the first half of the 1930s.[18] The struggles over class formation in a wave of strikes, mass demonstrations, and factory occupations prompted an extraordinary wave of social reform from a reluctant Roosevelt administration. The first two years of the first New Deal, 1933 and 1934, were more consistent with the pattern of the 1920s, when conservative national governments had systematically ignored labor's pleas for industrial justice, even though, under pressure, the president had included a nonenforceable provision of the National Industrial Recovery Act (NIRA), section 7(a), recognizing workers' right to organize unions of their own choosing.[19] In fact, both Socialists and Communists compared the first New Deal, which under the NIRA instituted industry boards to set prices and wages, with corporatism, a leading doctrine underlying fascist labor relations policy. Corporatism suppresses the structural antagonism between workers and employers and attempts to incorporate working-class discontent into a program of cooperation between labor and capital. The industry boards pitted a powerful association of employers that virtually dictated the terms of cooperation to a divided and largely disorganized and demoralized labor movement.

Despite their skepticism, the leaders of some of the more viable industrial unions seized on 7(a) to launch a major organizing campaign in the coal fields, men's and women's apparel industries, and textiles. The effort culminated in the largest number of strikes and most dramatic increase in union membership since the war. Organizers spread throughout the Northeast, some brandishing the slogan, "The President Wants You to Join the Union," which foreshadowed the coming alliance between the new industrial unions and the New Deal. In 1933, New York's two hundred thousand plus needle trades workers struck against wage cuts and for union recognition. Tens of thousands of shirt workers joined miners in the coal regions of Pennsylvania and West Virginia in a wave of strike activity and organizing. Smaller unions of autoworkers, retail employees, metal and electrical workers, engineers, and truck drivers began organizing drives that led to union recognition several years later.

The year 1934 was, in some respects, 1919 redux but on a wider scale. Spurred by a teamsters' strike led by members of the dissident Trotskyist Communist League of America, in fairly short order the city of Minneapolis was in the throes of a general strike that resulted in sweeping victory for the workers and made the city a union town that rivaled New York and San Francisco in density of union organization.[20] Similarly, labor radicals in or close to the CP led longshoremen in a complete shutdown of the port of San Francisco. In response to efforts by the stevedore companies and city government to force the workers back to work without recognition of their union, the city's labor movement responded with a general strike that embraced some 80 percent of the factories and service industries. The fledgling longshore union won recognition and soon broke from the conservative, racket-ridden AFL International Longshoremen's Association to establish the International Longshoremen's and Warehousemen's Union, which became the launching pad for organizing drives of the newly formed Committee for Industrial Organization on the West Coast. In Toledo, organizers of the American Workers' Party assisted in the organization and strike of workers in the large Electric Auto-Lite plant, which spread to a near-general strike.

The most dramatic event of 1934 was the national strike by four hundred thousand textile workers, especially in the South, against what they perceived to be the discriminatory policies of the NIRA in the industry. Roosevelt reacted to the walkout by promising leaders of the AFL United Textile Workers who called the strike that he would conduct a survey to determine the injustices and eventually mediate their differences with employers. Having crippled production in dozens of plants, workers returned to work without achieving their aims, confident that the president would come to their aid. Roosevelt reneged on his pledge. The union was unable to protect or support from seven thousand to fifteen thousand union activists discharged during the poststrike employer crackdown. The AFL was unwilling either to pour resources in to supplement those of its almost bankrupt affiliate or to hold the Roosevelt administration accountable on its promises. The result was that textile unionism in the South was set back fifty years.[21]

Yet the handwriting was on the wall. The long quiescent industrial working class was lifting the scales from its eyes. In a wave of strikes, demonstrations, and accelerated union enrollment it demanded a measure of industrial democracy—the right of workers to control the conditions of work—and a measure of economic redistribution in the forms of higher wages and the creation of a social wage—the phalanx of state-financed benefits such as pensions, unemployment insurance, and health care programs that comprise the welfare state. They struck for union recognition and, in 1936 and 1937, staged factory occupations in rubber, auto, and a number of other sectors that electrified American workers and struck fear in the ranks of the ruling circles. These struggles caught the Roosevelt administration, the employers, and the AFL leadership by surprise because with Congress's approval of the National Labor Relations Act (NLRA)—the same year that the Supreme Court declared unconstitutional the jewel of the first New Deal, the NIRA—politicians, AFL leaders, and corporations believed order would be restored to industrial and labor relations. Sen. Robert F. Wagner of New York had introduced the legislation at the behest of Roosevelt and the AFL leadership, who believed the law would furnish a framework for labor peace and would help quell what some had termed an incipient revolution in America's key production and transportation industries.

The thrust of the new labor law was to put teeth into section 7(a), which declared the right of workers to form unions "of their own choosing" (a less than oblique reference to the company unions of the American Plan), by establishing quasi-judicial procedures for insuring the right of workers to organize. The new Labor Board not only heard cases of unfair labor practices by employers, but had the power to issue compliance orders against those found guilty. The union was selected by a majority of employees within a given unit, and on penalty of being held in contempt, the employer was compelled to bargain with the union (although not to conclude an agreement). The board was empowered to resolve questions of jurisdiction between rival unions and determine appropriate units for the purposes of collective bargaining; it copied the American electoral system's secret ballot vote for union recognition and its winner-take-all basis for certification. That is, only one union could represent employees within a board-determined bargaining unit.

This provision differed not only from the previous pattern of American labor relations, in which more than one union represented workers of the same employer, but also from many European labor relations practices that awarded proportional representation (PR) to competing unions, depending on their share of the vote. The unions welcomed the winner-take-all system. Most leaders believed it was necessary to prevent company unions from gaining power in the plants. Roosevelt exacted a price for giving up PR and outlawing company unions: union autonomy would be constrained by a system of rules governing representation elections and by placing collective bargaining under the law. This tacit bargain proved a slippery slope that soon tightened government control over every aspect of labor relations.[22] The American Civil Liberties Union (ACLU) was among the few prolabor organizations that saw these ominous tendencies in the NLRA and opposed its enactment. Many socialists shared the ACLU's skepticism, but no other major organization on the Left actively opposed the bill. At the time of its passage the Communists and the Socialists attributed the enactment of the Wagner Act and Social Security to Roosevelt's political need to make concessions to an insurgent working class. But the Left failed to grasp the significance of what Roosevelt had "conceded." While other countries had adopted national pension and health schemes and codes to protect health and safety conditions at the workplace, the American restrictions on labor's ability to employ a wide array of weapons to advance its interests was more typical of authoritarian countries than liberal democracies.

But labor's top leadership was jubilant. AFL president William Green hailed the Wagner Act as "labor's magna carta," a euphemism that helped shape the dominant narrative of the 1930s. While it would take more than two years for the Supreme Court to dispose of constitutional challenges to the law—during which some of the most militant and far-reaching demonstrations of labor's power to act outside the law's guarantees were displayed—the fact that the events of 1933–37 that shaped labor relations for the most of the remainder of the century occurred outside the framework of the law remains a hidden story save for a few radical labor activists, historians, and legal experts. Green, who had been appalled by most of the strikes, demonstrations, and sit-ins of the period and whose AFL had, for all practical purposes, abandoned the millions of unemployed who demonstrated for jobs and relief, had the last word. His declaration about the significance of the law became the main story that was repeated by many of his industrial union adversaries, by the leading school textbooks, and by most historians of the New Deal. The workers themselves got little credit for the wave of organizing that preceded and followed the act. Despite widespread strikes and factory occupations in almost every major industrial center, the accepted narrative was that labor was more or less flat on its back before the law's administration and that unions grew only within the frame of the Roosevelt coalition and the New Deal.[23]

Even in the ranks of labor Roosevelt has basked in the sun and enjoys the stature of a deity. Although radicals remained skeptical and sometimes sharply critical of the administration and its labor policies, by 1936 many union leaders who had rejected the Democratic presidential candidate and had supported the 1932 presidential campaign of the socialist Norman Thomas or William Z. Foster's Communist candidacy became fervent New Dealers. A lifelong Republican, CIO president John L. Lewis joined the Roosevelt coalition the same year and, despite lingering reservations, the overwhelming majority of rank-and-file union members flocked to the president. Reflecting the gap between electoral and industrial struggle, on the shop floor and the picket line throughout 1936 and 1937 workers defied the president's anxious pleas to end their rebellions. They may have welcomed the second New Deal of social reform, but they were unwilling to surrender their right to engage in direct action.

Some corporate leaders like Myron C. Taylor of U.S. Steel, William Knudsen of General Motors, Harvey Firestone and the executives of Akron's rubber corporations, which had been shut down by strikers in 1936, swiftly sought to stem the tide of labor unrest by signing union recognition agreements covering all of their plants. The swiftness of their surrender was attributable to the workers' solidarity, but it was also a signal to the Roosevelt administration that a powerful fraction of capital was willing to compromise with organized labor in order to avert a widening struggle that could have led to class formation. Others, including Ford, remained unrepentant; employers of the so-called Little Steel corporations, Weirton, National, and Inland Steel, greeted a demonstration by Chicago steelworkers in May 1937 with bullets and tear gas in what historians describe as the Memorial Day Massacre. General Electric, perhaps the most sophisticated antiunion corporation in the country, forced the United Electrical Workers to recruit members on a plant-by-plant basis, and IBM and Kodak have succeeded in keeping unionism at bay to this day.

The conjunction of the introduction of new labor relations law and a fissure in the ranks of big capital contributed to the ability of Roosevelt to craft a coalition that included both progressives and conservatives in the ranks of organized labor's leadership. Some erstwhile socialists like Clothing Workers' president Sidney Hillman were predisposed to join the New Deal, and innovations in labor-management relations within the Men's Clothing Industry paved the way for both the NIRA and the political coalition around Roosevelt that Hillman helped craft in the late 1920s. After two decades of industrial strife Hillman became convinced that the union had to alter its combative stance during economic downturns for the industry in order to protect its members from hardship. He had been a pioneer in organizing employers into an association that bargained collectively with the union rather than as individual companies. In return the union took "responsibility" for the economic health of the whole industry. As it revived after the depression-wrought decline of the early 1930s, the union was prepared to use its growing strength to regulate piece rates and other shop floor conditions in a manner that would benefit both workers and the employer. The union used its financial power through the Amalgamated Bank to assist employers unable to obtain loans from commercial banks at reasonable rates and provided industrial engineers and other technical support and became the industry's de facto lobby in state capitals and in Washington.[24]

These precedents proved compatible with objectives of the Industrial Recovery Act. Although he had provided financial and organizing support to the ill-fated textile strike of 1934 and, throughout the 1930s, proved a stalwart of the CIO's organizing drives, Hillman was no longer convinced that labor was served by socialist politics. The defection of Hillman and the ILGWU's David Dubinsky from the Socialist Party to the Roosevelt camp was an important step in the process of the integration into the New Deal of organized labor's most radical battalions. Hillman gave strong support to the Roosevelt coalition, but, mindful of strong rank-and-file socialist and class political views, he kept the union's distance from the New York Democratic Party. He helped form the New York State American Labor Party in order to signal the independence of radicals and progressives from the corruption-ridden and largely conservative Democrats.

John L. Lewis, an old business unionist with ties to the Republican Party, became a fervent New Dealer, primarily because he believed that government intervention in labor relations was as inevitable as it was desirable and that the threat to the labor establishment posed by Communists and other radicals would grow unless the moderate heads of organized labor and enlightened members of the business elite took the initiative to head them off at the pass. He had endured a significant challenge from radicals in his own union that nearly defeated him in 1927. And concerned the events of 1934 might overtake the mainstream in the AFL he argued if fellow union leaders did not leap to the forefront of organizing in the mass production industries they might eventually lose everything to the Left. At the same time, he was a warm supporter of bringing order to labor and supported the Wagner Act. In a speech to San Francisco's Commonwealth Club on October 10, 1934, Lewis warned his listeners that if the leaders of the financial elite did not bend to organized labor, the Morgan-Dupont-Rockefeller triumvirate's "indefensible tactics would inevitably cause 'an industrial revolt attended by the menace of Communism or Fascism.'" He went on to declare that collective bargaining would come about "sooner or later if the economic system as we now know it is to endure" and warned that capital would commit "a social blunder which may lead to the toppling over of our whole economic edifice."[25]

Lewis's biographers tend to dismiss these statements as a rhetorical gesture aimed at softening business's opposition to union organization. But like Hillman, Lewis had reason to fear the Left. He observed that, despite the opposition of William Green and the leaders of the House of Labor, many of the major struggles were conducted in the main by the Left, but they were symptoms of the growing confidence of the labor Left to work outside the sponsorship of the AFL. One hundred thousand autoworkers joined "federal locals"—unions that directly affiliated with the AFL rather than with the weak United Auto Workers (UAW) union—and thousands more had joined independent unions. After being rebuffed by the mainstream AFL leadership in 1935, Lewis and Hillman formed an AFL Committee for Industrial Organization (CIO), and Lewis quickly invited Communists as well as independent radicals like Powers Hapgood and his own nemesis, John Brophy, to join the crusade to organize the unorganized.[26]

Barely tolerating the CIO, top AFL leaders still insisted that newly organized workers be recruited to the respective craft unions. When AFL president William Green sent a representative, Francis Dillon, to run the fledgling UAW, the relationship became more strained. Lewis was not fast to provoke a separation from labor's mainstream because he believed the industrial union forces were simply too weak. But he captured the initiative and, together with Hillman, invited the Left to sign on to the organizing crusade. With the help of the Communists, who by 1935 discovered the virtues of coalitions with their erstwhile union adversaries as well as with what they termed progressive sections of the political directorate, the coalition steered the new labor movement into the New Deal, leaving socialists and independent radicals out in the cold. It was not until 1938 that the CIO unions were expelled from the AFL and formed their own organization. But after the 1937 sit-down strikes by the UAW, the CIO had already moderated its militance. Deterred by the Supreme Court, which declared the sit-down strike illegal, CIO unions all but abandoned factory occupations and, after Roosevelt began to resist further social reforms in favor of the rearmament program, union leaders rebuffed pressure emanating from many local councils urging the formation of a labor party and began to feel comfortable with the Labor Board and its protections.

The third major partner in forging labor's participation in the New Deal was the CP, which, by 1936, claimed more than twenty-five thousand members, four times their strength at the onset of the Depression. More than half of these were activists, largely in the trade union movement. Communists played key roles in the formation of some of the leading industrial unions of the time: auto, electrical, packinghouse, mine-mill—the union of nonferrous metal mining and refining—transit, West Coast longshore, and two major seafaring unions, the National Maritime Union and the Marine Cooks and Stewards. When the CIO formed in 1938, CP-led unions comprised about a third of its four million members and were part of a unity leadership in the UAW and packinghouse workers. Of the major affiliates, only the mineworkers, steelworkers, clothing, and textile workers were led by anti-Communist factions.

The conversion of the Communists from earlier intransigence to a willingness to enter the mainstream of the labor movement has been attributed by historians to the abrupt aboutface brought on by Stalin's fear of the consequences of Hitler's rise to power, especially in the Soviet Union. Indeed, this was a major motive of the CP's attempt to form antifascist coalitions with the Social Democrats in Europe and with the Socialist Party and progressive trade unions and black and women's leaders in the United States. But the CP's shift was as much influenced by its isolation in the 1920s and early 1930s from labor and popular movements. The rise of fascism presented an opportunity to reverse the dire consequences of AFL exclusionary policies after 1922, policies that had driven the party, in desperation, to form their own unions, most of which failed to achieve stable membership and organization. By the time the CP joined the Roosevelt coalition it had already moved away considerably from its earlier isolation and sectarian rhetoric. While not fully accepted by many party activists, through the unions it influenced and led, Communists could offer real assistance to the labor movement and to the New Deal administration. This policy entailed new responsibilities and constraints. For example, there is little evidence that the party mounted criticism of the Labor Relations Act or its winner-take-all provision. And after having excoriated Roosevelt for the NIRA it muted its criticism during the 1936 elections. Nor did Communists maintain their skepticism toward the so-called right-wing leadership of the CIO, exemplified by Lewis and Hillman. Communists were reticent when it came to putting forward their own politics and programs, even though, on the whole, they retained considerable militancy on the shop floor and during organizing drives. At the national level, while urging Roosevelt to be more aggressively antifascist, popular front politics demanded that party leaders be conciliatory.[27]

Most historians and sociologists trace organized labor's subordination to restrictions placed on its freedom by the Taft-Hartley amendments passed by Congress in 1947. To be sure, the capitulation of organized labor to its key provisions amounted to a major retreat. But, apart from the Clothing Workers' social experiment in labor-management cooperation in the late 1920s, the beginning of labor's integration into the prevailing structure of corporate and political power was the leadership's embrace of the Wagner Act. This move was concomitant with the incorporation of both wings into the Roosevelt coalition, an alliance that all but scuttled the emerging movement within labor's ranks for the formation of a labor party. As the National Labor Relations Board went into operation, and the courts became more openly hostile to direct action, the institution of the labor-board supervised election gradually supplanted the strike weapon and other forms of direct action as the chief method by which workers gained union recognition. More to the point, the NLRA introduced a new, dominant theme in labor relations: it was no longer the direct intervention of the workers themselves upon which unions relied to solve grievances and win economic gains. The 1940s was a decade that, under the rule of law, witnessed the maturation of bureaucratic unionism in the CIO.

Although nominally voluntary organizations, unions in almost every respect were now largely regulated within the framework of the state.[28] Coverage by the law extended some rights but vastly increased union responsibilities. The collective agreement, once a simple declaration of the employers' obligation to recognize the union as bargaining agent supplemented by a wage chart for different occupations and by certain specified union rights, now became a Bible of labor relations. The contract now contained numerous articles covering many aspects of management-labor relations ranging from whether the union had the right to negotiate such changes as technological innovations to management's obligations to provide towels and showers. Union representatives, from chairs of grievance committees to shop floor stewards, began to carry the contract booklet in their pockets, and many became expert interpreters of its many provisions.

Even before the Taft-Hartley amendments of 1947, the White House and the courts tried to make sure that worker upsurge would not recur anytime soon. Between 1937 and the end of World War II, the Supreme Court ruled that factory occupations to gain union recognition were illegal; employers were granted the right to seek court injunctions restraining union members from mass picketing in order to prevent strikebreakers from performing their work; and President Roosevelt imposed a wartime wage freeze and sought a voluntary no-strike pledge from unions. When it refused to honor the pledge, the Courts fined the miners' union and jailed its leader, John L. Lewis. But the war did not entirely abolish the strike weapon: fresh from their sit-downs and strikes militant autoworkers ignored their leaders and protested wage freezes, even as companies raked in record profits; the strike movements in the electrical industry evoked disciplinary action by their Communist-dominated union, and workers in aircraft, shipbuilding, and other sectors staged job actions and "quicky walkouts."[29]

A year after the war's end, industrial unions staged the most sweeping strike movement in American history. In 1946 to win their demand for a 30 percent wage increase to make up for the draconian wartime wage freeze, workers staged strikes in virtually every major American industry. While most fell short of this objective, in nearly all of the settlements they won at least eighteen cents, or 18 percent.[30] By 1946, spurred by CIO energy and organizing acumen, the AFL became the main gainer from the upsurge in union membership, in some cases because it offered employers a softer alternative to its more militant adversary. Taken together with the independent unions, the two major union federations had organized nearly 30 percent of the labor force (in one of the textbooks cited earlier the authors' lament that only 28 percent had been organized). Considering that only a handful of federal, state, and local public employees and almost none of the health care industry had been unionized, the extent of union membership in the private sector labor force was almost 50 percent, the highest density among industrial countries. (By 1953 the figure had dropped to 35 percent.)

The Taft-Hartley provisions attached to the NLRA were enacted to throttle labor's awesome power. They were also aimed at ejecting the Communists from the labor movement, in the wake of the incipient Cold War and their entrenched power within the CIO. Indeed, the considerable wartime disruptions of industrial production and the mass strikes of 1946 were sufficient causes for alarm in the corporate boardrooms as well as among reactionary lawmakers. Riding the wave of business-generated antilabor propaganda on the promise of curbing organized labor's growing political and industrial power, in 1946 the Republicans captured both houses of Congress and promptly passed legislation that represented a major reversal of union power. In an early indication of the political environment that was to mark the Cold War, among other egregious provisions it barred Communists from holding union office, prevented unions from conducting sympathy strikes and secondary boycotts, and gave the president the right to declare an eighty-day cooling off period during which a strike was prohibited when, in his opinion, it threatened national security. After making some noises in opposition to what Lewis, by now a pariah in the labor movement, termed a "slave labor act," a rightward-drifting labor leadership quickly marched in lockstep behind what was widely recognized as a bipartisan, Cold War antilabor measure.[31]

By the late 1940s, in return for the employers' agreement to refrain from locking out employees, unions increasingly signed clauses that limited workers' right to strike to the expiration of the contract (such clauses had been introduced as a wartime expedient). In the best cases, notably the contracts negotiated with the Big Three electrical manufacturing companies, the dominant union in the industry, the United Electrical Workers, refused to sign the no-strike pledge. After a rash of wildcat (illegal) strikes following the union's signing of a five-year no-strike agreement in 1950, the UAW restored the right to strike in cases of discriminatory discharge, health and safety complaints, and some other issues. But by the early 1950s, 97 percent of industrial union contracts stipulated severe penalties if union members struck for any reason during the life of the agreement, which gradually was extended to three, four, and five years. To compensate for surrendering the right to strike the typical contract contains a procedure for resolving grievances whose final step is arbitration if the parties cannot agree. Reliance on mediation and arbitration is consonant with the belief in a mutual labor and management interest to maintain class peace.

Labor's post–World War II decline was a result of the logic inherent in its integration by the New Deal exemplified by the NLRA as well as its firm adherence to the Cold War objectives of U.S. foreign policy, an adherence that time and again tempered labor's militancy and thwarted the political independence of leaders such as UAW president Walter Reuther. The doctrine that labor organizations and labor relations should be regulated by the state and that workers' autonomy should be subject to regulatory law was consistent with the corporatist concept that drove the first New Deal. That Roosevelt was compelled to grant labor more rights is a tribute to the impact of struggles labor conducted outside the framework of law. But the regulation of labor relations inevitably restricts workers' freedom, in the first place to withhold their labor when they are aggrieved, and to prevent strikebreaking. The most effective means is through direct action such as factory occupations, mass picketing, measures to prevent truck and rail deliveries and to undertake acts of solidarity such as sympathy walkouts, boycotts, and to refuse to cross picket lines. Although onerous in comparison to the original language of the NLRA, the Taft-Hartley amendments may be seen as an extension of regulation imposed by the act and by various Supreme Court decisions rather than as the key legislation that reversed labor's rights. These fundamental rights were surrendered when organized labor agreed to become subjects of a law that regulated industrial and labor relations.

This tale raises the basic question, Why did the leaders of an insurgent labor movement readily accept the Wagner Act and, in the crucial years between 1937 and 1945, gradually adjust their trade union practice to the restrictions placed on their autonomy? To begin with, Hillman's and Lewis's enthusiastic support of the New Deal were a logical extension of their respective histories of collaboration with employers and the state. Although the Communists were skeptical of Roosevelt's motives in backing the Wagner Act, they hesitated to oppose the bill itself lest their strategy of, first, supporting Lewis's efforts to organize the millions of unorganized industrial workers and, second, forging a Center-Left alliance in the labor movement be scuttled. Perhaps more to the point, they were afraid of being left out in the cold. But these predispositions do not explain why the militants, including non-Communists, overcame their skepticism and, with the exception of some Left-socialists, fell in line.

The gradual move by Communists away from the Left in favor of an alliance with the Center immeasurably weakened the prospective opposition to the gradual emergence of bureaucratic unionism as the main form in labor's ranks. Indeed, the bureaucratization of labor's practice was not visible during the heady days of organizing and mass strikes, and the no-strike pledge could be rationalized as a wartime expedient, although rank-and-file workers in several key industrial sectors were not at all willing to submit. The sufficient condition for labor's ultimate integration, which preconfigured its inability to defeat and to repeal the Taft-Hartley amendments, was that it tended to narrate its victories on the shop floor and the institution of a plethora of gains in the social wage, such as Social Security, in terms that gave credit to Roosevelt and the New Deal and to the leadership of the unions rather than to the initiative of the rank and file. For many trade union leaders, including the Communists, preserving the Roosevelt coalition became their primary objective. But many enjoyed the relative comfort of legality and sincerely believed that the workers and their unions needed the law for protection against the inevitable employer offensives, let alone to expand. In time, the leadership consolidated its relationships with the political directorate and a segment of the corporate capital and began to form a distinct, albeit subordinate social formation within the ruling circles. When, beginning in the late 1950s, struggles over class were initiated by dissidents marching under the flags of union and industrial democracy and militancy erupted, a section of the leadership felt compelled to preserve their power positions.

Labor's leadership had successfully promoted the benefits of the law to the rank and file and elevated the contract to the law of labor relations. It encouraged the view that the grievance procedure provided by the agreement was effective for winning shop floor justice. Although the CIO unions were eager to train an army of stewards to administer grievances and local leaders to negotiate local agreements, they were reluctant to conduct political and ideological education because they had acquired a paranoid fear of union democracy and rank-and-file power. In multiplant chains of large corporations, the national agreement took labor out of competition with itself by establishing uniform wage and benefits standards; the local leadership dealt with such issues as working conditions. But when locals insisted that the national agreement await settlement of local issues, conflict broke out between the central offices and the locals. Even companywide bargaining committees composed of local representatives were often unable to stay the hand of increasingly powerful top officials. By the 1950s the only recourse for dissidents was to throw the rascals out in the international unions. When the rebels succeeded, they soon found that their wiggle room had been restricted by the law, by the imperatives of the contract and its administration, and by the imperatives of bureaucratic unionism. And the perks of union office should not be underestimated. Trips to conferences, meetings with top elected and government officials, and a style of life made possible by generous expense accounts and salaries well beyond those earned by shop floor workers were the oil that greased union machine politics within labor's ranks. Notwithstanding their desire to break with past union practices, lacking a politics and an analysis of the basis of the weakness of the union bureaucracy at the bargaining table, it was a relatively short step to occupy the positions of their predecessors.

But I believe any adequate account has to assess the effect of the absence of a truly inclusive labor communications network that informed and educated the rank and file and its local leadership. In time international union newspapers and other communications and education media became more or less overt advertisements for the leadership and its policies. Union education and media apparatuses were systematically marginalized by the business unions. Even in the progressive unions their scope and content were restricted to the messages that the leadership wanted to convey; with only a few exceptions the voices of the membership were absent in the labor press, except to extoll the union's achievements or to echo its perspectives. In almost no major union newspaper, magazine, or electronic communication could sustained criticism be discerned. Even now there are few op-ed columns in union newspapers. Most union radio stations built during the organizing phase were gradually sold, some to public radio stations. Union research departments were mostly data collection agencies for supporting contract negotiations.

By 1950, the CIO unions, most of which were less than fifteen years old, began to resemble their AFL antagonists. As the leadership became more entrenched they took on the features of a class or social formation that was structurally separated from the membership. They had become business unions, organizations that sold labor at the highest possible price and constructed themselves as the main vehicle for disciplining the often unruly rank and file. Hence unions became what Louis Althusser termed "an ideological state apparatus" rather than a class movement. The willful abdication of responsibility to provide vehicles for countercommunication with members and the general public left the rank and file subject to the influences of the commercial media. Responding to Richard Nixon's so-called southern strategy (read racism) and his appeal to the silent majority to reject social movements like feminism, by the late 1960s a growing segment of union members were voting Republican. A decade later the media were filled with stories of a new constituency of working-class Reagan Democrats, many of whom were union members. Since 1980, an overtly conservative coalition of corporations and a considerable fraction of the white male working class have driven electoral politics. The midterm elections of 1994, which elected the first Republican Congress since 1946, drove the point home. It was not until 1995 when, under the leadership of John Sweeney, the AFL-CIO began to confront these defections that the tide shifted, but only a little. Even as blacks, Latinos, and women compose a near majority of union members and issues like abortion, sexual freedom, the persistence of racial discrimination and stigmatization, and education continue to roil politics, the AFL-CIO and its affiliates tread gingerly over what they consider to be the minefield of social issues. Taken together with the weak labor media effort, such cautious behavior only shows that labor still has no viable strategy for overcoming its largely self-induced marginalization during the last quarter of the twentieth century.

Class discourse reemerged in the 1990s under the influence of two closely related developments: the overt exercise by transnational corporations of blatant power to determine the fate of nations, including the United States. This power was manifested in the political struggles that occurred around issues of trade when, in 1993, a waffling Clinton administration felt itself unable to resist the proposal for a North American Free Trade Agreement (NAFTA) and, fearing corporate reprisals, was unable to craft a reasonable universal health plan. What ignited class discourse was not these acts alone but the acceleration of strikes and demonstrations that for the first time in decades directly confronted capital's power. The nationwide Teamsters' strike at United Parcel Service in 1997 was followed by the Seattle demonstrations of 1999 against the WTO, in which unions participated in alliance with environmentalists and student groups. In 2000, along with growing protests at an international level (demonstrations were staged against the IMF and WB in Prague, London, and other cities), similar actions were conducted in Washington and at the two major parties' conventions in Philadelphia and Los Angeles. Yet, having poured its hopes and millions of dollars into the attempt to elect a centrist Democrat to the White House, labor's officialdom finds itself at bay in the aftermath of Al Gore's defeat and the AFL-CIO's inability to make the difference in enough congressional races. Clearly, the baby steps of labor's revival have come to a halt because unions are still not convinced that a broadly based democratic movement is necessary to reverse its long-term slide.[32]

4

DOES THE UNITED STATES HAVE A RULING CLASS?

CLASS AND FRACTION

In *The Communist Manifesto* Marx and Engels specify the phrase, "The history of all hitherto existing societies is the history of class struggle: Freeman and slave, patrician and plebeian, lord and serf, guild master and journeyman, in a word, oppressor and oppressed stood in constant opposition to one another, carried on an uninterrupted, now hidden, now open fight, a fight that each time ended either in a revolutionary reconstitution of society at large or in the common ruin of the contending classes."

But in each prior epoch there were gradations within the classes. After providing some detail about these gradations—actually internal hierarchies that in some instances, particularly feudalism, might be considered castes within social classes—the writers make the astounding statement that in the "epoch of the bourgeoisie" these gradations tend to disappear and class antagonisms have been "simplified" into two great classes: "bourgeoisie and proletarians."[1]

The *Manifesto* was written in January 1848 and was followed in June of the same year by the Parisian workers' insurrection, which Engels called "the first great battle between the proletariat and the bourgeoisie."[2] But when, four years later, Marx revisited French politics he recognized that these gradations had not disappeared. He discovered the political salience of differences within as well as between the oppressor class and the oppressed classes. Commenting on the formation of a bourgeois republic to replace

Louis Phillipe's "bourgeois monarchy," an event that was, in his view, a direct result of the insurrection against the monarchy's anti-working-class policies, Marx enumerates the class fractions that stood on the republic's side in its repression of the uprising: "the aristocracy of finance, the industrial bourgeoisie, the middle class, the petty bourgeois, the army, the *lumpenproletariat* organized as the Mobile Guard, the intellectual lights, the clergy and the rural population."[3] Thus when Marx must address the specific political/historical actors the gradations are needed to describe events and situations. Some of them, such as the army, do not correspond to the class model proposed earlier.

A manifesto is a call to action and, for this reason, must operate at a fairly high level of abstraction. The long historical perspective inevitably varies from how events are played out in a particular situation. Although the intermediate classes between workers and capitalists have not entirely disappeared in advanced capitalist societies, the *tendency,* especially in the twentieth century, was toward the simplification of which Marx and Engels spoke, and was no more evident than in the United States. In many communities, try to buy a carton of milk or a loaf of bread in a small grocery store; supermarkets have penetrated even geographically remote rural areas. An important component of the national culture, the independent small farmer, has often been reduced to a part-time operator and spends most of the time working for wages in a factory, driving a truck, or working in a retail establishment. There are fewer than a million full-time farm owners in the United States—many of them large and medium-sized corporations—who, thanks to technological innovation, together supply the nutritional needs of more than 260 million Americans and manage to export at least a third of the annual product.[4] In the United States, where New Deal–era farm subsidies were severely cut during the 1980s and 1990s, national farm organizations have been dominated by corporate agricultural interests; only at the state level do small and medium individual farm operators retain some political influence. Moreover, small merchants are chronically underorganized and have been overwhelmed by corporatization, not only of food, but also of clothing, appliances, and electronics retailing. Those who earn a medical or law degree have a 65 percent chance of becoming a salaried employee of a hospital, Health Maintenance Organization (HMO), or a law firm for most or all of their working lives. The self-employed engineer is now a rarity. In sum, only if one determines class chiefly by income can the simplification thesis be refuted. The rapidity of these changes varies depending on the national context, particularly its culture. French consumers, for example, have resisted the supermarket despite repeated attempts to institute it on a large scale, and a sizable sector of independent small and medium farms remains, although there are recent incursions by American wine corporations such as Gallo to foster partnerships.

No less than in 1850, today gradations, or what I have termed fractions, within social formations or classes remain and are constituent of economic, political, and social power, especially in the ranks of financial and industrial capital. The term *bourgeoisie* as a description of the leading protagonist of power in late capitalist societies conceals more than it reveals. It is not enough to enumerate the sectors of capital (aristocracy of finance, industrial bourgeoisie) to map power. Absent a direct threat to the system as a whole by insurrections or wars, which remarkably concentrate the loyalties of different fractions, the ruling circles are invariably fractious. Since the 1970s these fractions are engaged in intra- as well as interclass combat on the basis of divergent interests and ideologies, and this struggle is expressed in and through the contending electoral parties, within the national state, and within the institutions of global capital.[5]

How is economic and political rule exercised? In societies in which economic and political power depends on the consent of the underlying population, it is rare that agents of capital such as corporate officials rule directly. Most elected public officials, even those who hold presidential office, are traditionally recruited from the professional or entrepreneurial middle classes, and, even in this age of wealthy office seekers who are willing to spend millions of dollars of their own money to get elected, the electorate remains suspicious that they are merely buying the election. The state, conceived as both the institutions of government and those of major domains such as education, religion, and labor that provide the ethical and political legitimacy for the dominant social formation, is constituted as an autonomous constellation of institutions precisely because the exercise of naked economic self-interest weakens the authority of the socioeconomic system. But the state is constituted as well as a system of rules, the obedience to which is the social glue for reproduction of capital and labor. These rules are not merely convenient fictions but are the results of a series of struggles and compromises made in the past by contending forces. To the extent that the forces observe these rules, the system is stable.

The term *ruling* class signifies the power bloc that at any given historical period exercises economic and political dominance and ideological hegemony over the society as a whole and over the class within which it functions. The word *bloc* indicates that power is almost always constituted by struggles that lead to the formation of alliances, the outcomes of which are not determined in advance, although in contemporary economically and technologically developed countries the dominant fraction of capital tends to play the leading role together with the top layer of the permanent political class. Whether other institutions like the military, major research universities, and powerful labor unions share power is a historical/empirical question. Surely war is an event that generally alters the composition of economic and social power. Another is the relation of forces in struggles between capital and labor. And to the degree that the expanded capital accumulation increasingly relies on institutionalized scientific and technological knowledge, those who administer the production of knowledge may gain entry into the power bloc.

In the Cold War era C. Wright Mills argued that power in America was constituted by an alliance of major private corporations, the military, and the political directorate. But in a social system in which capitalism, whatever its modalities, remains the driving force, it is evident that capital and its leading fraction tend to be dominant to the degree that the state and its institutions, at both the national and global spheres, provide the indispensable legal and political framework for rule and can do so only under conditions of relative autonomy, capital must subject itself to the mediations of law, policy, and the accumulated rules of economic engagement. Similarly, the military, trade unions, and other potential power shapers bring to the table conditions arising from their own histories and institutional rules that configure and impose some limits on the scope of capital's autonomy.[6]

For this reason the ruling class in liberal democratic countries must be an alliance. The class that rules operates within the boundaries and conditions established by historical memory and by those institutions of the national state and of the global state invested with the task of regulation of relations among contending and complementary social formations and, in the case of civil courts, relations within the constituent fractions of power. That these rules generally favor large shareholders in leading corporations does not imply that any single capitalist or corporation, no matter how powerful in economic terms, is exempt from their enforcement. For example, the prospective breakup of the largest computer software company, Microsoft, and the earlier government-sponsored agreement to disaggregate AT&T—the virtual monopoly in national telecommunications—were vigorously contested.

Second, the faction of government currently in power puts its own stamp on the facts. Despite its pursuit of Microsoft's monopolistic business practices, the Clinton administration was relatively indifferent to the bevy of mergers and acquisitions that occurred during its watch. And there is the interpretation of evidence and of law by a phalanx of judges with varying degrees of power in the juridical hierarchy. What remains constant, however, are the boundary conditions, namely, that in no event—short of a catastrophic depression in which capital itself has decided to abandon a given sector—will telecommunications and computer software or any other major industry revert to public ownership regardless of the finding of virtual monopoly power by a single corporation or a small cabal of corporations over the market. The customary remedy is to break up the corporation into smaller units in order to foster competition from other sectors of capital. That the evolution of the disaggregated industry may, eventually, lead to mergers and acquisitions that reinstate the status quo ante in an era of neoliberal economic policy may receive little attention from government agencies.

In order to delineate power in society it is necessary to work at a lower level of abstraction than the largest historical divisions suggested by Marx and Engels. And, despite my previous incantation against the tendency of many to draw class maps as a substitute for historical and political analysis of class relations, I offer a historically situated class map. But in the course of mapping the ruling circles it is necessary to address, in some detail, the political theory of pluralism, according to which there are no ruling circles but only a liberal democratic state that reflects, more or less imperfectly, the multitude of interest groups that vie with each other for specific pieces of power within the framework of liberal democracy.

PLURALISM AND ITS DISCONTENTS

Pluralism is the theoretical expression of the combined theses of American exceptionalism and American classlessness. It is the common sense of contemporary American politics and of American political culture. Its premise is that the economic and social reproduction of the capitalist system is the fundamental basis of the unity of the state. Pluralism's theoretical model presupposes that the political sphere operates according to market principles. In concert with its positivist assumptions, what you see is what you get, that is, the visible is the only meaning of the real, and such abstractions as capitalism, class, and class struggle have nothing to do with social reality. And we can make inferences only from observed facts, where fact refers to the results of surveys worked up by statistical methods rather than to theoretical reflection or historical analysis. The undeniable fractions within social formations reflected through specific expressed interests are taken as sufficient reason to abandon classes as an analytic category.[7]

In addition, pluralist doctrine proposes a model of power that radically separates the political from the economic. While some of its more sophisticated versions acknowledge that giant financial and industrial corporations may, in certain sectors, dominate the markets for capital and for goods, pluralists insist that the institutions of large-scale capital in liberal democratic societies do not and cannot dominate the state and politics. Pluralists cite the multiple instances in which Congress and the judiciary have defeated or ignored the legislative programs of business groups. Because they reject the distinction in social theory between the visible and the invisible, the formal institutions of liberal democracy, including its regulatory agencies (which, in some instances, limit the scope of oligopolistic market domination), are taken as sufficient cause for the claim that, far from being an instrument of capital, the state is a mediator or, occasionally, an arbiter between competing interests. While in some sectors a few large corporations that dominate the market try to influence national and local governments and often get their way, they are seen as only one among a plurality of interest groups that seek political influence.

The absence of visible class politics in the United States—particularly the fact that workers and their organizations have not formed labor or socialist parties that, in their own name, contend for political power—has prompted some writers to declare that *pluralism* best describes American political power. Politics may be understood in the mathematical metaphor of a parallelogram of contending forces, none of which holds, in advance, decisive power. According to this conception, beneath the episodic act by individuals of voting, interest groups underlie local as well as national politics. Citizens typically act through nonpartisan organizations to advance their specific issues. They lobby, engage in public relations campaigns, occasionally endorse candidates who support their issues, often ignore candidates' positions on issues not of their immediate concern, and try to motivate their constituents to take action on behalf of their agendas.

Of course unions are just one, albeit a powerful, example of these organizations. Like other interest groups, the labor movement usually sets a few key legislative priorities to carry to local, state, and especially national legislative and political arenas. Although the pluralists acknowledge no coherent capitalist class, they cite business groups that, no less than unions, have a definite legislative and political agenda and may impose their will on the political system, but usually only in alliance with other groups. And traditional farmers' organizations have marched and lobbied on foreign and domestic issues they believe are of concern to the economic interests of their constituents. But according to pluralist lights, most interest groups are not driven by economic interest alone. Economic interests often overlap with professional and social belief systems that might include economics but are not confined to them. For example, until recently the American Medical Association (AMA), the traditional organization of self-employed physicians, crafted its opposition to federal health programs such as socialized medicine on professional and moral as well as economic grounds: it viewed socialized medicine as government interference with the patient-client relationship and a threat to physicians' autonomy in performing their professional duties, including the right to set fees for service. For more than a half century after it defeated New Deal proposals to insert national health insurance into the Social Security system in 1935, representative bodies could enact no health policy or program the AMA opposed. One may point to other organizations dedicated to single issues, such as gun control and antidrunk driving legislation, that cross class and status boundaries. The proliferation and influence of these groups are often cited to refute the alleged economic determinism of class theory.

The political theory of pluralism flourished in the post–World War II era, when the United States emerged as the leading capitalist power. In the wake of European devastation the United States remained untouched by the ravages of physical destruction and sustained relatively mild losses on the battlefield. The war had another effect. Contrary to gloomy expectations of the resumption of the depression, after the war and partially because of it a large portion of America's citizens experienced unprecedented prosperity. The years between 1948 and 1970 appeared to repudiate predictions of a new economic crisis and the idea that class struggle propelled politics. America embarked on a roll of government-supported private spending that appeared to benefit nearly all social formations of society, including those that had experienced the late 1920s and 1930s as an unmitigated economic disaster.[8]

Even the new radical social movements of the 1960s and 1970s could be framed by pluralist analysis. The emergence of the student, civil rights, and feminist movements during this period was, for some writers, proof that class did not define the most dynamic political forces. Some erstwhile marxists went so far as to cite the new social movements as sufficient reason to abandon class as a explanatory category altogether.[9] Others argued that, save the underclass of permanently poor blacks and Latinos who had been left out of the prosperity, the divisions within the traditional working class could be better described in race and sex/gender terms than as class fractions.[10]

Perhaps the most sophisticated theories viewed the plurality of interests in American politics as a symptom of the emergence of mass society in which problems of production had been displaced to issues of consumption. Suburbanization of a considerable proportion of the American population, it was argued, effectively eliminated housing segregation on the basis of economic class. And the advent of education as a path to social mobility, especially the postwar influx of millions of veterans from predominantly working-class backgrounds into institutions of higher education, supported the conclusion that America had become a meritocratic society in which credentials rather than the social conditions of birth determined an individual's life chances. These theories reinforced the proposition that, in political terms, Americans affiliated with their status group (professions, social and cultural organizations, guildlike crafts, and so on) rather than with their class.

The thesis of suburban mix of disparate economic and social formations did not survive the 1950s.[11] By the sixties, sociologists observed suburban class and race segregation. Owning a one-family home and a late-model car did not qualify a working-class aspirant for admission into either the country club or neighborhoods where the price of a house was for all practical intents a restrictive covenant along class lines. Some workers might play golf with managers and self-employed professionals, but when they left the course each went back to their own neighborhood. Some suburbs were constructed by developers and planners as working-class settlements; the only middle-class residents were small shopkeepers or those who had traditionally lived there. It was fairly plain that within and between communities in the areas of massive suburban development class segregation was alive and well.[12]

In pluralist thinking, the complexity of interest group politics demonstrates one more aspect of American exceptionalism. When actors in other liberal democratic states experience ideological splits, they tend to form new political parties, and their programs are clearly linked to class interests. In contrast, American political parties are typically coalitions of disparate interest groups; further, in an age when media play an enormous political role, as primaries have displaced party conventions as the main arena of candidate selection, the parties themselves have yielded to candidate-based organizations and to the primacy of the so-called congressional parties, which deal directly with interest groups. The second pluralist contention suggests that although these groups may be incessantly in conflict, compromise and consensus mark American politics and make for the extraordinary stability of the political system. Hence the slogan that most outcomes of political conflict are win-win, at least for all but the most economically and socially abject.

Pluralism's legitimacy relies largely on the common sense that the labor question is separate from sex and race. Reflecting the refusal of the labor movement to link the politics of production with the politics of consumption and with the cultural question, pluralism identifies labor relations with conflicts at the workplace rather than with questions of power in every aspect of social life. Since the concept of the alienation, let alone the exploitation, of labor as a characteristic feature of capitalist production is denied on the scientific ground that such relations cannot be reduced to measurable things, the idea that workers who may enjoy the benefits of middle-class consumption are in the ranks of the oppressed seems an ideological fantasy. In concert with the dominant social and political thought, race and sex are understood as essential, irreducible characteristics, especially in the era of so-called identity politics. Thus the problem of race and sex discrimination in employment can be resolved without a restructuring of the workplace and of prevailing social relations. Many who equate democracy with its representative institutions and juridical and legislative expressions remain convinced that the Civil and Voting Rights Acts of the 1960s were sufficient to end discrimination; the laws prompted many conservatives to declare the abolition of race and sex bias, and liberals sincerely believe that its persistence is a matter of enforcement by legal bodies or an unfortunate sedimentation of older, irrational attitudes.

Insofar as class is recognized within the pluralist framework, it becomes the domain of white men and the labor movement and is acknowledged in terms of "job property rights." Indeed, such statements seem vindicated by years of exclusion by many unions of blacks and women.[13] In many respects unions have been, and often have remained, white male job monopolies. But in the wake of deindustrialization and deregulation, which have decimated many of labor's traditional strongholds, and of recent union efforts to organize the working poor, blacks, Latinos, and women are rapidly overtaking, at least numerically, the historic dominance of white men. Blacks and women are indeed workers as well as oppressed social formations. They are more prone to union organization than any other fraction of the working class, precisely because they face the double burden of low wages and the stigma associated with color and sex.[14]

But the sweeping argument that political parties are coalitions of interest groups must address the increasing ideological coherence of the Republican Party and the failure of the Democrats to constitute a genuine opposition. The insurgence of the Right since the mid-1960s has gradually driven the moderate wing out of the party. Moreover, since the 1970s, the Democrats have converged with the Republicans on several crucial fronts, especially in their embrace of neo-Smithian economics, according to which the market must be allowed to govern economic relations free of government regulation. Consequently, social services like health and education, which since the Depression were largely treated as public goods, must now be subject to the same rules of investment, cost containment, and profitability that govern any private enterprise. Excepted, of course, are the regulatory functions of the Federal Reserve, the Securities and Exchange Commission, and the Food and Drug Administration, which are institutions that capital supports, a tacit recognition that the unfettered free market is not always in its interest.

Some differences remain between the two parties, especially on the so-called social issues. Having caved in on health—indeed, the failed Clinton national health plan was based on managed care administered by private HMOs and private insurance companies—the Democrats are still committed to public education and opposed, in the main, to privatization proposals. But the persistence of some disputes between the major parties, mostly matters of emphasis rather than principle, does not erase the fact that on a wide array of burning economic questions the parties differ only marginally. Since 1990 the Democrats have been recipients of contributions from the giant corporations almost in the same volume as Republicans.

Within the framework of its blatant big business orientation the Republican Party remains a coalition: of the social Right, including abortion opponents, privatizers of public goods, supporters of "faith-based" publicly financed social services, and other interests linked to fundamentalist Christian churches; the embattled middle class of farmers, professionals, and merchants in small towns and rural areas; and the most powerful fractions of capital, finance and industrial and regional financial capital. These partners are not always in agreement about social issues; it is arguable that among leading executives of the financial services sector Republican loyalties have weakened precisely because of the growing influence of fundamentalist Christian organizations and because the White House and congressional leadership, which are closely allied to the social Right, seem intransigent on some issues that propelled the bipartisan internationalism of the post–

World War II period. In the post–Cold War period the party has shifted somewhat, with the backing of the financial sector, toward supporting the interests of industrial capital, especially steel, oil, and coal mining, which have lost ground to international competitors in the era of the strong dollar. Yet President George W. Bush took pains on the eve of the Genoa G8 meetings in 2001 to assure his partners, as every national administration since World War II has, that the U.S. government condemns critics of free trade and passionately adheres to the neoliberal policies of the WB and IMF. These tensions do not undermine the party's ideological unity.

Republicans have faithfully brought agendas of various corporate capitalist fractions to legislative bodies: deregulation of business at all levels of enterprises and trade; tax reduction for wealthy individuals and corporations; the revival of the near-dormant nuclear energy industry; limitations and abrogation of labor's right to organize and bargain collectively; a land policy favoring commercial and industrial development at the expense of conservation and other proenvironment policies; elimination of income support to the chronically unemployed; reduced federal aid to education and health; privatization of the main federal pension program, Social Security; limitations on the right of aggrieved individuals to sue employers and corporations who provide services; in addition, as social programs are reduced, they are joined by the Democrats in favoring increases in the repressive functions of the state, expressed in the dubious drug wars in the name of fighting crime, more funds for surveillance of ordinary citizens, and the expansion of federal and local police forces. Since the World Trade Center attacks of September 11, 2001, the GOP, with virtually unanimous congressional Democratic support, has been in the forefront in its advocacy of extending the permanent war economy with a massive arms buildup era. The Bush administration has made this a cornerstone of its program. It has proposed instituting a missile defense shield in violation of antinuclear missile treaties negotiated since the early 1980s with other nuclear powers by Republican and Democratic administrations alike.

The Democrats have all but abandoned their only distinctive political doctrine, the social welfare state developed during the second New Deal. The two pillars were public income support for those adversely affected by the vicissitudes of the labor market and the expansion of public goods. The Democrats still adhere to a modest defense of labor's rights without drawing out the implications of this position for its free trade policies. For the heart of laborism is that workers, through their unions, are constituted to limit capital's freedom to put labor in competition with itself globally as well as within the nation-state. Having presided over the enactment and implementation of NAFTA and sponsored its extension to Asia and Latin America, the Clinton administration gave only a rhetorical nod to AFL-CIO demands that these agreements include labor protections; and it collided with the federation on its insistence that Congress's ability to amend any agreement be sharply curtailed by granting the executive branch fast track powers that would limit congressional action to simple approval or disapproval of trade agreements.

Deregulation of banking and transportation, the most anti-working-class measure of the postwar era, was an initiative of the Democratic Carter administration. The respective bills were sponsored by the liberals Ted Kennedy and Henry Reuss and passed by a Democratic Congress. Within a few years of its adoption, deregulation created a huge nonunion sector in the trucking industry by abolishing the tradition of articulating wages to regulated interstate freight rates. Even as Congress closed some loopholes for the rich and for large corporations, a bipartisan measure to deprogressivize federal income taxes was crafted by Democratic Senator Bill Bradley. And it was the Clinton administration that placed paying down the debt, a warhorse of fiscal conservatism, as the major domestic policy of its second term, just as Clinton signed welfare reform legislation in 1996 that eliminated guaranteed income supports for the unemployed and the indigent by placing a time limit on such assistance. Nor are the Democrats prone to propose spending measures to address such issues as poverty, unemployment, universal health care (except a health system that would be administered by the private sector), or a vast expansion of federal aid to education. In sum, as James Truslow Adams once remarked, the business of the American government is business, and this statement is more true today of both parties than at any time since the Coolidge years.

I am not claiming that all American affairs of state and politics that have economic dimension are merely an efflux of the will of capital. On questions of land policy environmentalists have won a few rounds in the face of implacable opposition from organized business interests, especially lumber and oil; given the militancy of the movement, the Democrats have generally supported restrictions on resource development in the remaining forest and wilderness areas such as Alaska, Colorado, and elsewhere. And the perennial proposals advanced by conservatives, and also by some securities and investment banking interests, to privatize Social Security have been thwarted, or at least postponed, largely because of the formidable electoral strength of organized labor and retirees. Nevertheless, Democratic presidential candidate Al Gore in 2000 was willing to consider "experimenting" with a voluntary program to use some Social Security money to establish private individual investment portfolios. The foregoing inventory suggests that, although issues associated with sexual and race freedom do cleave our polity in a distinct manner that cuts across economic formations, capital remains the decisive element in how America is ruled.

The composition of the power bloc and the relations among its components depend on historical conditions. In the post–Cold War era, as the military has been subsumed under civilian control, it is no longer constituent of the ruling class, although George W. Bush's avowal of permanent war may alter this judgment. Since the last quarter of the twentieth century, the U.S. ruling class consists of the dominant fraction of capital, finance capital; the political directorate, that is, the permanent national political class, some of whom are intellectuals who shuttle back and forth into universities and policy think tanks like the Brookings Institution and the Conference Board, but also the more openly ideological Heritage Foundation and the American Enterprise Institute; and others, such as the Clinton administration's Treasury secretary, Robert Rubin, who are recruited from and return to high corporate managerial positions, especially but not exclusively national corporate law firms and financial institutions.

The top research universities—including most Ivy League schools, elite private colleges, MIT, major public research universities, and some quasi-public research universities such as Cornell and Penn State—constitute important institutions of ruling class formation. In the past they were chiefly institutions for the social reproduction of the higher circles and constituted the networks for recruitment into corporate and government bureaucracies, leading corporate law firms, and intellectual fields like economics and political science that, with some exceptions, have become the technical and policy disciplines of social rule. But in the past half century, as they have become important sources of the production of scientific, technical, economic, and administrative knowledge, the leading research universities are increasingly integrated into the sinews of rule. Their corporatization in recent years signifies not only a tendency to forge partnerships with leading industrial corporations, especially of biotechnology and information, but also to structure their own governance in the template of corporate hierarchy.[15] They raise tens, sometimes hundreds, of millions of dollars from their alumni, many of whom are perched at the top of the institutions of the power bloc, and from research partnerships with the government and private corporations. The cumulative effect of these relationships has been a decisive shift of university power. This trend has gone far to destroy traditional academic culture, according to which universities are sites of critical inquiry. On the contrary, as key producers of technoscientific knowledge, these institutions enjoy affiliations that are closer to those of ruling circles than to the collegium, a shift reflected in the fact that high university officials are, more and more, recruited from the corporate boardrooms and high-level political and government offices.

Class power sets the framework of what is politically possible. If any branch of government is prone to "think outside the box," the ruling circles will quickly signal their readiness to take action to thwart such decisions (an exception occurs in time of war, when the executive branch may exercise emergency powers). Such action may entail capital strike or capital flight. This framework applies to both Right and Left-Liberal policies and programs, even though, in recent years, it is usually the hard Right, when it seizes the reins of government, that may stretch the boundaries, at least for a time. It is not unreasonable to read the five to four Supreme Court ruling of December 2000 that stopped the recount of Florida presidential ballots as a kind of right-wing coup. Bush's victory has been interpreted by some commentators as an extraordinary violation of democratic freedoms rather than a symptom of a larger shift. On the contrary, it illustrates a central feature of American liberal representative government: there is always a danger that the rules can be broken when the dominant power bloc determines its vital interests are at stake in a given election. When the practical "left" side of the political spectrum—which questions the efficacy of the market in achieving the goals of social justice and thereby advocates government intervention to modify the deleterious effect of corporate power and provide for those unable to fare well otherwise—gains national and local political office, it governs on the expectation that it will have thoroughly internalized the boundaries of the invisible box of acceptable economic and political action. In an intellectual and political environment in which the concepts of popular democracy, public goods, and public authority have been systematically delegitimized, the practical left is generally unable to challenge even the most outrageous right-wing power plays.

For instance, having exhausted his legal options, Gore, in the interest of preserving political stability, not only threw in the towel but instructed trade union and liberal supporters to refrain from taking to the streets. And the decision by Democratic vice presidential candidate Sen. Joseph Lieberman of Connecticut that military voters who cast their ballots after the official deadline "should be given the benefit of the doubt" reveals the degree to which the Democrats have been subordinated. Given that Bush's victory in Florida, which decided the election by a handful of votes, occurred in the face of the wholesale disallowment by election officials of ballots cast in some heavily pro-Gore districts, the Democrats, to have any hope of winning, should have charged the Right with stealing the election.[16] Instead, unsure of their legitimacy and directed by their conservative wing, the Democrats completely acquiesced to the most brazen abrogation of democracy since the Republicans sold Reconstruction in 1876.

Contrary to pluralist claims that rely heavily on the fractious struggles over social issues in the past four decades, I would argue that since the ruling fractions have no firm position on social issues, the practical left enjoys a wider field of action. Under certain circumstances, especially the effort to prevent social unrest and thwart the Right's coalition, a segment of the ruling class sided with social liberals on such issues as civil rights, abortion, and easing punitive drug laws. But when the authoritarian Right can plausibly abrogate democratic processes, the practical left is generally in no position to defend popular sovereignty, nor does big capital seem to read these abrogations as violations of its own interests.

A HISTORICAL MAP OF CLASS POWER

I will now attempt to draw a map of the ruling class. The difference between this map and those offered by most social cartographers is that it is temporal as well as spatial. My purpose is to identify, in historical/temporal perspective, the composition of that class that wields the heaviest economic and political weight in alliance with the fraction of the political directorate that administers the institutions of rule. But rule exceeds the exercise of naked economic and political power. It also entails the struggle among contending forces over setting the rules by which conflicts are resolved. The power bloc at any time may not correspond to its antecedents and may be displaced through struggles over the composition of ruling formations. The struggles over ruling class formation are no less intense than those conducted within the formations of labor and other oppressed and exploited groups. Acting on behalf of certain interests, who controls the decisive levers of economic, political, and social power changes according to the outcomes of struggles within capital as well as between capital and labor. Nor is the state—the constellation of institutions responsible for the maintenance of economic, political, and social stability—always subservient in its day-to-day activities to specific business groups. Just as the structure of the working and middle classes is constantly evolving, so the constellation of social formations that constitute, in the most general terms, social rule is subject to historical determinations that bear on relations within and between classes. We cannot understand power relations unless we understand their history. At the national level whatever formations constituted the rulers at the turn of the twentieth century may, at the dawn of the twenty-first, have disappeared, been relegated to middle levels of power, or been eased into the margins.

Take the diminished economic and political position of the steel and rail industries in the century since the apex of the industrializing era. A little more than a century ago there was no more powerful figure in American popular culture and politics as well as industry than Andrew Carnegie, poised on the edge of creating the mammoth United States Steel Corporation. Similarly, the preeminent rail magnate, Jay Gould, stood at the pinnacle of the economy. Because the federal government's imposition of eminent domain to clear rail passages was crucial to creating a national rail system, Gould, Jim Hill, and other rail titans were president-makers and all but set land policy. So powerful were the rail corporations that the U.S. army spent much of the post–Civil War years expropriating these lands destined for rail and agricultural development from Native American tribes.[17] As late as the 1940s the figures of U.S. Steel's Myron C. Taylor and National Steel's Tom Girdler were prominent representations of the power of steel to shape the nation's fate. Today, steel corporations have been consigned to secondary importance; even if they succeed in aligning themselves with the prevailing political directorate on trade issues, it may no longer be said that "as steel goes, so goes the nation." Steel has suffered from a fifty-year history of mismanagement and international competition whose technology outstripped a relatively archaic U.S. industry. Once dozens of communities depended on steel for their economic lifeblood and created a culture around the mill. In addition to electricity and home heating, steel constituted the basic link of the coal industry to the economy, and many mines were owned directly by steel corporations. But steel's eclipse at the top is only the most visible of the shifts in power relations from industrial to financial corporations.

Railroads no longer drive America's economic expansion. Rails are still important, but trucks and airplanes have largely displaced them for shipping goods and carrying passengers. And our sense of place is no longer exclusively geographic. Other means of communications—telegraph, telephone, radio, television—have altered the significance of travel over geographic space. The discovery and dissemination of cyberspace, the virtual domain of the Internet, has just begun to affect air and auto travel and the character of distribution and consumption. So social power is highly volatile, depending on how circuits of capital are arranged, the nature of international as well as domestic competition within and between business sectors, and cultural and technological changes, which are both linked to these and independent of them.

In contrast to the media and other popular representations of power, which are usually embodied by individuals who hold corporate and political office, in the concept of social rule offered here many of these individuals are understood as bureaucrats. Management's power is temporary, limited to the offices they hold. Although they are usually personally wealthy and hold securities and stocks as perks of office, when they retire or are replaced they typically take only themselves and their personal wealth with them. Corporate power resides in the institution and its largest stakeholders: groups that control quantities of invested capital. What is the institution that holds power? Is the president or CEO of a small or medium-sized corporation who is manufacturing a new product for information industries part of the ruling class? They are part of the bourgeoisie but are not included in the system of rule. In most cases these smaller firms are capitalized by banks or venture capitalists, who in the face of capital shortages or economic downturn lend them money or provide it in return for a share of the business. In the recent past, entrepreneurs of startup companies in the information sector were forced to share ownership with their creditors.

In 1932, A. A. Berle and Gardner Means theorized that the evolution of capitalism from family-owned businesses to large corporations as the characteristic economic unit had resulted in the separation of ownership from management. Their study, *The Modern Corporation and Private Property,* drew from earlier speculations that, although corporations were still formally owned by shareholders, the huge quantities of capital required by these institutions resulted in widespread dissemination of shares such that no single individual or group typically held the majority of stocks. Shareholders ostensibly owned the firm, but managers were in control. James Burnham extended the argument by claiming that the class of salaried managers was virtually autonomous from the legal corporate owners. Responsible for raising capital, finding the design and industrial labor to produce the commodity, choosing methods of marketing and distribution, and delivering profits in the form of dividends, they had rapidly displaced the old barons of industry at the commanding heights of power. In sum, he argued, the corporate form of organization had altered more than the distribution of market share between the largest corporations and smaller companies. It had transformed capitalism itself. The prophets of the "managerial revolution" claimed that capitalism was in the process of self-transformation; Berle's question was whether private property in the decisive industries still described the economic system. For if in the modern corporation the labor of management was now invested in salaried professionals whose collective knowledge necessarily far exceeded that possessed by the individual entrepreneur or even the large investor, wasn't it possible that the nature of property had unalterably changed or rather that the relation of ownership and control was severed?[18]

Burnham argued that top managers had become a new ruling class. Berle, along with other progressive economists such as Rexford Guy Tugwell and administrators such as Thurman Arnold, tried, through antitrust and federal regulatory powers, to enlist state authority to hold these huge corporations they purportedly ran accountable to the public. Differing from the pluralists, for whom economic concentration had no particular consequences for political power, some students of corporate capitalism increasingly recognized that despite the high measure of control exercised by top managers over the functions of large corporations, the visible hand of financial capital, particularly the large investment banks and the insurance companies, was, not too subtly, behind the ostensibly autonomous corporate bureaucracy as well. As has become crystal clear since the 1990s, when the top-level salaried professional managers falter, boards of directors dominated by investment capital do not hesitate to replace them. If the bottom line of quarterly profits has assumed unprecedented authority over the operation of corporations in every sector of the economy and may lead to layoffs across the spectrum of employees, including managers, then the concept of managerial autonomy, except in a fairly restricted sense, disappears.

More convincing are those who, noting the differentiation of financial and industrial capital in mature capitalist societies, argue for the persistence of capitalist rule. In 1909, the Austrian marxist Rudolph Hilferding noted the merger of industrial and banking capital into a new sphere, finance capital. American journalists—among them Ida Tarbell, Henry Demarest Lloyd, Ferdinand Lundberg, and Gustavus Myers—documented the growing concentration and centralization of capital in the industries that constituted America's economic lifeblood.[19] Others, such as Lincoln Steffens, showed the link between the monopolies and the political process and, in a vein similar to that of some current criticisms, argued that American democracy was profoundly undermined by the corruption of politicians by capitalist tycoons who freely offered bribes, including campaign contributions, in return for executive and legislative decisions that directly benefited them.[20]

THE MYTH OF THE FREE MARKET

Neither capital's concentration nor the predominance of the modern corporation is part of the eternal essence of capitalism or its market. In his classic refutation of the commonly held idea, following Adam Smith's economic doctrine, that capitalism functions best under the regime of the free market and that "state intervention" in the economy is a relatively late development in the history of the capitalist system, Karl Polanyi showed that the terms of economic production and trade invariably entail the involvement of the state. At no time since the inception of capitalism has the market functioned without its assistance. Under conditions in which the state has been relegated, relatively speaking, to Smith's ideal "nightwatchman," that is, limited to protecting property and national sovereignty from those who would steal it, the market does not provide the conditions for economic stability, let alone growth. Polanyi's chief illustration is the close relationship of state and capital in late eighteenth- and nineteenth-century Europe, not only in that the state provided capital with the material infrastructure for the movement of goods and means of communication, such as a publicly run postal system, but also, he argues, in that capital relied on the state to play an important role in economic development by, among other means, transferring funds through the tax system.[21]

Far from remaining an exception to this relationship, the development of the United States demonstrates that its economic system since the continent's settlement in the sixteenth and seventeenth centuries was deeply intertwined with the mercantilist policies of the colonial, and then with the independent, American state. During the founding years of the American Republic, the agrarian yeoman middle class as well as the slaveholding planter class relied on the state to supply the primary means of communications, such as roads; later the state secured the right-of-way for rail transportation and, since it controls airspace, air transportation. Business interests were assisted as well as constrained by tariffs and other terms of trade. Since the early twentieth century in most countries, including the United States, the state regulates to a greater or lesser extent interest rates on loan capital and, even under neoliberal regimes that officially adopt the nightwatchman metaphor, intervenes monetarily or fiscally to thwart the market's supposed natural tendencies toward recession and depression. Although in early America Smith's followers held the reins of political power and resisted the program of the state's close integration with business interests, they rarely hesitated to mobilize the state on their behalf. One of the most ardent supporters of the ideology of market liberalism, President Thomas Jefferson, sponsored several expeditions to claim and eventually develop vast territories in the West and Southwest for the United States and was the guiding force for the Louisiana Purchase of 1805, in which France sold millions of acres of land to the U.S. government. The Louisiana Purchase was the first in a century of state-sponsored territorial acquisition, many of which entailed war and other forms of military intervention.[22]

Relying on the slave trade, with its most important products, cotton and tobacco, America remained an agricultural society whose surpluses were traded with England and other European powers in return for manufactured products. Technological development that originated in the United States was focused largely on steam engines for the ships and trains that took its agricultural products to internal and world markets and on farm equipment, such as Eli Whitney's cotton gin, which improved the productivity of slave labor. The slaveholders and their party, the Democrats, dominated national politics until the Civil War. Despite the "peculiar institution" of a slave mode of production amid a society of free labor, slaveholder power was linked to market capitalism. Although this mode was not based on wage labor, the crops the slaves planted, harvested, and processed were destined for exchange; the proceeds accumulated by the owners were not entirely absorbed by the slaveholders' personal consumption. They were invested in farm equipment and used to pay the costs of maintaining their unpaid labor force.

The South fought hard to preserve a national free trade policy. Since Europe, especially England, was the center of global manufacturing and had no significant international competition for its products, southerners wanted to lower trade barriers to discourage the appearance of such competition and to facilitate the import of cheap manufactured products. These policies were opposed by the owners of the incipient textile and iron manufacturing industries in the United States, which had begun to expand in the late 1830s. They wanted higher tariffs in order to protect themselves against much stronger European and French competitors, but lost most of the battles in Congress before 1850, when, to some extent, the tide began to turn.[23]

Charles Beard called the Civil War the "second democratic revolution" because it completed the unfinished promise of freedom for all Americans mandated by the Declaration of Independence.[24] In the complex of its overdetermined causes and consequences, none exceeds in significance the fact that the Civil War set right the gross injustice of the Constitution and of the American legal system, which had sanctioned slavery. African American freedom was systematically abrogated by the southern ruling class after the Republicans, who either formally or informally controlled the national state from the Civil War until Woodrow Wilson's election in 1912, scuttled Reconstruction in 1876 and returned the former slaveholders to power. In the Hayes-Tilden compromise, the Grant administration agreed to withdraw the Army of Occupation that had, for a brief historical moment, insured the integrity of the democratic laws enacted by the new, radical-dominated black state legislatures, a signal event in the long history of capital's record of limiting or abrogating democracy when its interests required such action.[25]

War is a boon to capital accumulation; the state becomes the investor by letting contracts to private corporations that reap most of the benefits. In the previous two decades the American bourgeoisie had already developed coal, textile, iron, and shipbuilding industries. But the proliferation of government contracts for every manner of war matériel, from clothing to arms, ships to metal parts for machinery, greatly expanded and accelerated its economic reach. The Civil War consolidated the national market under the political and economic hegemony of an industrial capitalist class which had financed and otherwise promoted the war, in alliance with radical politicians committed to the utter destruction of the South's planter aristocracy. Relentless in the pursuit of political domination in the service of the accumulation of large-scale industrial capital, rails—which entailed the development of mining, metallurgy, and a large military force—became the basis for the formation of a new ruling class during the war, and the national state became the sufficient condition for the consolidation of its power. As America rapidly evolved into a world economic and military power in the last quarter of the nineteenth century, the national state assumed new prominence.[26]

As powerful as industrial capital had become, it was unable to underwrite business expansion purely on the basis of its own surplus. Only a few decades after the Civil War, to the Carnegies and the Hills were added the proprietors of large investment banking corporations, among them the Harrimans, Mellons, and the Morgans, some of whom, like Rockefeller, were important industrial capitalists as well. Together they openly took control of the Republican Party. Until Wilson's election to the White House in 1912 even some free market liberals regarded the gilded age of big business domination of politics and government as a blatant power grab. Not only progressives but conservatives recognized that the drive for business expansion at home and abroad propelled American politics and culture, and, in its wake, courts and local governments suppressed the rights of labor, farmers, and other small proprietors.

Those who would challenge the proprietors of the Gilded Age were forced to break with the two parties in order to gain some purchase on national power, let alone reverse the historic ascendancy of what were commonly known as the robber barons, not only for their ruthless exploitation of natural resources and of labor but also for their brazen program of buying and selling politicians and the judiciary at the national as well as the local level. The populist, progressive, labor, and socialist movements achieved some success in curbing the unbridled power of capital by winning legislative backing for the establishment of antitrust and other regulatory agencies. Some have claimed that these reforms were in the interest of capital itself and were supported by some of the largest corporations because they recognized the destructiveness of the unfettered monopoly and the ultimate inefficiency of the system of political spoils and corruption they had fostered in the past. But it would be a serious error to confine an account of this period to the conflicts and their resolution within the ruling circles alone, particularly in midwestern and southern agricultural areas.[27]

In the American West and South small farmers were being reduced, de facto, to wage workers by rail and processing corporations whose real home was on Wall Street. The farmers protested the subservience of the two major parties to big business and created their own political parties. In some instances, farmers' alliances created a new political force, the People's Party, which won office in hundreds of local elections in southern and western farm states and took over some statehouses as well. But these victories were accompanied by a large-scale farmers' cooperative movement to replace farmers' reliance on food processing corporations, which, in alliance with the railroads, were bleeding them to economic death. Even so the party was unable to stem the power of rail and processing corporations to fix prices. In what may have been one of the most significant miscalculations in the history of American politics, the People's Party in 1896 supported William Jennings Bryan, the Democratic presidential nominee, who opposed the GOP's hard money policies based on the gold standard and who by favoring free silver in order to raise farm prices gave a national voice to anti–big business anger. When Bryan was defeated, the party gradually disappeared. In the first decade of the new century some farmers, especially in the Southwest, briefly supported the Socialists. But in South Dakota, Nebraska, and Kansas powerful farmers' organizations decided to take over the Republican Party and make it a populist bulwark, a strategy that, undergirded by sustained farmer-control over processing and distribution, succeeded until World War II.

THE POWER OF FINANCE CAPITAL

Power in the twentieth century may be described as the now-allied/now-conflicted relations between industrial and financial capital. The first fight was resolved in many economic sectors by the merger of the two capitals, but these mergers were generally under the dominance of the investment bankers and the large insurance companies. Within the corporation, however, conflict broke out between large investors who sat on the board of directors, older owners who were sometimes reduced to impotence, and the professional managers, who operated the day-to-day business. Strategic issues such as mergers and acquisitions with competitors that might affect the company's short-term profit, cash flow, and debt situation, for example, divided the managers from the investors. In general, finance capital cared only about the bottom line, leaving to managers the tasks associated with design, production, distribution, and sales, which were of a technical nature. Unlike early industrialists, who were committed to their sector and to their product, financiers moved money according to the narrow criterion of whether profits were to be had, even if it might destroy a corporation or industry. Corporate management came under intense pressure to deliver profits to shareholders as well as to accumulate capital for upgrading and expanding plant, labor, and products. In the main, the period between the two world wars witnessed a growth of financial capital proportional to the United States' growth into a world military and economic power. Many industrial corporations, especially oil, chemical, steel, and electrical, were enmeshed in global trust arrangements with capitalists in other countries, and finance capital viewed the world, as much as the nation, as its investment oyster.

Aggressive free trade internationalism reached an early apex during the New Deal, when, despite the Depression's damper on internal capital investment, U.S. global investments boomed in raw materials like copper and oil and in Japanese, German, and English manufacturing companies. These years were marked by heightened American interest in what was then known as the Far East (now Southeast Asia), which consisted mainly, but not exclusively, of China and Japan; in patent, pricing, and other agreements with German and British steel and chemical producers; and, in the epoch of the emergence of oil as the leading energy resource for industrial and home use, in large-scale military and economic interventions in Latin America and intensified economic diplomacy in the so-called middle east, the site of apparently limitless oil reserves. In each region the state was vitally implicated in fostering corporate interests and was prepared to deploy armed forces to slake capital's global thirst for sources of raw materials.[28]

TECHNOLOGY AND CORPORATE POWER

The years between 1880 and World War I witnessed three crucial technological revolutions—electrical, transportation, and chemical—that permanently altered the structure of capital, transformed the relations between knowledge and production, changed our collective sense of time, and altered the perception of the physical geography of the globe. These revolutions broke the traditional pattern of economic development in a number of ways, not the least of which was to provide a channel for the power of finance capital. Marshaling the natural resources of water, coal, and eventually oil, industrialists within a few decades turned electric power into the leading motor of production of nearly all commodities as well as a major component of cultural change. It was a source of innovation in the labor process, making possible the introduction of the assembly line, but, together with scientific discoveries in electromagnetism, it was also the condition for the invention of self-generated artificial light, the telegraph and telephone, radio, and film; and, perhaps equally important, it changed our sense of time. Day and night no longer divided work from leisure. Under electrical illumination the workplace could function twenty-four hours a day. Electric light changed our waking and sleeping routines and our relation to food. Electrically powered refrigeration transformed the food processing industry; in its home applications, food could be stored longer, and that reduced time spent shopping, making people's lives easier (as well as more dangerous because the more people relied on processed food the less nutritional value it provided).[29]

The development of the automobile and of motorized airplanes effected a massive transformation of transportation, creating in its wake vastly expanded networks of roads in the air as well as on land surface. Our perception of space and time utterly changed; within a few decades of the introduction of the car, truck, and airplane for everyday use, travel that once had taken days and months could now be completed in hours. The railroad found itself in serious crisis. In the years immediately preceding World War II most rail lines were privately owned but could no longer turn a profit without substantial state subsidies. So capital migrated to greener pastures and, consistent with the precepts of "lemon" socialism, only then did public ownership of trains and buses, except for freight lines, become politically viable. But in the 1960s and 1970s, despite the consolidation of local routes into a single national rail system, a congressional leadership under the tutelage of car and oil corporations, which fiercely defended the priority of highway construction, became firmly committed to privately owned transportation systems. Congress imposed permanent austerity on the railroad and appropriated tens of billions of dollars for road construction, to this day the most reliable federal and state-generated jobs program.

The chemical revolution radically reduced our reliance on nonrenewable natural resources for many aspects of our sustenance, at least in the short run. The synthetic processes of chemistry enabled substitution of artificial products for relatively scarce natural goods. Supported by government subsidies, farmers could purchase chemical fertilizers rather than relying on manure. Chemicals had a wide variety of industrial and home uses, especially cleaning; and during World War II the military found many new uses for chemical products, the most far-reaching of which was Lucite, or plastics, which, with the use of federal funds, was developed for aircraft parts during the metal shortages. Once a government-held patent that was turned over to private enterprise, plastics rapidly replaced many other scarce or more expensive materials, most famously leather, cotton, and wool. The introduction of synthetic fibers into textile manufacture made the production of cheap but perfectly serviceable clothing possible. By the 1960s they were commonplace around the globe. The only problem with these innovations is that they also altered our collective relation to the various ecosystems upon which life depends. It turns out that plastic is not really biodegradable and damages water and air.

The industrializing era was based on the achievements of artisanal production and in its early incarnation was continuous with the practices of such production. Textile technology had advanced from the hand-operated single loom to the self-acting "mule," which enabled a single worker to tend many machines. But before the 1880s, shipbuilding, machine manufacture, puddling, refining, and mold making—the three basic processes of iron production—and mining, among leading manufacturing industries, were largely ensconced in older craft techniques. Even the emergence of the steel industry, which developed some new technologies, mainly the Bessemer and open-hearth furnaces, and incorporated some scientific knowledge, principally chemistry and the new science of metallurgy, still bore the mark of the artisanal mode of production.[30]

But electricity and the internal combustion engine, which allowed automobiles and aircraft to propel themselves without relying on animals, and the development of wide uses for chemicals signaled a rupture with craft-based knowledge. They did not evolve from earlier modes of production and for this reason had to be propelled anew, largely without the collective experience of the artisans. These new industries were, from the start, emanations of financial and industrial capitalists such as Dupont and Rockefeller, who were pioneers in the industrial applications of scientific knowledge, but also investment banks such as Mellon and Morgan. The enterprises created to build the plants, recruit the labor, and develop the markets were, with few exceptions—notably Henry Ford and the earliest auto pioneers, most of whom rapidly discovered the limits of their resources to survive the market—public corporations rather than individual family-owned firms. In many cases their early managers were engineers, such as Alfred P. Sloan of General Motors and Walter P. Chrysler, and inventors like Alexander Graham Bell and Thomas Edison, who never ceased to rue his demise under the hammer of the corporate form of industrial organization.

The inventor became the folk hero of capitalism precisely at the moment when science displaced craft as the basis of technological innovation. The celebrity of Bell, Edison, Ford, and the Wright brothers identified their work with the American tradition of tinkerers; all of them were mechanics rather than engineers or scientists. Yet the infrastructure of the twentieth-century technological revolution was science, not craft. Virtually unknown are the names of, for example, Willard Gibbs, whose contributions to electromagnetic theory were both substantial and widely known, the German émigré Charles Steinmetz, who set up General Electric's laboratories and directed much of its early research in the development of electric machinery, and the countless engineers at Bell Labs who until the 1990s were responsible for developing much of communications technology. But the concept that capital has been the main spur to technologies that, in the words of a popular General Electric slogan, "Bring good things to life" or, in the Dupont version, afford "better living through chemistry" is one of the underpinnings of the American ideology. And that the knowledge producers were salaried employees, not the abstraction of the corporation, is conveniently omitted.

In sum, the new industries emanating from inventions and scientific discoveries, some of which languished until banks made their capital available to convert the new knowledge into commercially viable products, became a platform for the rise of finance capital. Corporations like AT&T, General Electric, General Motors, Westinghouse, DuPont—which, as Hercules Powder Company, began as a producer of gunpowder and ammunition during the Civil War—Union Carbide, Allied Chemical, and virtually the entire aircraft industry were run by managers but controlled by investment bankers. After World War I corporate organization rapidly became the preferred form for the retail and wholesale sector as department store chains gradually displaced the small clothing and appliance store, supermarkets became the characteristic grocery, and the recently arrived information industries for which computer-based technologies are central were founded. These corporations remained the heart of the permanent war economy after 1938 and emerged from World War II more powerful than ever. Their future became even more bright as the Cold War provided a seemingly endless stream of defense contracts, many of which were on a cost-plus basis, meaning that profits were virtually guaranteed by the Department of Defense. So much for the free market.

INFORMATION: THE NEW ECONOMY?

The media hype of the 1980s and 1990s was that applications of computer-mediated technologies in every nook and cranny of American life—homes as well as businesses and nearly every institution of government, health, and education—constituted a new economy. Prophets of the new economy justified their claims by citing business applications which literally turned commercial and industrial practices upside down within a quarter century after their introduction; the mass production and consumption of personal computers (PCs) that eventually reached into virtually every upper-middle-class household and many in those of other social classes as well; and most spectacularly, the Internet, which had not only changed the culture of everyday life but had permanently altered capitalism. According to the mantra, the information superhighway will produce so much wealth and good jobs that recession, let alone depression, would eventually become a faint memory. The new information economy restores what big capital had almost destroyed: individual entrepreneurship. But the proliferation of startup firms, colloquially labeled dot.coms after the syntactical protocols of the worldwide net, was heralded as nothing less than a rebirth of competitive capitalism. Adam Smith was reborn as a high-tech guru for a trail of wildly optimistic economists in universities, corporations, and government agencies.

Yet by 2000 many who had been persuaded that, beyond their multiple business applications and cultural innovations, computer-mediated information technologies ushered in a qualitatively different economic and social system, were having second thoughts. It turns out the information revolution was continuous with the relations between capital and applied scientific and technical knowledge current at the turn of the twentieth century. Finance capital lay at the root of the emergence of this sector. In most respects the computer hardware and software corporations have been treated as a major venue for investment. As long as they made money, not even the sky was the limit. But when the PC sector reached a plateau in the late 1990s, the flow of capital became finite, and a restructuring of the industry occurred.

In the 1950s and 1960s, electronic engineers and computer hackers-cum-entrepreneurs compressed and reproduced the two-hundred-year history of American capitalism in a few decades. Like Edison and the Wright brothers before them, many of the computer industry's pioneers had their production and research facilities in garages, lofts, small offices, or their homes. Many were able to produce prototypes of computers, operating systems, new applications, and other peripheral programs. Some were even able to take the next step, manufacturing a commercially viable product. But by the mid-1970s it was plain that, as large corporations entered every aspect of the industry, without significant infusions of capital their best option to avert a personal crash was to sell the patents for their inventions to one of the larger electronics corporations. IBM was the leading, but by no means the only, large corporation that acted both as rescuer and financier; when some of these companies' top officials recognized that the large corporation may be an inhospitable environment for innovation they encouraged some of their most talented engineers, computer scientists, and technicians to start businesses on the explicit agreement that, in return for its investment, it would be the sole customer for the product, or at least would have first refusal on patents.

Owing to its historic dominance of the industry, IBM was in a position to hold computer makers hostage to its preferred operating system, DOS. This dominance extended from its original mainframe business developed in the 1930s and 1940s to the PC, which it introduced in the 1970s but chose, much to its regret, to license to others rather than hold for itself as a production monopoly. In time there were a dozen or more leading computer brands, some of which were Japanese or European, but only two key operating systems, one developed by IBM-linked scientists and engineers and the other the much less used, but substantial, Apple. By the eighties, Microsoft had transfigured DOS into Windows and Intel had become the eight-hundred-pound gorilla of the chip industry. Apple, which suffered from this growing monopolization of the PC industry by IBM's PC-based hardware and Microsoft's software, had lost much ground in the PC market, even though it was used in some offices by architects, designers, and a relatively small coterie of individual users who have become a high-tech subculture. Teetering on the brink of collapse by the precipitous fall of its market share to less than 9 percent, Apple was forced to cut a deal in 1998 with Microsoft in order to recapitalize; it rehired one of its founders, Steve Jobs.

Twenty-five years after the introduction of the PC, the market is apparently locked up by a few giant corporations. Although the oligarchic network of computer software corporations has periodically been challenged over the past fifteen years by such well-financed competitors as Sun Microsystems, who offer software they claim is more reliable and easier to use than Microsoft's Windows, the computer hardware makers have demurred. Under the threat of losing their access to Windows, computer manufacturers, except for some firms specializing in business machines, have refused to do business with software corporations that would displace Windows in PCs. Startups are most successful in the peripherals, repair and services. The computer resembles the automobile business: a handful of giants and thousands of tiny service companies making their living by picking up the pieces. In the main, the early pioneer hackers were bought out or failed and became managers for one or another of the big computer and software makers. Even when they started their own businesses they often had to deal with IBM or Microsoft by sharing their patents to finance the operation.

After failing to stem Microsoft's dominance in the marketplace, competitors mounted several legal challenges to this state of affairs. For example, in 1999 Netscape, a pioneer Internet server, brought suit and other servers complained that Microsoft has acted as a bully by requiring computer makers to build in its Internet server to the exclusion of others and was thereby engaging in monopolistic behavior. The Justice Department was prompted to investigate and finally brought an antimonopoly suit against the software giant. The government won the first round in its effort to force a breakup of the company into several separate corporations, but a federal judge's initial order for Microsoft's breakup was reversed on appeal. The Bush administration and eighteen states announced, in July 2001, they would not challenge the ruling.

During the second half of 2000 it became apparent that the information sector was subject to the same forces as the older industrial domains. PC sales began to drop, and a similar slump soon hit the mainframe business. The decade-long campaign by Microsoft to convince users that the latest version of Windows was absolutely indispensable began to fall on deaf ears; after the truly dramatic change from Windows 3.1 to Windows 95 users saw little difference in subsequent versions. In any case, the factors that produced the economic slowdown of 2000–01—huge credit card debt amid income stagnation and overproduction of almost every major commodity resulted in declining investment—manifested in a veritable crash in most technology stocks. The technology-heavy NASDAQ exchange lost 60 percent of its value between March 2000, when it reached 5000, and a year later. By spring 2002 it had lost almost 10 percent more. The largest chip, hardware, and software producers announced they would lay off between 10 percent and 25 percent of their workforces, and, as hundreds of small dot.coms declared bankruptcy, no big corporate daddy was prepared to rescue them. The new economy looked very much like just another sector of capitalist industry. But having been so lavishly oversold (an illusion that was shared by many investment bankers and employees of computer and information-based companies as well), the new economy experienced a bust that was deeper than that in traditional production and service industries, which were facing similar stagnation in investment.

5
NATIONAL AND INTERNATIONAL BLOCS

At the height of the Cold War in 1956, C. Wright Mills identified three principal institutional orders in the constitution of the power elite: the large corporations, the national political directorate, and the military. Mills's designation of the military as a national power institution corresponded to its enhanced and relatively autonomous role in creating and sustaining the permanent war economy, a judgment later vindicated by Dwight Eisenhower's valedictory warning that a military-industrial complex was threatening democracy. But the emergence of a powerful military was crucially dependent upon the division of the world into two primary military superpowers. With the collapse of the Soviet bloc in 1991, the installation of the United States as the only military force capable of negotiating enforceable international agreements, and the relative reductions in military spending during the Clinton administration, the power of the military and of the alliances it had cemented with sections of capital were once again subsumed under civilian political control.[1]

Statecraft as well as economic relations since World War II have become global in a new way. The Marshall Plan, by which the United States, investment banks, and industrial corporations made extensive loans to and investments in British, German, Japanese, and Italian corporations and to governments, was among the earliest postwar efforts at economic and political integration, although these measures were sold on humanitarian and democratic, anti-Communist grounds. Aimed at stopping Soviet expansion, the

Truman Doctrine meant, in practical terms, that the European and American military would now be integrated as well. The third leg of the alliance was the effort to hammer out common policies between national states concerning hot spots in the developing countries, where nationalist revolutions, often led by Communists or nonaligned political movements, threatened the economic interests and political domination of the anti-Communist Western alliance. Because the West European powers were unable to maintain their own colonies these efforts were far less successful than economic and military integration. As France, the Netherlands, Belgium, and Portugal faltered, in some cases through military defeat at the hands of insurgent armies and armed civilian populations, the United States assumed the main military and political burden of counterrevolution in such areas as Africa, the Middle East, and Southeast Asia.

The old imperialism was marked by extensive colonization and by capital investment associated with the development of extractive industries: mining, oil fields, and agricultural products such as food and cotton. But successful struggles for national political independence did not produce economic autarky. The new globalism was characteristically neocolonial; relations were marked by the persistence of economic dependency. After a newly independent India and some African nation-states proclaimed a policy of nonalignment with the two great powers, by the late 1970s most third world countries had slowly gravitated toward one or the other of the two great power blocs. For different reasons India and China maintained their own versions of nonalignment. In the case of India, during the reign of the Congress Party—which, led by Gandhi, had sparked the independence from Britain—this entailed a loose favored-nation relation with the Soviet Union for a large portion of the period before the latter's collapse. But even before 1991, Western powers led by the United States had established a new institutional framework. The U.S.-dominated WB and IMF were prime vehicles in the restructuring of economic and political relations on the basis of a global economic regime in which free trade, unfettered investment, and transformation of the old dictatorships into liberal democracies (the latter introduced under the sign of achieving a stable investment climate) became the preconditions for economic development.

Most Latin American countries had been formally independent before World War II, but had been subsumed under the American empire since the Spanish-American War. Their economies were chiefly oriented to extractive industries—mainly metals, oil, and agriculture—and the United States was their primary trading partner. Mexico, Brazil, and Argentina were partial exceptions to this rule. Although by no means democratic in nature—indeed, after the initial democratic upsurge they had long-term authoritarian governments—each had experienced a successful nationalist revolution whose primary aim had been to establish a framework for economic as well as political autonomy on the basis of mixed private and public enterprises. Under the impetus of world economic crisis and domestic political challenge from the Left, however, these three largest states in the region have, under the auspices of U.S.-based bank loans, become clients of the American empire.

On the other hand, Cuba, which had broken from the United States after its revolution of 1959 against the client-government of Fulgencio Batista, was the single successful effort in the Americas to resist U.S. military and economic domination. But its alliance with the Soviet Union, forged in the aftermath of the Eisenhower and Kennedy administrations' firm refusal to recognize its autonomy within the framework of the American empire, fell victim to its protector's collapse. Plagued by a U.S. blockade and its increasing isolation within the Americas after the failure of the Salvadoran, Chilean, and Nicaraguan nationalist and socialist insurgencies to overcome the subversion of their governments, Cuba has struggled, with remarkable success, to preserve its independence. But in concert with other prolonged examples of independence from neocolonial relations, it has paid the steep price of deferral of democracy and of economic well-being for most of its people. In its effort to overcome the effects of the blockade, the Cuban government has entered the world market on capitalist terms, a bargain that has produced a two-tier economic system and undermined its fierce attempt to maintain rough equality among its people.

While it would be a mistake to overstate the trend toward globalization, there is no doubt that the global integration of production, distribution, and marketing and the integration of financial and industrial capital mean that economic tremors in one part of the world will, sooner or later, be felt in another. When a long-term economic slump afflicted most countries of Western Europe in the early 1970s, within a few years the United States was in the throes of its most serious economic downturn since the Depression. The weakest of the big three automakers, Chrysler, almost collapsed in 1979. Only when the Auto Workers made wage and work-rule concessions and the federal government agreed to raise a billion dollars in direct subsidies was the company saved. The world slump prompted transnational corporations and key nation-states to create a new global state. The constituents of this state are the international economic institutions, such as the WB and the IMF, transnational but invariably nationally based capital, and (contrary to some who proclaim the demise of the nation-state) the states that contain the seven largest capitalist economies. Since the war the imperatives of international relations, including the deployment of large military forces around the world, often in combat situations, have consistently placed limits on what nonmilitary programs the American state can achieve at home. The leading world financial as well as military power placed most of the domestic priorities of labor, liberals, and the black freedom movements on permanent hold; when these were tested in Congress, almost without exception they were defeated.[2]

The twin programs of neoliberal economic policies and anti-Communist globalization that were forged within the United States during the Cold War era became a model for subsequent moves by the West in the direction of establishing a new world order. Under Democratic as well as Republican administrations the postwar era was marked by policies that concentrated federal spending on fulfilling America's global commitments: before 1990 to defend the "free world" and subsequently to foster the program of the global state. This policy was promulgated at a time when the welter of depression-driven and wartime-deferred social needs such as housing and health care became an urgent domestic political priority. Rather than undertaking welfare state expansion in the fifteen years immediately following the war, the state actively intervened by providing federal funds for urban renewal and low interest loans for home buyers to assist banks, insurance companies, and the construction industry to build millions of privately owned homes. Perceiving that the political arena was all but foreclosed to them, the most powerful unions negotiated what I term the private welfare state through collective bargaining: company-paid pensions, health care, and social services. Consequently their main business with Congress and the national administration was to press for defense contracts for firms with whom they held collective bargaining agreements.[3]

Led by UAW president Walter Reuther, the labor-liberal faction of the Democratic Party became allies of the dominant power bloc's program of solving such social problems as employment, discrimination, and inequality through policies of economic growth. Reuther advocated job creation rather than confrontation with the white male labor monopolies that excluded blacks and women. He even coined the phrase "reverse discrimination" to characterize left-wing proposals to negotiate special agreements with employers to promote blacks outside the traditional seniority system, which in many industries ensured that, as the last hired, blacks would be the first fired. That federal policies linked to the growth strategy imperiled the environment, were fueled by a commitment to the permanent war economy, and entailed the spread of U.S. influence—primarily by military means, including spying and ideological cold war, on a world scale—did not detain progressives like Reuther. In fact, Reuther was an indefatigable lobbyist on behalf of defense contractors, many of whom negotiated collective labor agreements with the UAW and other industrial unions. Reuther himself became disenchanted by some of the excesses of American foreign policy during the Vietnam War era. But his and other progressives' belated recognition of the destructive aspects of U.S. commitment to thwart revolution in developing countries cannot efface the record: American labor leaders stood beside the leading fractions of capital and the political directorate in promulgating what Eisenhower had warned against: the domination of American politics and culture by global interests of American corporations.[4]

EMPIRE OR NEW IMPERIALISM?

During the 1960s some intellectuals linked to the mass anti–Vietnam War movement explained U.S. involvement in the network of Southeast Asia wars as an instance of imperialism. On the description of the long march by the Vietnamese and their Communist leadership as a prolonged military and political struggle for national independence—first from the Dutch and then from France, which held the nation as a colony—they interpreted Eisenhower's decision to pick up where the badly battered French military left off as an unwarranted abrogation of the right of colonial nations to self-determination. Many tried to find economic motives for the escalation begun under the Kennedy administration. While there are always economic factors in the conduct of wars, the chief reason the United States became embroiled in what became its most colossal military and moral defeat of the Cold War was chiefly strategic and political. Consistent with its foreign policy, whose chief focus was on fighting "Communist expansion" even if it entailed tactical support for dictatorships, the United States assumed the role of protector of a succession of weak, antidemocratic, but anti-Communist regimes by intervening to thwart the self-determination of the Vietnamese people, especially when they had apparently chosen to live under Communist rule. While it is doubtful the United States sought to make Vietnam its colony, as it had in Korea and in Central and Latin America, the government followed a policy of dominating weaker nations for political, strategic, and economic advantage.

The United States never held a large number of direct colonies, a fact that prompted many political leaders to declare it the great exception to colonialism. Yet the Monroe Doctrine became for 150 years a rallying cry for American economic and military engagement in Central and South America and remained a hallmark of American foreign policy until the 1990s. As the recent attempt by Puerto Ricans to prevent the navy from continuing to use the island of Vieques as a bombing range indicates, the U.S. government retains something of a colonialist mentality. Moreover, contrary to the claims of various American national administrations, the United States has rarely been at peace. Even the collapse of East European Communism and the rapid integration of China into the world market have failed to stem the steady tide of American military intervention in the affairs of weaker, quasi-sovereign nations.

Although the rhetoric of anticommunism has largely given way to the rhetoric of human rights as a justification for these involvements, for many on the Left events like the Gulf War are merely further examples of the same old imperialist adventures. But according to Antonio Negri and his American collaborator, Michael Hardt, the Vietnam War was the last great battle of the old imperialism. In their view we have entered the era of empire, a "supranational" center consisting of networks of transnational corporations and advanced capitalist nations led by the one remaining superpower, the United States. In this globalized economic and political system a genuine world market has been created, national boundaries are increasingly porous, and a new system of "imperial authority" is in the process of taking hold. The new paradigm of empire "is both system and hierarchy, centralized construction of norms and far reaching production of legitimacy, spread out over world space." The invocation of human rights is not merely a fig leaf for the imperium; it is part of an effort to create enforceable international law in which the institutions of empire take precedence over formerly sovereign states, in short, assume the role of world court as well as policeman. The interests of empire are also invoked in the economic arena; it may be noted that the American president has been largely refashioned as a high-level trade representative for the transnationals.[5]

Hardt and Negri insist that the intensity of U.S. interventions is consistent with the project of creating a system in which disputes between nations can be adjudicated by a legitimate international authority and by consensus, upon which world policing may be promulgated to contain them. Even though there are no institutions in place—most of the initiatives remain ad hoc—the authors announce the existence of a dominant "system totality" or logic that, however invisible, regulates the new economic and political order that has taken hold almost everywhere. The new paradigm of empire has gained enormous strength since the collapse of the Soviet Union but is not the direct result of Cold War triumph. In my view, it emerged organically within the old system as a result of the tremendous power of the postwar labor movements to bid up both money wages and the social wage; the pressure of national liberation movements on the old imperialism; and the gradual delegitimation of the authority of national states and their institutions to maintain internal cultural as well as political discipline.

Having increased its power at the industrial workplace, by the 1960s labor was engaged in what Negri had previously termed "the refusal to work."[6] Even as mass consumption was rising, productivity eroded and profits in some instances actually declined. The nation-state, which since the great eighteenth- and nineteenth-century revolutions had, through education, the granting of citizenship to the lower social classes, and imperial ideologies such as racism and patriotism, effectively enforced internalized mass discipline, was increasingly unable to command popular allegiance as, one after another, their efforts to thwart national liberation movements ran afoul. Things came to a head in 1968 and 1969 when mass strikes, notably in France and Italy, almost toppled sitting governments; in Mexico and the United States, too, disruptions and mass demonstrations threatened the stability of the ruling regimes. But the conjunction of economic crisis and the crisis of rule was an occasion for renewal, not breakdown.[7]

The renewal was signaled by President Richard Nixon's abrogation of the Bretton Woods agreement in the early 1970s, by which the dollar rather than gold became the universal money standard. Weakened by international competition and rising costs of production and of governance, the United States was no longer able to contain world prices by monetary means and preserve the system of internal trade regulation. Now the dollar floated along with other currencies. In quick succession the U.S. Congress removed most major regulatory controls: on banks, trucking and other transportation, and most antitrust restraints. The price of fuel and of many other products now floated in the market. Nixon started the process of ending the stubborn legacy of the New Deal, but the so-called Reagan revolution, of which the Clinton administration seemed an ambivalent supplicant, greatly accelerated the changes. The doctrine of Keynesianism—which proclaimed that, because capitalism tended toward equilibrium but fell short of a level of full employment, governments must intervene directly to stimulate economic growth and employment—was declared dead. The free market and with it the idea that government should, as much as possible, stay out of the economy, except to regulate the supply of money and credit in order to stimulate investment and stem inflationary tendencies, became the new religion.

A key element in the new corporate strategy was to reduce wages through curbing the power of organized labor. Battered by the deterritorialization of industrial production as corporations removed plants offshore, to rural southern areas within the United States, and around the globe and by the relentless antilabor policies of the Nixon and Reagan administrations, by the 1980s organized labor in all major industrial countries was in full retreat. In the United States and the United Kingdom unions proved unable to protect many features of the social wage won during the 1930s and the early postwar years. In the United States, even as its density shrunk by half, the AFL-CIO became, at least at the electoral level, identical with the Democrats, whose race to the center-right quickened, paradoxically, in proportion as unions donated ever more funds and workers to its campaigns. Although the power of labor in other countries took a longer time to diminish, most European workers' movements, too, experienced years of agony in the eighties and nineties. Even when labor-backed socialist governments took power in France, Germany, and Italy, welfare state erosion, the decline of union membership owing to heavy losses in the old material goods industries, and the rise of the largely nonunion information and communications sectors reduced not only the power of organized labor but also, with few exceptions, its will to resist their governments' neoliberal economic policies. In fact, when the conservative governments of Great Britain and France were finally turned out of power, the Labour Party in Britain and the Socialist Party in France largely embraced neoliberal policies and were unable to initiate bold new social programs.

The stunning exception has been the enactment by law of shorter hours in France, an initiative that was forced on the government by intense trade union movement pressure. During the struggle, employer associations raised all of the usual objections to shorter hours: because the proposed legislation entailed increasing salaries to compensate for shorter hours, the reduced workweek would hurt France's competitive position; capital flight would be almost inevitable; and the delicate balance of European Union labor standards would be disrupted. In a rare moment of courage and solidarity, the unions stood unbowed beneath these claims, and the Socialist government refused to heed employers' threats. France is no worse off because of the reductions in part because the German metalworkers' union IGMetall, the largest and most powerful in the West, was simultaneously waging a victorious battle for the thirty-five-hour week. Similar campaigns were conducted in Belgium and Italy with limited success. The successful struggle in France against deep cuts in public services and for shorter hours demonstrated a maxim that has not yet occurred to trade unionists in the United States, namely, that workers and their unions can engage in offensive struggles despite times of economic hardship and severe membership losses. Although deindustrialization has seriously afflicted France, private sector union membership has declined to less than 10 percent of the workforce, and unemployment hovers permanently above 10 percent, the ideological power of the labor movement remains formidable. Thus numbers or union density do not tell the whole story. For even when American unions represented a third of the labor force they were unable to win substantial social gains because of their ideological and political subordination to the ruling circles.

For some observers globalization was the major mechanism through which to solve the crisis. Three key transformations have occurred since the 1960s: (a) the economic shift from the dominance of industrial production to information; (b) the integration of the world market so that, with global communications, industrial deterritorialization, and accelerated world investment and trade, the lines between inside and outside are blurred; (c) and the decline of the nation-state as the core of political sovereignty and as a mediator of economic and political protest. The introduction of new scientifically based technologies led to the creation of entirely new communications and information industries and have largely replaced the old regime of Taylorist and Fordist production. Fordism has been replaced with what has been termed Toyotaism or post-Fordism. One of the characteristic features of the new production methods is "flexible specialization" or "just in time" production. Employers in auto and other mass production industries no longer accumulate large parts inventories. Through computerized information technologies management is able to compress the time between the provision of raw materials to the shop floor and the actual production process. While this method cuts down costs of storage and production of unused parts in several instances, it has made possible more effective job actions by disgruntled workers. The entire labor process is disrupted when a department or section of a factory walks out for any reason; because there is no inventory the time required to resume production is much greater than in the old production regime.

But the technological revolution has had another effect. Information technology signifies the advent of "immaterial" production and with it the emergence of the knowledgeable worker who integrates knowledge, skill, and labor, what Robert Reich has designated "symbolic-analytic services," that is, activities that entail "problem-solving" and "brokering" once performed chiefly by managers. Some optimists have predicted a flattening out of the corporate bureaucracies as middle managers are replaced by qualified self-managed workers. The central actor in this new immaterial production no longer stands as a cog in the labor process but is at the center of it. Since these workers are, contrary to popular belief, not immune to the vagaries of exploitation (many of them work on a part-time, contingent, and temporary basis, even in software heartlands), they are among the potential actors in a potentially revived labor movement. Globalism is not primarily a regime of goods production but, with the aid of science, leads to a new paradigm of the relations of humans to their evolutionary partners and to the physical universe. Nature, too, has been integrated into the new system: witness the emergence of industries based on biotechnology that treat life itself as a new field for investment and production. The body is now commodified.[8]

Nation-states, which emerged from the decline of the feudal monarchies and aristocracies and their replacement by liberal democratic systems, captured the collective imaginations of national liberation movements. Despite their relative loss of sovereignty, they still perform important tasks for the empire. Without nation-states the control of whole populations would be impossible. Yet imperialism has died precisely because nations are no longer the key mediators of international economics and politics. The nation may still ignite fierce loyalties among subordinate peoples, but for Hardt and Negri they are no longer truly independent of the new world order. Almost none of these nations afforded the majority of their populations decent living standards. In the year 2000 a third of the world's labor force remained unemployed and underemployed, and tens of millions migrated in order to make a living. The term *third world* describes the past. Having been subordinated to empire, these nations no longer express an alternative. But for Hardt and Negri this situation is no occasion for nostalgia. A new proletariat is emerging on a world scale out of the enormous expropriation of peasants by the new enclosures, a proletariat that may become one of the constituents of resistance and power against empire. The old distinction between industrial production and agriculture has been sundered as hundreds of millions of people are herded into cities in their own countries and, more to the point, in the advanced societies to work in the manufacturing sites of the empire. Those who remain on the land are increasingly subject to capitalist industrial methods; emulating the United States, these nations have turned their farms into factories in the field.

Although *Empire* sometimes strays from its central theme, it is a bold move away from established doctrine. The insistence on a new world is promulgated with energy and conviction. Especially striking is the authors' renunciation of the tendency of many writers on globalization to focus exclusively on the top, leaving the impression that what happens down below, to ordinary people, follows automatically from what the great powers do. In the final chapters they try to craft a new theory of historical actors, and here they stumble, sometimes badly. The main problem is that they tend to overstate their case. From these incontrovertible observations that the traditional forces of resistance have lost their punch the authors conclude that there are no more institutional "mediations"; power must be confronted directly. Not so fast.

One of the serious omissions in *Empire*'s analysis is a discussion of the WTO, the IMF, and the WB. Lacking an institutional perspective—except with respect to law—Hardt and Negri are unable to anticipate how the movement they would bring into being may actually mount effective resistance. Although not obliged to provide a program for a movement, the authors offer indicators of which social forces may politically take on the colossus. Having argued that the classes of historical capitalism, which relied on the mediating role of the nation-state, and institutions such as trade unions and political parties are no longer reliable forces of combat, they are left with the postmodern equivalent of the nineteenth-century proletariat, the "insurgent multitude." In the final chapters of the book, incisive prose gives way to hyperbole, the sharp delineation of historical actors melts into a vague politics of hope. Insisting that resistance precedes power, the authors advocate direct confrontation "and with adequate consciousness the central repressive operations of Empire" to achieve "global citizenship." At the end, the authors celebrate the "nomadic [communist] revolutionary" as the most likely protagonist of the struggle.

The Seattle demonstrations against the WT0 in December 1999, the subsequent anti-IMF and WB activities in Washington, Prague, and Quebec, and the protests at the G8 (the seven largest industrialized countries plus Russia) meeting in Genoa in summer 2001 tell a somewhat different story. The fifty thousand demonstrators who disrupted the Seattle WTO meetings and virtually shut down the city consisted in definite social groups: in the first place, a considerable fraction of the labor movement, including some of its top leaders, who were concerned that lower wages and human rights violations would not only undermine their standards, but also intensify exploitation in the empire's factories; students who had been protesting sweatshop labor for years and were forcing their universities to cease buying from them; and the still-numerous, if battered, detachment of environmentalists—together a burgeoning alliance that appears to have continued. These developments shed a brilliant light on the the existence of resistance to empire but also on the problem of theories that wax in high abstractions. For it is not clear that, as the authors claim, mediations have exhausted themselves, and for this reason it may be argued that some of the traditional forces of the opposition retain at least a measure of life. While direct confrontation is, in my view, one appropriate strategy of social struggle today, it does not relieve us of the obligation to continue to take the long march through institutions, to test their mettle. After all, "appropriate consciousness" does not appear spontaneously; it emerges when people, nomads or not, discover the limits of the old. And the only way they can understand the nature of the new empire is to experience the frustrations associated with attempts to achieve reforms within the nation-state, even as the impulse to forge an international labor/environmentalist alliance proceeds.

Perhaps more to the point, Hardt and Negri underestimate the role of the leading nation-states in constituting the empire's institutional infrastructure and completely deny their relative autonomy. Those who announce the end of the nation-state as a significant force do not comprehend that the nation-state is a constituent of globalization. As the divisiveness over global warming indicates, even when elements of transnational capital, Japan, and most European powers are willing to entertain significant controls over carbon dioxide emissions (greenhouse gasses), the Kyoto Treaty, at best a compromise that environmentalists term a first step, has experienced years of deadlock. In meetings at Bonn in 2001 to hammer out an agreement among the leading players, the United States and Italy, while ostensibly agreeing with its objectives, bluntly rejected the treaty, and other participants quibbled with some of provisions that they believed might hurt their domestic economies.[9] At the same time, a meeting of the G8 in Genoa failed to conclude major agreements on forgiving third world debt, addressing global warming, or modifying trade agreements to protect workers. One might argue this is a temporary glitch in the steamroller of empire. Yet a closer examination of the composition of the leading institutions of which it is comprised paint another picture. Nation-states are part of the constituent power of the new global order.

One of the most striking examples of the growth of transnationalism or globalization, mergers between two ostensibly intranational corporations in 2001 crossed national boundaries and to some extent have modified the concept of national sovereignty. The action by the European Union (EU) in opposing the proposed merger of General Electric and Honeywell must be taken seriously. In the era of transnationalism it is no longer possible for nation-states to approve or disapprove such economic alliances without consultation with other power blocs, a message that American politicians have been slow to absorb. That national sovereignty has thereby been partially abrogated, there is no doubt. That such veritable vetoes by foreign powers will exacerbate nationalism is probable. But the EU's contention that corporations based in the United States that produce and distribute complementary products can constitute a global monopoly threatening the interest of transnational competitors and must be prohibited from taking such action is a novel wrinkle in the evolving story of international economic and political relations. Will such provocations prompt retaliation by the U.S. government in concert with U.S.-based transnationals such as GE? Are we witnessing a new stage of inter-national rivalry? Was the assertion of U.S. hegemony over world economic and political affairs premature? It is probably too early to tell, but what is clear is that neither the transparent picture of pluralism nor the verities of the old marxisms that posited a renewed Pax (corporate) Americana are sufficient to explain the new global configuration.

Within the system of liberal democratic capitalism the state's autonomy is a necessary condition of its role in ensuring a measure of inter- and intraclass regulation of sufficient authority to curb acts of creative destruction that threaten the general capitalist interest. As long as it operates within the bounds of the general systemic interest, its range of decision making may be quite broad and independent of even the most important fractions of the capitalist class. And what that systemic interest actually is may be hotly contested on ideological as well as economic and political criteria, so that there are times when the state acts in a nonrational manner, at least from some perspectives: witness the rejection by Microsoft and its CEO, Bill Gates, of a district court's finding that it had violated antimonopoly statutes. Rationality is, after all, subject to partisanship, as when, in 2001, a fraction of industrial and finance capital joined to oppose the proposed sharp reduction of the estate tax during the administration of George W. Bush. That this powerful group of leading capitalists lost the legislative battle illustrates that a struggle was under way within the ruling formation over an important domain of politics, tax policy.

One of the more significant indications of the operational autonomy of the American government was Bush's appointment of Paul O'Neill, CEO of the leading aluminum producer, Alcoa, as secretary of the treasury. Traditionally the office is occupied either by a visible figure in the financial services sector, such as Henry Morgenthau, Jr., during the Roosevelt administration, C. Douglas Dillon, in Eisenhower's term, or Robert Rubin, Clinton's choice, each of whom was a principal in a leading Wall Street investment banking firm; or by an economist who is closely linked to finance capital, like the labor economist George Schultz, who served several Republican administrations, and Lawrence Summers, who succeeded Rubin after serving as his undersecretary for seven years. (Shultz is only one of several labor economists who rose to high office in the political directorate. One may mention Harvard's John Dunlop and the legal scholar Archibald Cox, both of whom played an important role in taming postwar labor.) After his tenure in the Clinton administration Summers went on to become president of Harvard University, not only a leading research institution but for decades the source of a number of pivotal figures at the top of Democratic and, to a lesser extent, Republican administrations.

O'Neill is not only a "dangerous crank" (according to the journalist William Greider) for his open hostility to social security and other public goods and for his off-the-cuff suggestions that corporate taxes be abolished. He is also unusual for being tied mainly to the production sector rather than to financial corporations, connections that may signal that the traditional bipartisan free trade internationalism may be challenged by the Bush administration. In spring 2001, the administration began negotiations with the steel industry and the United Steelworkers, who were seeking import quotas. This protectionist measure was scorned by several previous presidents and by finance, which incessantly warns of retaliation by trading partners. In a move widely interpreted as a strategy to split sections of labor from the Democratic Party, Bush imposed a 30 percent tariff on steel imports, thereby risking a trade war with European allies. Similarly, during his first European trip, Bush, arguing that his first priority is economic growth, played the nationalist and productivist card by openly defying entreaties from European leaders to sign the Kyoto Treaty, which begins to address the dangers posed by global warming. Moreover, the Bush administration has announced it would deal with the developing energy crisis in the United States not by investing in alternative and renewable energy technologies, but by providing federal assistance to expand the use of nonrenewable fuels such as coal and oil to solve the long-term shortage of electric power.

Viewing O'Neill's appointment in the context of a rift between financial and industrial capital and the internationalist and nationalist wings of the conservative hegemony, we may discern how the invisible becomes visible.[10] For despite his successful campaign pose as a "compassionate" conservative, a code word for moderate, Bush has surrounded himself with a nationalist coterie: top officials like O'Neill, Vice President Dick Cheney, who is acting as perhaps the key operative in this administration, and especially Secretary of Defense Donald Rumsfeld, the point person in the war in Afghanistan, who wants to create a defensive missile shield around the United States in violation of established international treaties. Yet at international meetings Bush maintains a strong free trade line. In the face of powerful antiglobalization demonstrations at the Genoa G8 meeting, Bush took the trouble to denounce the protesters three times by declaring free trade was the best strategy to help poor countries. This contradiction is more than a sign of conflicting rhetorics of an otherwise reactionary administration: it is an indication of the limits to national sovereignty in the new empire.

Needless to say, as the nationalist and right-wing character of this administration comes to the surface, the foreign policy establishment, which has been internationalist for more than a half century, leaders of financial corporations, and members of both political parties who have hewed to the line have become nervous that this administration is attempting to shift power decisively by, among other tactics, winning over the beleaguered but still substantial fractions of industrial capital and integrating some ailing industrial unions into a new coalition with the social Right. The defection from the Republican Party of Sen. James Jeffords, a moderate from Vermont, is only the most visible sign of the erosion of the party's moderate wing. It is socially liberal, but fiscally conservative and, above all, internationalist. Jeffords's leaving reflects not only Vermont's social liberalism but the interests of its farm sector, which has been a major supporter of international trade. This leaves the fundamentalist Christian Right, traditional conservatives who form the constituents of the National Association of Manufacturers, and the mainstream farm organizations, hardly a majority, to form the Republican alliance. Obviously, if this program is to succeed Bush—who, in his response to the growing shortage of electrical energy, has signaled his attraction to a program of internal industrial development in traditional industries like coal-driven power plants—in attempting to bring back the Reagan Democrats would be forced to make concessions on trade policy to his new partners in organized labor. Such a shift from the bipartisan free trade program of the government could further strain relations between the United States and Western Europe. At the same time, Bush has already incurred the enmity of financial capital and of the leaders of the information sector, whose interests he seems to hold in low regard in part because they have shown strong loyalty to the internationalist wing of the Democrats.

THE END OF THE NATION-STATE?

Contrary to the emerging conventional wisdom, according to which globalization signals the end of the sovereignty of national states—indeed, some argue that states are no longer important powers—national states play an important part in processes of globalization. First, they have been key instrumentalities in paring the welfare state programs that resulted from the class compromise forged in the postwar era. And they are crucial in the task of the social control of workers, immigrants, and others affected by the erosion of the social wage. The WB, IMF, and WTO—the constituent leadership of which includes representatives of the principal states and the main international financial institutions—are charged with regulating the relations between the industrially developed world by reproducing the conditions of domination and dependence. In Russia and elsewhere, the IMF and WB have directed the transition from state-owned to privately owned and operated enterprises. These market policies, termed structural adjustment, entailed the imposition of systematic austerity measures: radically altering and otherwise reducing the broad welfare state; controlling the labor force by lowering its living standards; renouncing many labor and health protections, a policy that, together with reduced wages and lower quality of life, has in ten years lowered life expectancy by more than a decade. Russians, especially Russian men, can be expected to live on the average fewer than sixty years, a life span equal to that in a third world society.

Russia has assumed sizable portions of accumulated debt and is still required to pay on time. In order to ante up the cash, Russia has caused its people to suffer. The populations of many other former Communist states have felt the pain, too, as have those in Africa, including in recent years postapartheid South Africa, and in Latin America, which in many social as well as economic policies remains under the control of the WB and IMF. For as South Africa, to take one example, has discovered in regard to the promise of land reform—which along with labor rights, social freedom, and an expanded welfare state was at the heart of the program of the key movement in the liberation struggle, the African National Congress—if the IMF and WB disapprove of such programs the country may be deprived of funds for development. As Argentina, Brazil, and Mexico have discovered, only if the state agrees to neoliberal austerity measures can it expect aid.

Within the governing bodies of the IMF, WB, and WTO, the American secretary of treasury plays a key role in mobilizing finance capital for their activities. As we have seen, the American secretary has conventionally been part of the financial institutions upon which these agencies depend. But since their budgets and thus the funds they are able to disperse are dependent upon banks and other financial institutions and on the national states that compose their governing bodies, there is always a question of how much autonomy they enjoy or how much capital they will be able to mobilize. While there is little question that, in their policies as well as their functions, these international agencies embody the neoliberal orientation of global capitalist interests, at any given moment such issues as which countries they will support and how are subject to the politics of nation-states as well as of the transnational banks and other financial institutions from whom they must receive support.

Although the U.S. government has played a leading role in these organizations, and the national administrations of both parties have supported their general policies, European states participate as well. Yet the states are constrained, not the least by international economic and political relations that increasingly impinge on their autonomy: which indicates the dual nature of these states. Collectively they are among the central players in globality and are committed to neoliberal control over international relations. On the other hand, since there is no legal and juridical concept of global citizenship or global regulation the polity remains, for the time being, confined to the framework of nation-states. This contradiction is played out in the conflict between the policies of fiscal austerity in the United States and Western Europe and the demands of the citizens of those states. In all of these countries since 1990 labor movements have engaged in strikes and other forms of protest against attempts by conservative and social-democratic governments alike to reduce the scope and size of the social wage. While these struggles have been most visible in France and Spain, German and Greek unions have found themselves in conflict with their own labor-supported governments. In the United States the production unions declined in reaction to the deterritorialization of industrial production and progressive unions became more critical of free trade agreements, some urging the government to protect certain industries such as steel from international competition.

Of course in the United States, Canada, and Western Europe, the neoliberal global capitalist state has encountered most resistance from environmentalists, trade unionists, and mostly young proponents (some of whom are anarchists) of labor rights in what they call the global sweatshop—clothing and shoe plants in Southeast Asia and Latin America that force workers to endure nearly intolerable working conditions and pay extremely low wages. No meeting of the IMF, WTO, or WB or of the general policy organization of the seven leading industrialized nations can expect to be free of mass demonstrations by tens of thousands of protesters demanding a voice in determining the policies of these institutions. The resister alliances have become so ubiquitous and effective in challenging the taken-for-granted assumption that capital has the divine right to go anywhere it pleases in the pursuit of profits free of labor regulation and trade unions and environmental protections that the institutions of empire have had to resort to force in order to hold their meetings. They have obliged host nation-states to front a shield of repression to keep the horde at bay. The decade-long effort to subject the global state to a new, as-yet unarticulated concept of global citizenship has met with some success: the Kyoto Treaty; pledges by the IMF and WB to protect workers' rights in forging new trade agreements (concessions that activists regard with more than a little skepticism); and, beginning with the environment summit in Brazil in 1996, promises that the global ruling institutions will consult with nongovernmental organizations (NGOs) on development policies. In fact, the reneging on the agreement by transnational capital and participant nations to involve the NGOs at the Brazil conference was a kind of parting of the ways for many from their naïve belief that the system would reform itself. What occurred subsequently in Seattle, Washington, Prague, Quebec, and Genoa was a symptom of the widening cleavage between the exemplars of incipient global citizenship and the empire.

The concrete program of the alliance is still framed in terms of structural reform. The imperative demands of the movements arrayed against global power—democratic participation, relief for countries whose economic and social institutions are crumbling under the burden of excessive accumulated debt, and a sharp reversal of ecologically disastrous development policies—have failed to produce a productive response from the global powers, even though in some countries, notably Germany, Italy, Greece, and Spain, Green parties are an institutional force for reform. The slow pace of change has led to profound, potentially grave consequences. In 2001, the United Nations issued a report, subsequently supported by one thousand of the world's leading scientists, that in the twenty-first century global warming will lead to a serious crisis for world agriculture, create a water shortage for large portions of the world, and make some areas, especially in the southern hemisphere, unable to sustain life. The wide chasm that separates the antiglobalization movements from the global state and its components has led a significant segment of the movement to link its demands with an anticapitalist ideology, which still lacks a program. In the next two chapters I want to examine these movements as instances of struggles over class formation. As before, historical as well as theoretical and structural features of these struggles will be explored in following chapters.[11]

6

THE NEW SOCIAL MOVEMENTS AND CLASS

Every great social movement must experience three stages: ridicule, discussion, adoption.

—John Stuart Mill

Stuart Hall has argued that "social movements are the modality in which class politics are enacted."[1] The ordinarily assumed distinctions between workers' movements and social movements may instead be understood as different modalities of class movements. This formulation presupposes that, although property relations are salient to all social movements, class is a concept of historically constituted power and powerlessness rather than being confined to ownership of property alone. For example, we are currently witnessing a left, socially conservative tendency to marginalize or to condemn movements for sexual freedom in its feminist or gay modalities as distractions from or obstructions of class—where *class* is coded entirely in economic terms; and, on the other hand, a tendency to subsume social movements under the sign of bio-identities. What unites these conceptions is that both insist on their absolute separation from class politics. Lacking the concept of the unity of social and cultural divisions around the axis of power, they cannot grasp the notion of modality and must present difference in terms of irreconcilable binaries. Binary thinking excludes overlap and multiple identities and replaces complexity with grids of inclusion and exclusion.

Just as capital is divided into class fractions, so the class that stands opposed to capital is divided. These fractions possess economic, political, and social attributes that are conditioned by specific historical situations; their course is constituted by struggles over class formation among contentious fractions as well as struggles against capital. Thus, women, blacks, and the physically disabled are, in the overwhelming majority, wageworkers, but all of them stand in a specific relation of subordination to the power bloc. Given that these formations, when organized in social movements, seek to overturn or otherwise modify existing power relations, we may, rather than reduce them to a function of biological or educational or occupational identity, term this specific relation a modality of class politics.

WHEN LABOR WAS A SOCIAL MOVEMENT

The history of social movements is a complex interplay between their autonomous demands and their dialogue with the prevailing power blocs. Social movements almost invariably arise from the arrogant rejection by the prevailing powers of politely delivered appeals to reason and to justice by the aggrieved. Revolution or radical confrontation against the ruling class almost always presents itself as a historical accident; habituated to subordination to established authority, the aggrieved frequently agonize before taking any drastic action. And the protagonists are invariably alliances between the modalities of insurgent class formations, like those movements for religious freedom that animated the English revolutions of the seventeenth century, which seemed, on the surface, to have no relation to the class politics. They were frequently wrapped in the cloak of universalism that proclaims the Rights of Man, independent of social class or station, but were often intertwined with Protestant doctrine that installed individuals to religious and civil sovereignty and claimed the inalienable right to liberty and property. The bourgeoisie's claim to economic and political power in the face of the absolute authority of the monarchy was often wrapped in the cloth of religious doctrines that affirmed the right of the individual to dissent. The struggle for religious freedom was not reducible to the demands of the emergent middle class for freedom to produce and exchange goods without interference from the monarchy. It had its own characteristics, but they were consistent with the broad demand for freedom that remained the hallmark of the bourgeois revolutions of the eighteenth and nineteenth centuries.[2]

For John Locke, individuals were constituted, under God, as the ultimate authority and, on the grounds of natural law, enjoyed an inalienable right to own their own labor. But if labor was inalienable from its owners, the freedom of workers to collectively withhold their labor power when they objected to the terms and conditions of employment offered by the proprietor remained a contested extension of Locke's theory. British and American courts frequently followed English common law, which judged strikes a restraint of trade and workers' demands for higher wages an imposition on the natural right of the employer to accumulate capital. In fact, Protestantism supplied crucial elements of justification for capital's claims on the state. Its political doctrine, namely, economic, social, and intellectual freedom, was provided by Locke. If the state will not relinquish these powers, then the prevailing political forms should be dissolved and replaced by one that is dominated by property owners, who, Locke asserted, were the only members of the society deserving of citizenship. As citizens, they should be empowered to choose their own instruments of political rule. Then, and only then, would citizens yield to the state's ultimate authority.[3]

From this followed the idea that propertyless wage earners and the unemployed should be deprived of the vote and, in the opinion of some of Locke's followers, even of the right to assembly for the purpose of seeking vindication of their grievances. As E. P. Thompson has shown, labor strife in the late eighteenth and early nineteenth centuries took the mode of a social movement for universal male suffrage as much as for workplace power against a now-dominant bourgeoisie that, having won economic and political rule, opposed labor's claim to share economic and social power.[4] The two and a half centuries that separated the seventeenth-century English revolutions and the Chartist achievement of "manhood" suffrage from the British and American feminists' movement for universal suffrage demonstrated that what for Locke and the English middle classes had been natural turned out to be historical.[5] What the male-dominated labor movement took as universal was understood by women to be partial. Yet while sizable sections of labor recognized women's suffrage as a class issue, industrial capitalists, both of the liberal as well as conservative wings, maintained their opposition. It was only when these apparently separate movements of labor and women joined, took to the streets, and, through intense direct action as well as public discussion, captured public opinion that sections of the liberal middle class and intelligentsia became convinced it was in their interest to support these demands and the ruling bourgeoisie yielded.[6]

But if workers' movements believed that voting rights were the necessary condition for freedom, trade unions were the sufficient condition. Industrial and craft workers' unions in England and the United States not only sought higher wages through measures to control the supply of labor, but also fought for power at the workplace. Workers discovered that only when labor organized as a social movement were they able to make long-term gains, even after they won "manhood" suffrage regardless of property qualification (in the United States universal manhood suffrage was enacted by Congress in 1828; in Britain it took fifty more years). When workers struck they were almost invariably subject to court injunction ordering them back to work on penalty of fines and imprisonment, a punishment borne by many labor activists with pride as well as with pain. Yet legal rights to strike and engage in job actions were not the condition of labor's capacity to take action; in fact, the post–Civil War American labor movement neither sought legislation to extend its rights nor relied on the courts to safeguard its strike weapon.

As we have seen, when the labor movement accepted the framework of law as a basis of labor struggle, early success soon gave way to compromise and retreat. From the simultaneous restrictions and opportunities on their scope of action provided by rights and by their ability to share in American prosperity, most unions drew the lesson that discretion and conformity to the restrictions imposed by a Cold War national state was their best course. The past fifty years have witnessed a slow and steady decline of organized labor's power as union density has slipped to about 13 percent. The decline led many to conclude that the labor movement had ceased to be a social movement; unions had become institutions of contract administration for a diminishing fraction of the wage-labor force, which often entailed taking responsibility for a labor contract that, among other things, disciplined recalcitrant workers. As an old movement it had been integrated into late capitalism.

Indeed, the achievements of postwar American Labor were purchased, in part, at the price of the relative deprivation of the rest of the working class. Although some gains made by unions, especially in wages, reverberated throughout the rest of the labor force, the private welfare state widened the benefits gap between unionized and nonunionized workers. The collective bargaining agreement, rather than the state, was the chief mechanism for providing the social wage for its constituents. Although AFL-CIO convention resolutions supported increased public spending for such programs as health care for the uninsured, higher pensions and broader coverage under the Social Security system, and improvements in the minimum wage, in practice labor's legislative clout was largely muted in some of these battles, especially health care and social security, because unions had become insurance companies that dispensed these benefits to members only.

In addition, the Cold War alliance between organized labor and the American state meant that unions were willing to postpone, perhaps indefinitely, their demands for guaranteed income, shorter working hours, and other historical aspirations of the labor movement. As an entailment of its new position as a partner of the American empire, Labor often found itself siding with capital and the liberal state in opposing revolutionary and radical movements abroad. Until 1995, when a new leadership took office, the AFL-CIO unequivocally sanctioned government policies such as neocolonialism; indeed, American unions supported U.S. involvement in the two great Cold War military conflicts: Korea and Southeast Asia. For the so-called new social movements this partnership indicated that although labor struggles had historically demonstrated that only from the standpoint of the outside could real change be made, union labor was now on the inside and could not be viewed as an ally. For activists in the feminist and black freedom movements it was evident that the ruling class and the political directorate were generally indifferent, even hostile, to their most comprehensive demands for freedom and equality. In the 1950s and 1960s they had become the outside mandated to change the system. As we shall see below, being sensitive to its alliance with the establishment, Labor stepped gingerly through what it perceived to be a series of land mines: while it could not oppose civil rights it would not support civil disobedience; although it supported equal pay for equal work, Labor was caught in the crosscurrents of sections of its socially conservative base in the building trades and some industrial unions and the growing number of women and blacks who were joining unions, especially public and private service sector organizations.[7]

The history of the black freedom movement exhibits some of the same overlapping characteristics. It was a social movement that confronted slavery simultaneously as a moral question and as a labor question. For many of its protagonists the abolition of slavery was a religious crusade; the idea that fellow human beings could legally be held as property in a free society was a violation of fundamental Christian teaching of the sanctity of the free individual. Indeed, the moral argument against slavery carried considerable weight in the court of public opinion prior to the Civil War. Those in the ranks of capital, however, as well as in the labor movement understood the struggle against slavery as a labor struggle. For them abolitionism was a modality of class politics. The antislavery slogan, "Free labor, free men, free soil" linked agrarian, radical, and labor movements. At a time when the United States was chiefly an agricultural country, slavery as a labor question was intertwined with the land issue. The availability of land being the natural condition for all types of farming, cattle ranchers and small farmers alike viewed the slave mode of production, which pressed to expand to free states and territories, as an obstacle to the growth of free-labor-based industrial capitalism. And workers' organizations viewed slave labor, potentially as well as actually, as a threat to their livelihood.[8]

Having fought for emancipation and subsequently been declared citizens by constitutional amendments, blacks soon discovered—when the two major parties betrayed Reconstruction—that segregation, discrimination, and social stigma survived as the ineluctable legacy of the hated slave mode of production. Their judgment was confirmed in 1896 by the Supreme Court decision in *Plessy v. Ferguson,* which asserted that "separate but equal" facilities fulfilled constitutional requirements, by the resumption of wanton lynching of black people, by the exclusion of blacks from industrial jobs in the North, except as strikebreakers, and by the reimposition of compulsory labor systems in southern plantations at the turn of the century. In response, a new black freedom movement emerged. This movement, which embraced a wide array of ideological and political tendencies, remained isolated from the main currents of radical and liberal thought and practice until the 1930s, when the "Negro question" became a subject of debate in labor and liberal circles. Among predominantly white organizations, only the communists and the tiny band of radical pacifists placed the struggle for black freedom at the top of the political agenda.[9] For as Harvard Sitkoff has shown, neither the major political parties nor, indeed, a significant fraction of capital was prepared to acknowledge the legitimacy of demands for full equality. For the next thirty years blacks and their allies debated whether the political institutions of the liberal state could deliver equality at all levels of social life or whether other means were necessary to attain genuine freedom.[10]

In fact, what concessions in employment, military, and school integration were actually made by the state were directly or indirectly the result of direct action such as sit-ins, boycotts, and demonstrations led by blacks themselves. But the struggle for equality was ineluctably bound with discrimination as a labor question. Only when A. Phillip Randolph threatened to stage a mass march on Washington in 1941 did President Roosevelt establish the Fair Employment Practices Commission (FEPC), which required defense contractors to hire blacks. The freedom rides to break the color bar in public accommodations conducted in the late 1940s by members of the pacifist-led Congress of Racial Equality (CORE), the War Resisters League (WRL), and the Fellowship of Reconciliation were largely ignored by the mainstream National Association for the Advancement of Colored People

(NAACP). In fact, WRL organizer Bayard Rustin refused to move to the back of the bus as early as 1942 and was part of a group of eight black and an equal number of white activists who tested the Supreme Court decision of 1946 against segregation in interstate transportation. These early freedom rides aimed at breaking segregated bus travel received almost no publicity. Nor did the Montgomery movement, whose reluctant tribune was the Rev. Martin Luther King, wait for the wheels of justice to grind before confronting segregation. But this time things were different. When Rosa Parks, a longtime activist, spurred the movement by committing an act of civil disobedience against a Jim Crow law, the reverberations were felt abroad. Whereas the media had been indifferent to the pioneers of direct action, this time, informed by Cold War imperatives in which the United States claimed the mantle of freedom against totalitarian Communist expansion, the world took notice, and the black freedom movement entered its brief but momentous stage of civil disobedience.[11]

THE RISE OF NEW SOCIAL MOVEMENTS

The last half of the twentieth century witnessed the rise of four great social movements in American political and social life. Each succeeded, at least for a time, in posing its demands in ways that cleaved the polity, and their achievement entailed a profound restructuring of important aspects of economic, political, and social life. Movements of black freedom, feminism, ecology, and the physically disabled were second waves, that is, they had been preceded by insurgencies whose histories, although venerated and recognized as pathbreaking, had weaknesses that needed to be corrected by a new generation. Perhaps the most important of these was that, having accepted the framework for change offered by liberal democratic states, the earlier movements were obliged, by the political context as much as by choice, to restrict their demands to the achievement of rights. Consequently, they focused most of their efforts on lobbying for legislation and, through litigation, on the courts.

In contrast, in their most dramatically effective period (the 1960s and early 1970s), the new social movements, though not turning their backs on efforts to influence the institutions of the liberal state, expended their energies mainly on direct action, tactics they learned quite consciously from the militant labor movement of the 1930s. The lunch counter sit-ins, the feminist protests at events like the Miss America contest, guerrilla acts such as bra burning, the massive blockades of nuclear facilities, and confrontations with lumber and oil companies brought to the surface the seething opposition to the social and economic consequences of unfettered capitalist, white, and male domination. Their demands were often incorporated in administrative reforms such as affirmative action and the Clean Air and Water Act, and in judicial decisions such as *Brown v. Board of Education* and *Roe v. Wade*—following the pragmatic dictum that the American way was "tinkering" with social institutions rather than overturning or radically altering them.[12] At least for a time, however, the intellectuals and activists linked to these movements offered a fundamental critique of incremental change and counterposed various versions of what they called radical social change, radical because it proposed new forms of governance that challenged, if not entirely rejected, the leading precepts of liberal democratic thought, particularly the conflation of representative institutions such as the legislative branch of government with democracy.

The emergence of new movements to a position of preeminence during the sixties and seventies resulted from a multiplicity of determinations. Activists were unpersuaded by the slogans of the American Celebration that peppered public speeches and were repeated with numbing regularity in classrooms and in the media. According to the mantra, the United States was the best of all possible worlds. Evidence, in the midst of unparalleled postwar prosperity, of material squalor among large sections of the population, particularly blacks; uninterrupted subordination of women to men in the home as well as in the paid workplace; the growing recognition that rampant industrialization, suburban sprawl, and the plunder of nature had produced a rapidly deteriorating physical environment that threatened human as well as animal and plant life; the gap between democratic promise and authoritarian political reality; all these factors turned many young people into skeptics, if not outright opponents, of the economic and political systems. Ironically, these young people emanated from some of the more privileged layers of the social structure. They were of a generation that had been informed that theirs was the first in human history to be permanently freed of material want. Perhaps for this reason it had become disillusioned with what its elders viewed as the proud and unique achievements of America: technological superiority, the cornucopia of goods, the permeable class structure. Many felt that what Herbert Croly once called the "promise of American life" of equality, freedom, and universal abundance had proven hollow and false.

But in economically and politically secure societies disillusion often takes the form of intellectual and political cynicism. Young people judged that

America had become what one writer called "an air conditioned nightmare" for the generation born between 1940 and 1950. But some found reason for hope. Tens of thousands of young people, and many of their elders inspired by them, began to believe they could actually change the world, not in the spirit of incremental reform consistent with the liberal tradition, but of radicalism, whose antecedents were the bourgeois and socialist revolutions. At first the rebellion was framed not in the lexicon of conventional marxism, but in the rhetoric of nonmarket libertarianism. The operative terms were the highly contested concepts of freedom and liberation, ideas that were claimed by liberals and radicals alike. But the student and youth movements endowed them with different, often antagonistic, meaning. In fact, the intellectual origins of the new radicalism can be traced to a critique of the contradictions between liberal practice and liberal profession. According to the political tendency known as New Left, liberal political philosophy contained authoritarian premises, the most flagrant of which was property rights, which entailed exclusion of the propertyless; but among other such premises were the feeling that democracy was identical to the institutions of representative government (in 1965 Staughton Lynd organized a Congress of Unrepresented People) and the idea that in America individual rights were sacrosanct in the practical sense.[13]

Blacks would not be assuaged by achieving supposed civil rights that provided only the legal framework for access to institutions, especially voting and education. Many were not content either to define equality by measures that afforded opportunities to enter the ranks of the professions or the technical occupations. The aspirations of the mostly student contingents of the southern black freedom movement during the early 1960s were not chiefly the right to bid for better positions in the existing occupational structure, as determined by whether a fraction of blacks could achieve middle-class status in consumption terms. They sought instead powers associated with freedom, a concept that connoted both freedom from such outrages as racially motivated discrimination and physical terror, but also individual and collective autonomy. The liberal establishment saw voting rights as a means to broaden the base of the Democratic Party and, perhaps equally important, to reduce, if not break, its reliance on the traditional rotten boroughs of the racist plantation aristocracy. If activist organizations such as the Student Nonviolent Coordinating Committee worked to register blacks to vote in rural southern counties, the intention was to provide one of the important conditions for creating independent political institutions that could contest the entrenched white agricultural and commercial power structure.[14]

While supporting mainstream feminist programs for more institutional access, radicals posed the fundamental aim of the movement to be liberation from male domination. For the first time in recent history the so-called private sphere of the home came under public scrutiny and entered the popular culture. For whether women were engaged in paid employment or not they always had full-time jobs. Second-wave feminism—so defined in contrast to the earlier suffrage-based movement—focused on the home, where women raised children, on the bedroom, where many suffered sexual misery, and on the kitchen, where they performed as cook and housecleaner while holding down part- and full-time paid work outside the home.[15]

Whereas mainstream environmentalism set goals of winning legislation to protect water and air quality and fought for policies that set aside some still undeveloped land for recreation or wildlife preservation, a growing body of scientific and political thought confronted some of the contradictory precepts of the Enlightenment, especially its ethic of viewing nature as fungible and the object of human dominion. For the first time since the early nineteenth-century's romantic rebellion against the satanic mills of capitalism, social ecology began to ask whether such concepts as development, industrialization, and even capitalism were ecologically sustainable.[16] And some, notably Murray Bookchin, linked the domination of nature to human domination.

Members of Students for a Democratic Society (SDS) began to challenge the claim that the institutions and processes of the liberal state were democratic at all. SDS's *Port Huron Statement,* which was widely circulated in the growing student and civil rights movements, charged that the American system of representative government excluded major segments of the population. *Port Huron* was first and foremost a reflection on the failure of representative democracy, the preferred political system of capitalism. It notes that many of the working class, especially the poor, are indifferent to the electoral system because they do not see themselves in it, even if they possess the suffrage. But at its core, *Port Huron*'s critique is that representatives were mainly beholden to large corporate interests and that both political parties were caught in these encumbrances; many, perhaps most, Americans were unrepresented in the political system. America needed a new "participatory democracy" in which the act of voting became only one of many means by which people could directly control the "decisions that affected their lives."[17]

In practice, participatory democracy entailed changing institutional power. Democracy meant that the people whose interests were most affected should make decisions about schools, health care, the industrial workplace, and other sites. And by the late 1960s the ideas of participatory democracy began to have some practical political effects. In New York and Chicago, government decentralized district administration of schools, and elected community school boards responded to activists' and parents' allegations that politically appointed central school boards were insensitive to local needs. While established politicians viewed with alarm the demand, forcefully advanced by the Black Panthers, for community control of the police, in cities with large black and Latino populations who were in the throes of full-scale rebellion against their social and economic subordination, government bodies eventually felt constrained by charges of police abuse to appoint civilian review boards. These were limited in their powers to investigating complaints but were rarely able to punish offenders. Yet under the burden of the huge Vietnam War budget and the government's fear that they had become hotbeds of protest, the small antipoverty programs initiated during the Kennedy and early Johnson years to forestall growing unrest were systematically cut back.

Women were increasingly critical of laws banning abortion and began to challenge their subordination to men in the nuclear family, in civil society, and in employment. Beginning in the 1960s, women massively entered the paid workplace, both as protest against the limits of unpaid labor at home and as a means to address the fact that a single wage earner could no longer earn the family wage. The new workplace, marked by the proliferation of part-time, temporary labor to allow women to take paid employment, was fundamentally sustained by the double shift in which women participated in unpaid and paid work. Feminists addressed the new structure of working time. Here feminist politics was a class politics directed not only to capital but also to the privileges of men. Hence for early radical feminists the "woman question" was posed as a labor question but in a new context. Attempting to forge "feminist historical materialism" in which such categories as labor, the mode of production, and class informed their arguments, writers like Shulamith Firestone and Nancy Hartsock insisted that women were a class that entailed a distinct standpoint and that the demands for equality disrupt not only the social conditions for the reproduction of capital but those of patriarchy as well. Feminist theory insisted that the claims of capitalism and its institutions to offer freedom and equality were simply a pretense: in reality, capitalism was sustained by the subordination of women to men as well as to capital.[18]

To illustrate the class dimension of the radical feminist politics, we might undertake a thought experiment. Suppose industrial and service workplaces adjusted working time to the demands of the household rather than the reverse. Work schedules would be adjusted to the requirement that men share all aspects of household labor, a situation that might result if women set the condition of cohabitation and of conjugal relations as a sharing with their male partners of all aspects of housework: child rearing, shopping, cooking, housecleaning, paying the bills, and other duties. The eight-, ten- and twelve-hour days many industrial and intellectual workers are obliged by their employers to endure would be put into question. Except for a selected group of occupations such as health, transportation, public safety, and continuous flow operations in industrial plants, the twenty-four-hour workplace would be relegated to the museum. Where both partners participated in paid labor the waged working day would be sharply curtailed. Both partners would have the prerogative of leaving their job as a matter of right when a child became ill or needed to be picked up from school early. In short, think of radical change as consisting in social arrangements in which the job is subordinate to life. Shared housework would surely raise the ante for increased public funding of child care, after-school activities, and other recreation programs. If men were faced with even a reduced double shift their indifference to child care might evaporate.

Through such tactics as mass demonstrations and political theater as well as legislation and lawsuits, radical women called public attention to the fact that, almost fifty years after passage of the Nineteenth Amendment, men still dominated the institutions of representative government as well as schools, health care agencies, and other workplaces like the home, where, overwhelmingly, women do the work. At the social level, spurred by their massive entrance into the paid labor force and by feminist propaganda that proclaimed their ability to liberate themselves from the yoke of male oppression, millions of women who in previous generations had little alternative but to suffer miserable marriages took the road of divorce. By 1970, almost 50 percent of marriages ended in divorce, and the number kept rising, even though divorce almost always results in both partners becoming poorer. With the routinization of single, mostly female parenthood and the disappearance of the radical phase of the feminist movement, the double shift in the past thirty years has become more ubiquitous, intensifying the class exploitation of women. In the absence of collective solutions to a social inequity, most women are forced to consider individual solutions within the private sphere. Of course, none of them are satisfactory.

One of the most effective instances of collective action was the movement of those coded by the industrial and political cultures as physically disabled. Like the black freedom and feminist movements, disabled people took to the streets to dramatize their demands. The wheelie demonstrations they conducted were indispensable preconditions for the enactment of the Americans with Disabilities Act (ADA), which required federal, state, city, and county governments to make public facilities accessible and barred employment discrimination on the basis of disability. The burden of radical democratic discourse was demands for freedom, equality, and power, both of the social and political kind and in the connotation of personal autonomy, not rights. Under the sign of access, these became embedded in material changes, including ramps, depressed street curbs to accommodate wheelchairs, public elevators in subway and train stations, designated parking spaces, and elevated and widened toilets in public rest rooms. The new movement did not rely exclusively on the conventional tools of petition and lobby but chose an in-your-face strategy instead. Of course, that the discourse of power was recoded as rights and became embodied in legislation speaks to the depth of the liberal political tradition in American life.

Even as many feminist and civil rights organizations were choosing, in the ebbing of their direct action phases, to transform themselves into lobbying and electoral organizations in the 1970s and early 1980s, movements for sexual freedom spearheaded by lesbian and gay insurgencies kept the tradition alive. In July 1969 police raided and shut down the Stonewall Inn, a private gay club in Greenwich Village. Instead of humbly accepting their fate, according to one reporter, "The queens had turned commandos and stood bra strap to bra strap against the invasion of the helmeted Tactical Patrol Force. . . . Queen Power reared its bleached blonde head in revolt. New York experienced its first homosexual riot. . . .

"'We may have lost the battle, sweets,' said a spokesperson . . . 'we've had all we can take from the Gestapo. We're putting our foot down once and for all.'" The Stonewall revolt heralded the explosion of one of the most vital social movements of the post-1960s decades. With the discovery of AIDS, which by the 1980s had reached epidemic proportions among gay men, the movement spawned a series of organizations ranging from the Gay Men's Health Crisis (GMHC) to the activist AIDS Coalition to Unleash Power (ACT UP), whose confrontational tactics earned it both widespread admiration and condemnation among political, religious, and scientific authorities.[19]

Spectacularly, ACT UP demonstrations at Saint Patrick's Cathedral, at federal agencies such as the Food and Drug Administration and the National Institutes of Health, and at the offices of leading politicians resulted in official scorn but eventually won the organization a place at the policy table. Among its boldest moves was to challenge the slow pace of clinical trials for anti-AIDS drugs performed by health institutions; it proposed changing other scientific procedures as well. Although ACT UP had the advice of scientific professionals, to the consternation of administrators the movement demanded that, as it was composed of afflicted and potentially afflicted victims of the epidemic, its voice be heard at every level of science and health policy. Eventually the group was able to negotiate the terms of AIDS policies. Branches sprung up throughout the country and by 1990 ACT UP was a force to be reckoned with in many cities, especially San Francisco, Philadelphia, and Washington. For a time it appeared that a new era of scientific citizenship was in the making; unfortunately, the movement did not conceptualize its gains in these terms and made decisions that were subject to criticism, even from within its own ranks. New York ACT UP soon fragmented and went from a movement that within a few years had attracted thousands of activists and tens of thousands of supporters to one that had dissipated its power.

It was a sign of the political and organizational immaturity of the new movements that they were unable to consolidate their temporary hegemony over the conversation by forging an enduring, interidentity alliance based on the concept of radical democratic change. Several national conferences, beginning with the Chicago Alternative Politics conference in 1967, were dedicated to finding ways to bind the civil rights, antiwar, and progressive labor movements into an enduring class alliance that could play an independent role in American politics. But divisions between blacks and whites, women and men, and young and old were barriers that prevented the cementing of any genuine unity. Roiled by the intervention of left sects in their ranks and by the disappointment that despite the massive movement against the Vietnam War the government remained committed to its policies, some in the key organizations such as SDS began to veer toward marxist-leninist sectarianism. After the ill-fated mass demonstrations against the liberal establishment that had promulgated the war at the Democratic National Convention in 1968 and the subsequent Days of Rage in Washington—a symptom of a badly divided and frustrated movement—SDS splintered into warring factions and soon disappeared.[20]

The black freedom movement split as well. Black power advocates like SNCC chair Stokely Carmichael renounced the integrationist goals of the civil rights movement and embraced nationalism and separatism. In the early 1970s, feminist separatism, led chiefly by a growing lesbian contingent, resulted in what its critics termed cultural feminism, a movement based on identity politics that emphasized such issues as opposition to pornography—where it found itself in an uneasy alliance with the Christian Right—and violence against women. Meanwhile, in the 1970s and 1980s organizations such as the National Organization for Women focused on securing passage of an Equal Rights Amendment. The author Betty Friedan urged the movement to turn away from the radical critique of the family and divisive issues like women's sexual freedom and concentrate on economic equality, which, she asserted, would make possible an alliance with organized labor and liberal politicians whom the women's movement needed if it was to close the income gap and gain social mobility.

By 1980, identity politics and moralism came to dominate most of the new social movements. The struggle for political class formation at first took the form of deepening fraction divisions. Even within the Democratic Party, which until the early eighties conceded some power to these fractions by holding a midterm issues convention dominated by the new movements, their organizations lost the initiative and yielded to an alliance of center-right, neoliberal politicos and intellectuals who have established ideological hegemony since the Reagan era.[21]

Yet the sad end of their radical phase did not exhaust the long-term impact of these and other social movements. Although their political demands were incorporated into watered-down liberal reforms, the ideological and cultural influences of these movements have left a permanent legacy. Despite relentless right-wing attacks that sometimes involved terror and even the murder of physicians, abortion remains legal because the overwhelming majority of women support it. Similarly, the popular revolt against processed food, a campaign that originated in the counterculture, has spread throughout the population. Further nuclear production, once portrayed by the industry and widely accepted as the future of energy policy, remains stalled after public interest activists conducted a sustained and largely successful education and action struggle to shut down defective plants and reverse government approvals of new facilities.[22]

But admittedly many social movements have lost their punch and have been absorbed by the liberal establishment. Not all of the movements have disappeared, but as they assumed institutional forms those that remain have mostly evolved into bureaucratic organizations concerned with defending legislative and juridical gains. Most have drifted back into the Democratic Party and have become important mobilizing agents for the national party. The legacy of the radical critiques of the social movements is their long-term cultural influence in bringing the politics of everyday life into the public sphere. Their success may be partially measured by the fact that neoliberal economic policies notwithstanding, the Democrats have remained progressive on most of the social issues. At the same time, the institutional forms of the movements have become more or less frozen. They inspire no imaginative or creative ideas, and, except for the new antiglobalization alliances discussed in chapter 5 (to which I will return in chapter 8) that in some instances include the labor movement, they forge no new public space.

Until the 1980s, most social movement activists were aware that if they followed the path of their forebears, who relied heavily on persuasion and remedies granting rights to the aggrieved, they would still be waiting, given the encrusted resistance of legislative and executive authorities to demands that propose genuine changes in the way the system operates. What the era of social movement activism after 1960 demonstrated was that changes in law follow mass organization and the movement's direct confrontations with established authority. On the one hand, the enactment of laws granting new rights are signs of the victories of movements from below. On the other hand, just as no good deed goes unpunished, no victory is without its elements of defeat. For in many cases the effect of the laws that resulted from popular insurgencies is to impose responsibilities for their enforcement on the legal subjects themselves, turning them from movements into administrators. And for many who participated in mass demonstrations that, in some cases, entailed being arrested and serving jail time, a legislative gain or a court victory seems to give them permission to return to their private pursuits; that is, until, as we have seen in the instance of abortion, the Right launches an all-out assault, and they are obliged to defend what they have won.[23]

SOCIAL THEORY AND SOCIAL MOVEMENTS

The strength of social movements since World War II, and their separation from the conventional labor and socialist movements, has generated a new branch in the social sciences that has attempted to theorize their advent as distinct from the labor and class questions. Social movement theory accepts both a pluralist and consumerist framework for these struggles. One strand, associated with Talcott Parsons, subsumed these movements under the rubric of collective behavior, a phrase that recalls Gustav LeBon's studies of the crowd or Freud's group psychology, both of which view mass upheavals as episodic outbursts of rage or as dangerous deviations from prevailing social norms. Following Max Weber's concept that classes or social formations that contest existing institutional power arrangements are contingent and temporary, the collective behavior school views movements in terms of action by a particular group around specific grievances; for the most part these movements are sporadic and disappear when their goals have been reached. Parents succeed or fail to change a school policy; neighbors organize to prevent city government from agreeing to the plans of a supermarket chain to establish a store with a huge parking lot in their community that will cause congestion and displace small proprietors who are willing to give credit; or workers may break a contractual prohibition against strikes and walk off the job to protest management's discharge of a fellow worker. These fights may be fierce and even politically consequential. Accordingly, when movements become organizations with bylaws and elected officers, they cease to be movements and take their place in the pluralist polity as just another interest group.[24]

But by the early 1960s, the emergence of mass national student, antiwar, and the black freedom movements produced more sophisticated conceptualizations by Charles Tilly, Sidney Tarrow, William Gamson, Alberto Melucci, Meyer Zald, and James McCarthy, among others. Reflecting their view that class and class struggle had either disappeared or was in abeyance in the wake of the political and economic entente between large fractions of the working class and their unions and the prevailing system, these writers tended to reify the break between labor and social movements. They define social movements in terms of physical identities such as race and sex and communities of interest grounded in common geographic space, profession, generation, or ideological perspectives. Even if they become important political and social forces they are not conceived in terms of challenging or changing prevailing power arrangements but are ultimately consonant with interest groups, as defined by pluralist political theory. Movements succeed or fail according to criteria of whether they can mobilize resources: for example, recruit a mass membership, gain media attention, acquire funds, and attract coalition partners to advance their aims. But for most writers the basic objectives of social movements are not linked to the class affiliations of their constituents.[25]

Social movements and class theory mirror each other. Despite the many rich descriptions of the practices of social movements, not only do the categories of political economy disappear in the discourse of social movement theory, but so do questions of structural power. Most writers on the labor movement may factor race and sex into their accounts of labor struggles, but the sites of their analysis are the workplace and the unions. They rarely address such issues as inadequate housing, the poor education blacks and other minorities suffer, abortion, or the so-called double shift of home and paid work most women endure. Nor do writers on the labor movement generally address environmental concerns or problems of the physically and mentally disabled within the framework of class analysis. Thus the divide between social movements and class is deeply embedded in recent labor studies as well.

Ernesto Laclau and Chantal Mouffe's influential *Hegemony and Socialist Strategy* (1987) raised the theoretical and political stakes of social movement theory by linking the emergence of the movements to the critique of marxist class reductionism and proposing a new paradigm of historical transformation in which the centrality of class and class struggle is explicitly abandoned. The tacit presupposition of previous theory that social movements were historically and logically separate from labor and class are accorded philosophical and theoretical status by Laclau and Mouffe. In effect, they codify the proposition that class is an expired social category and that the new social movements in which bio-identities are at the core marked a crucial shift. Following Michel Foucault's conception according to which language and discourse rather than the mode of material production and class relations constitute the sinews of social power, they go so far as to suggest that social relations (by which they invariably signify economic relations)—indeed, even the concept of the social as such—be abandoned or understood as derivative of the conflation of power and knowledge. But the authors go further and declare the divergence of the aims of the new social movements from those of the labor and socialist movements. In effect, they argue that the working class and its unions and political parties have been more or less permanently integrated into the power system. In their critique of the European and Latin American Communist movements that dominated Left politics until the collapse of the Soviet Union, they insist that "Socialism" should no longer be comprehended within leninist categories such as revolutionary dictatorship led by the working class, which was a bedrock of Communist ideology.

Reflecting their evaluation of the bankruptcy of the leading parties of socialism, the authors counterpose the strategy of "radical democracy" that they attribute to the new social movements. But it is never clear what they mean by radical democracy. They are unable to advance specific proposals because their theory presupposes the highly centralized institutional structures of European states. For the most part, radical democracy signifies to them struggles for space for marginal formations within the sphere of "civil society," a sphere which, in its Gramscian locution, is located between the economy and the state, the space of voluntary social organizations and institutions like schools. But whereas Gramsci's politics was anchored in the struggles of the working class and argued that its achievement of ideological hegemony within cultural spheres such as education and literature as much as in politics entailed the proposal of a new "common sense" in which the social question—by which he meant issues of economics, politics, and culture—is moved to the center of political discourse, Laclau's and Mouffe's proposal entails the displacement of existing "hegemonies" of Labor and capital. Their attempt to suggest a new common sense is a radically decentered ideological field in which no particular interest save that of democracy can be said to have priority.[26]

In the 1990s, in the wake of the collapse of Soviet Communism, *Hegemony and Socialist Strategy* became a standard reference for many intellectual radicals—academics and those within the new social movements, especially feminists, sexual freedom activists, and those concerned with reforming the prison system and other disciplinary institutions such as the schools. Laclau and Mouffe seemed to confirm the autonomy of social movements, the validity of struggles at the margins and of so-called marginal people. At the same time, in concert with Foucault's thesis, power was to be found everywhere but was most evident in the body, which encapsulated the displacement of class by bio-identities. In this they were among the social theorists, including, prominently, Judith Butler and Joan Scott, who gave new conceptual weight to identity politics.[27] History, indeed the past, could now be viewed as irrelevant when not destructive of the new formations. And while the authors were ostensibly indebted to the marxist tradition insofar as they retained some kind of socialist framework and asserted their affiliation with the work of Antonio Gramsci, for example, the effect of their postmodern theory was to provide a new version of political liberalism. For by affirming the primacy of human rights and by their renunciation of class formation and class struggle they had deprived themselves and the movements they extolled of the levers of power, except those of incremental reform. Moreover, by renouncing class analysis and substituting the indeterminate plurality of struggles based largely on bio-identities, they were unable to answer the question, What issues are worth fighting for?

Laclau and Mouffe are only among the most prominent of those who have told only half the story. Surely the accumulated events marking the gulf separating workers' movements from the autonomous social movements in the nineteenth and twentieth centuries were nothing short of a tragedy. The breach deprived both movements of the possibility of forging an alliance that could redefine freedom and effectively contest power. The workers' movements in the United States were damaged by this rift as much as the social movements. For example, when the alliance between a segment of organized Labor and capital began to unravel in the 1970s, the choice Labor had made after World War II to buy into the Cold War and into America's global expansion rather than to take the alternate path of opposition was so deeply ingrained in its institutional predispositions that the concept, let alone the practice, of forging relations with the burgeoning student, feminist, and the more militant wing of the black freedom movements was inconceivable. Except for a relatively small corps of progressive trade unionists and some of the newly organized public employees' unions, which were more sympathetic to feminism and to war opponents because many of their constituents were in the ranks of these movements, the mainstream of American Labor either sat out the 1960s or actively sided with the government and corporations in promoting war aims and, in consequence, fought against protesters. Equally important, organized Labor remained a bastion of conventional morality in the face of the emergence of the visible demands for sexual freedom by women and gays. And under the sign of saving jobs many unions responded to ecological efforts to limit the scope of despoliation of the natural environment by making alliances with their own employers. Even as the AFL-CIO joined forces with the liberal wing of the civil rights movement to advance its legislative program, Labor viewed the sit-ins, freedom rides, and other direct actions to break segregation with suspicion and antagonism. As a result, in the 1960s the gulf separating labor from the leading militant social movements became wider.

Even in retreat the unions clung to the fig leaf of class compromise rather than forging a bloc that could challenge and contest power. When the social contract it had entered with capital after the war was unilaterally abrogated, organized Labor found itself with few allies. Its isolation combined with a mentality that stubbornly clung to the all-but-destroyed postwar arrangements placed the unions in a defensive and increasingly conservative posture. As we have seen, in the 1980s unions entered into concessionary agreements that transferred the burden of the effects of global economic stagnation and crisis from employers to workers and, for the most part, responded repressively to rank-and-file attempts to resist this transfer. The mantra of union leadership was that in the face of economic turbulence saving jobs was the first priority. On the shop floor decades of gains in imposing contractual and informal limitations on the authority of management to set production norms, introduce labor-saving technologies, and control work environments with respect to health and safety were frequently given up in return for job security agreements.

But as collective bargaining turned into collective begging, the hard-won democratic character of the unions eroded as well. Unions that could no longer deliver in the pay envelope and had surrendered power on the shop floor attempted to retain membership loyalty by transforming themselves into organizations that dispensed members' services. The tendency toward the clientization of union members, already incipient in the bureaucratization of labor organizations—in which full-time staff rather than shop floor leaders effectively ran the union—became the norm in many public and service employees organizations; the proud democracies that had been established in many industrial unions during the organizing phase either disappeared or were watered down. Unions' constitutions mandated less frequent conventions and elections of officers. Rebellious local unions were often slapped with trusteeships that temporarily abrogated the prerogatives of their leadership. And even if these local unions were not taken over, international union auditing departments oversaw their funds, not only to detect corrupt practices but to restrict their autonomy.[28]

At the political level unions became even more dependent upon the Democratic Party and the liberal state, so that no calumny visited upon workers and their unions by Democratic administrations was too harsh to prevent the leadership from giving its wholehearted support to the dominant centrist wing of the party. Taken for granted as a political ally, with only tiny exceptions Labor's legislative program during the last four Democratic administrations remained unadopted by Democratic- as well as Republican-controlled Congresses. Organized labor was not outraged by Bill Clinton's decision to give the full weight of his administration to supporting free trade agreements such as NAFTA and the WTO; and when the president agreed to sign the Welfare Reform Act of 1996, the new, progressive AFL-CIO leadership under John Sweeney failed to raise its voice in dissent or mobilize its legions of activists and rank-and-file members. In the aftermath of the disappointing political defeat of its candidate for president in the elections of 2000, there were signs that Sweeney was toying with a new strategy. In spring 2001, the AFL-CIO executive council announced a new policy of nonpartisanship that implied it would support worthy Republicans. A few months later organized Labor formally endorsed a new round of protests scheduled for fall announced by opponents of the neoliberal policies of the IMF and the WB; but the War Against Terrorism resulting from the September 11 events prompted cancellation of its plans to participate in the protests.

It remains to be seen whether unions can recover from decades of class compromise and political distance from the Left. At a time when globalism signifies, in the first place, massive new enclosures, that is, the displacement of hundreds of millions of people from the land and from the factories; a time when sections of the labor movements of advanced industrial societies, including those in the United States, are for the first time in nearly a century beginning to recognize the urgent need for international solidarity among all who oppose multinational corporate and state power, the hegemonic status of identity politics within social and political discourse transformed the "social" question, which has historically denoted the struggle for the emancipation of labor from class exploitation, into a question of identity. Now the worker becomes only one among the plurality of identities arrayed throughout the cultural and political field with no particular privileged position with respect to historical transformation. With Foucault many argue that history may not be understood in terms of stages or of successive modes of production but should be conceived as a series of discontinuous "discursive formations" marked by specific configurations of knowledge/power. So knowledge, not labor, becomes the linchpin of power.[29]

In turn, postmodern and poststructuralist thought deconstructs the goal of "emancipation" by showing that those who adhere to this goal are infected with the virus of essentialism. Since they are anticipatory concepts and, in traditional social theory, connote a preconceived goal of social struggles, independent of the actual course of these struggles, those who invoke emancipation, liberation, and freedom in relation to workers and other social movements are condemned for utopianism, or harkening back to the tragic experience of Communism, many now agree with Isaiah Berlin the idea of "positive" freedom is inherently authoritarian. Many of these persuasions do not hesitate to conflate utopianism—indeed, the centrality of the labor question—with Stalinism and other heinous versions of marxism.[30] As a result, we have experienced a weird convergence of some of radical postmarxian philosophy and social theory with conventional liberalism; like the trajectory of a good portion of literary radicals after World War II some have found themselves verging on neoconservatism or Right libertarianism.

RECLAIMING CLASS

There is a long way to go before American labor becomes a class-oriented social movement again. While the AFL-CIO has supported the principle of equal pay for equal work and has opposed discrimination in employment and education, it remains neutral on issues of sexual freedom that animated feminism and has abjured support of the gay and lesbian struggles on the basis that many of the members objected on religious grounds to homosexuality, as they do to abortion.Thus, bereft of a broad alliance capable of challenging capital's power, in the last half of the twentieth century the struggle for class formation was severely impaired. The consequence of the schism was that the movements lost a powerful ally, but in addition Labor was backed into the corner of being viewed within the framework of interest group politics; the labor question was narrowed to issues of wages, benefits, and job security, and women and racial minorities were invited to join unions, provided they kept other issues at home. Yet the class dimension of race and sex will not disappear. While one may not reduce the demands of women, blacks, and those with physical disabilities to their economic dimension, neither can the millions of blacks and women who are relegated to second-class positions within the occupational structure be ignored. Moreover, as I shall argue below, as necessary as they are, rights or the struggle for space within civil society do not and cannot embrace the totality of their demands.

In this connection, most social movements since the late 1970s have consigned the class demands of their broad constituencies to the back burner. It is not only because the officers, staff, and membership of many movements remain solidly ensconced in the professional/managerial fractions—lawyers and physicians, ministers, engineers and computer technicians and teachers. One might speculate that the marginalization of traditional issues such as economic equality in the civil rights organizations and in those of mainstream environmentalism and feminism is related to the fact that corporations have played an increasing role in providing financial support to some organizations. It might be too crude to claim that these groups are hesitant to bite the hand that feeds them, but the record of the last two conservative-dominated decades of the twentieth century is fairly plain: if civil rights organizations address employment discrimination it is usually confined to affirmative action programs, which large corporations and major universities have gladly embraced since the 1970s. Women's organizations have been more concerned with penetrating the so-called glass ceiling that inhibits women managers from rising to the top of the corporate hierarchy than with raising the bottom of workers in food service, health care, and retail establishments, who earn wages that revolve closely around the minimum wage. NOW, the feminist organization with the largest membership, has been largely absent from the recently resurgent labor struggles, many of which are directed to the working and living conditions of working women. And the mainstream environmental groups, such as the Sierra Club, have increasingly developed ties with corporations, many of whom are the leading polluters, on the premise that if they are to achieve meaningful reform they must make a deal with prevailing powers. As exemplified by the civil rights leader Jesse Jackson's recent strategy of hobnobbing with high corporate executives in order to win some concessions in hiring, taken together these compromises signal that once vital social movements have taken sides in the class fight—and it is not on the side of labor.

When theory reifies the division between class and social movements it tends to ratify the limits of both. In this sense, in the main body of social movement theory, as well as in the perspectives of the activists themselves, we witness a retreat from the emancipatory vision, first enunciated by all movements of anticapitalist opposition of the unity of the exploited, the traditional core of the labor question, and the oppressed, the rubric under which blacks, women, and the disabled created social movements. Many intellectuals who had become disillusioned with the vanguardism of Left formations rediscovered the wonders of liberalism, albeit in widely divergent versions. Laclau and Mouffe were the most theoretically rigorous, but their conclusions varied little from those of the rest. It was a subtle drift from postmodern and poststructuralist perspectives that radically decentered social structure, to pluralism. In the process the overlaps between class and identities based on biophysical distinction were easily ignored. Having determined that the economic dimensions of the social question had been solved in late capitalist regimes or were subject to solution without specifically addressing the relation of class to social inequalities and social stigma, these intellectuals found it relatively easy to ignore, if not deny, the fact that the overwhelming majority of the activists as well as the constituents of all of the new social movements were wageworkers whose supposed middle-class status was based on conventional accounts such as income, education, and occupation.

The authors of what became popularly known as the "Port Authority Statement," a reference to their New York origins and to the more famous declaration, the SDS activists Robert Gottlieb, David Gilbert, and Gerry Tenney theorized in class terms the emergence of the relatively recent social layer of salaried professional and technical workers. They suggested that in advanced capitalist societies the labor question was now a struggle for emancipation, not from labor itself, but from the authority of capitalist management. Drawing on the pioneering work of Serge Mallet and André Gorz, they argued that the social position of educated workers, especially in the advanced technological sectors, should be understood as a new working class rather than adjuncts to management and members of the middle class. What distinguished the demands of this formation from those of industrial workers was that they were most concerned with the quality of their working lives—whether they enjoyed autonomy in the performance of their work commensurate with their education and knowledge rather than chiefly with job security and with wages.[31]

The dispute as to whether intellectual labor was a new middle class, as Nicos Poulantzas insisted, or a new working class has never been resolved, but the indisputable facts are these: in the 1990s some of the most dynamic union organizations have emerged from the grievances of intellectual labor, for example, in higher education, especially by adjunct professors and graduate assistants, independent as well as salaried physicians and nurses, and, most recently, technicians and engineers in the information industry. Moreover, it is this social layer that has supplied the preponderance of leaders and activists, for all of the new social movements arose in the wake of the expansion of three main institutional sites: the rise of the information industries; the rapid development of the welfare state during and after the 1960s; and the enormous growth of higher education in American life that, as we have seen, became a major industry after World War II.

Most activists in the new social movements, indeed, in any civic activity within the liberal state, are recruited from educated professional and technical social formations. In addition to possessing educational credentials and incomes that are considerably greater than those of industrial and service workers, they are a major component of the politically active base of the liberal state. In fact, the legitimacy of the state depends on their participation. They have grown up in the belief that distinctions between the two main political parties matter and that voting is a relevant political choice. They tend to follow the activities of various legislative and executive bodies with keen interest and have been habituated emotionally as well as intellectually to respond powerfully to public events. These habits are reinforced by their predominant social and professional networks, consisting of people like themselves, people who share the same upbringing, professional backgrounds, and education. Collectively, their political philosophy tends, except in extraordinary times, to converge with classical liberal theory; in general they are susceptible to arguments that equate social change with incremental reform and hold, albeit implicitly, to Locke's doctrine of inalienable rights based on natural law. In turn, they have a healthy sense of entitlement, which helps them react to evidence that state and corporate institutions often violate the human rights of ordinary citizens as well as of political opponents; except, of course, when in times of war they perceive their country has been attacked or is otherwise endangered by a foreign power. During these times many liberals are prone to accept the doctrine that human rights may be suspended for the duration and, as in the case of the recent war against Afghanistan's Taliban regime, failed to raise their collective voices against the federal government's indefinite detainment of more than eleven hundred foreign nationals from the Middle East and Central Asia.

While many people whose lack of education and of socially privileged background have, out of fear, inhibited their willingness to question, much less challenge, the authority of the state and of the large corporate enterprises, the activists' sense of entitlement makes them aggressive in the face of official perfidy. They are not only in, but of, the moral and political system so that whatever their ideological objections to the system, beneath this layer lurks a great sense of justice and injustice; their outrages are motivated by that sense of fairness that distinguishes many decent people. When they form organizations that seek redress of social and political wrongs they retain faith in the power of reason to overcome ingrained intellectual as well as economic and political resistance. These beliefs may be shaken in their student days; some even proclaim their intellectual and political radicalism and, for a time, may adopt the judgment of radicals throughout history that, far from being joined at the hip with democracy, the history and practices of capitalism and of the liberal state show that the system is amenable to democratic processes only when forced to yield from below. But the conditions of everyday life and of their histories reveal themselves in times of the movement's ebb.

Among these is that as we grow older we take on work and family responsibilities. Except for the relatively few—and then for only a limited period of their lives—dedicating large amounts of energy and time to political activity is experienced as an enormous sacrifice of other equally pressing tasks. These predispositions are rarely enunciated by their bearers. On the contrary, many shift their field of activity to places like schools, professional associations, or unions that are more integrated with the rest of their lives. Their intellectual radicalism may not have diminished, but their predispositions and everyday routines make participation in demonstrations, which often entails traveling long distances, impractical. That explains in part why most radical social movements are generational; they embrace the young and the old but rarely those in the throes of the seasons of life that may be constrained by the demands of career and child rearing.

Although most of the new social movements have, in the past three decades, reverted like the labor movement did in the 1930s to rights discourses, sometimes in radical guise, their initial thrust was directed to addressing traditional demands by direct action rather than by relying on the institutions of the liberal state. What is significant about a sit-in, a rent strike, a boycott, or a mass march? These are tactics that signify rejection of a strategy to win gains by exclusive reliance on legal processes and the slow and often ineffectual procedures afforded by law to adjudicate grievances. As Martin Luther King proclaimed in defense of the use of civil disobedience and challenging the abstraction of the sovereignty of law, the oppressed have no obligation to obey an immoral law. If the law is to be changed, he implied, let those in authority accommodate to us. And perhaps more important, the movements raised new questions connected to some of the hidden or taken-for-granted aspects of social life. For example, whereas the subordination of women to men in the home was mostly a topic of closed door discussions by discontented women, the new feminist movement in the 1960s subjected such questions—who performs child rearing and housework? what are sexual relations?—to public discussion and debate, especially at a time when more women were entering the paid workplace and found themselves working a double shift. Similarly, the idea that people who have what the mainstream regard as severe physical impairments were incapable of participating in public life, hold a full-time job, or become educated at every level of the academic hierarchy was part of the culture and was accepted, however reluctantly, by its victims.

And of course, until the 1970s homosexual practices, when not directly suppressed by police and courts and deemed illegal by state laws banning sodomy (many states still have these laws on the books), were exercised underground. Although the material achievements of the movement of those with physical disabilities were visibly linked to rights—of access, against employment and education discrimination, and other familiar demands for equal opportunity—in order to get that far they had to challenge the stigma of being considered less than human; in this sense, the struggle resembled that of the black freedom movement. There is perhaps no greater obstacle to equality—except for the color bar—than being deracinated. Blacks lost their name and with it their past; the physical stigmata make their bearer invisible in ordinary society. However sincere the empathy, one is noticed only to be dismissed from membership. For many the proper response to the disabled is to make a charitable contribution.[32]

The cultural unconscious is the most powerful ally of the myriad of organizations that raise money for the infirm. By expiating our collective unease concerning the fragility of our own bodies, they permit us to forget, at least in the course of the everyday, that the line between the normal and the pathological is at bottom arbitrary. We can be rendered infirm in an instant by serendipity: an automobile accident, a household fall, some unexplained virus that suddenly afflicts a limb or some other organ, a chronic ailment that turns acute. Of course, the aging know these things best, but, until recently, their complaints were routinely ignored because they reminded us of our own bleak future. The illusion of eternal youth pervades our public culture. The same generative force of the power of religion—our inability to face our mortality—makes us blind to the fact that mental and physical well-being possesses historicity: the bed- or wheelchair-ridden person before us is a reminder of what we would otherwise deny. Only by consigning the "other" to the periphery can we maintain the illusion that we will not be identified with them.

The stigma of physical disability was so great that Franklin D. Roosevelt, who became paralyzed in adulthood, spent most of his subsequent years disguising the fact that he could walk only haltingly and aided by prosthetic devices. Every public appearance he made was carefully staged to present the illusion of physical normalcy. Although still unacknowledged by most students of social movements, the many decades of struggle conducted by people with physical and, more recently, mental and emotional disabilities—beginning with the militant efforts of Helen Keller early in the century—constituted one of the radical social movements of the twentieth century because it challenged our collective conceptions of the distinction between the normal and the pathological. What we saw were the visible signs of the movement's power: the transformation of public accommodations to make them accessible and the amending of antidiscrimination laws to guarantee the employment and educational rights of the so-called handicapped. But the hardest task entailed a process of changing the public perception that those who do not meet the historically constituted standard of normalcy were inferior, from which followed their justifiable exclusion from many institutions of economic and public life. Needless to say, the fight is not over, least of all the effort to change perception as well as to persuade those suffering the stigma and the hardships of disability, mental as well as physical, to take control of their destiny. More than a half century elapsed after Roosevelt's death before the public recognized and accepted the fact that he had infantile paralysis, a recognition that was inscribed in a new national statue of the president that depicts him in a wheelchair. But even the ADA, which places some legal bars on discrimination in education, public accommodations, and employment and has produced a sea change in everyday life, has proven inadequate to secure genuine equality.[33]

Many school systems still balk at providing enough trained teachers, equipment, and facilities for disabled students. Most disabled workers languish in low-paying jobs or remain for years in so-called sheltered workshops because most employers remain reluctant to hire them, regardless of evidence of their skills. Others hesitate to spend the money necessary to make the workplace accessible to these workers. Many communities in this country have no accessible public accommodations. Like every rights-directed antidiscrimination statute, the provisions of ADA require political will and staff if they are to be enforced. But given the ingrained prejudices of our culture, political will often requires direct action to awaken it, especially when fractions of capital have brought suits to the Supreme Court that restrict their obligations under the act.

Taken together, these movements have succeeded, to a degree, in changing the lives of millions: although their most radical class demands remain unfulfilled, the feminist movement has altered everyday language, sharply curtailed sexist practices at work and in public life, opened some of the doors to professions like law and medicine once reserved for men (but still not engineering and, in science, only biology) and narrowed the wage gap. Yet joblessness among women remains higher than that of men; their living and working conditions tend, in growing numbers, to veer toward economic and social disaster. The relative indifference of the organized women's movement to these situations forecasts no immediate relief, except insofar as the working poor mobilize in limited numbers to join the unions. Similarly, legal rights to education and employment notwithstanding, the most basic program of the black freedom movement remains a distant shore even as the black professional, managerial, and technical fractions have grown. In some ways, the black working class as a whole is worse off than it was in 1970. Unemployment among blacks remains twice that of whites, millions are stuck in deindustrialized urban areas where wages revolving around the federal minimum wage still predominate and schools have become the institutional sites of the stigmata that ensure that most black youth will remain poor. In an environment in which poverty and unemployment have become ordinary, as William DiFazio has argued, and in which the functions of local and state government are focused on terrorizing the victims of an increasingly iniquitous economic and political system, there is little evidence that civil rights organizations or unions are prepared to mount meaningful resistance.[34]

This litany will be challenged by official statistics and by the optimistic judgment of many economists and leaders of rights movements who have evaluated the 1990s boom as an instance of win-win results. The disparity between the two viewpoints may be ascribed not to objective criteria but to social and political standpoint. That prior to the recession of 2000–02 black unemployment was somewhat reduced there is no doubt. But that the labor they must accept, in an era in which federal income guarantees have all but been abolished, does not permit a decent living standard is ignored by these economists. Even poverty statistics are skewed by the politically generated grossly low poverty line established by the federal government, a line which is less than half that proposed by independent investigators.[35] And optimists don't bother to rationalize the snail's pace of the narrowing of the income gap between men and women, which stands at 80 percent; after several decades of annual raises of 1 percent, the gap has stabilized during the "boom," a testament to the proposition that economic growth is disconnected with equality. In fact, the market is by no means an equalizer. Lifting all boats may leave many passengers under water. Only when movements struggle on a class basis—which invariably entails playing the zero sum game—do the fractions that are left behind begin to catch up.

7
ECOLOGY AND CLASS

We are finally coming to recognize that the natural environment is the exploited proletariat, the downtrodden nigger of everybody's industrial system.

—Theodore Roszak

THE DOMINATION OF NATURE

The great achievement of the ecology movement has been to promote a general understanding that human relations with the natural environment are vital to the shaping of human social relations. In turn, social relations alter the natural environment. In this regard relations of power play a decisive role. Who was to make the decisions about how to fill the space left vacant by the terrorist attack on the World Trade Center was determined, to a large degree, by which interests succeeded in setting the priorities. What is still less understood is that the built environment that sustains our mode of life and, indeed, the totality of our surroundings, including what we code as nature, is mediated by labor. The construction of our built environment as well as our primary relation to what we call the external environment is intrinsic to labor. The production of the built environment is, at the same time, the production of social space. When a construction project displaces residents and their homes not only is physical space altered but a new social space is created as well. When people form a neighborhood movement to force authorities to build affordable housing rather than office buildings or luxury apartments on vacant or condemned land, they as well as the construction workers are producing space.

The materialist insight that humankind is part of natural history refutes the humanist illusion that somehow we stand above the material world. This illusion forgets that we are biologically constituted beings and that labor, the process by which we negotiate with nature and thereby transform human nature as well, is the condition of what we take as specifically human. Thus the labor question is not only socially but ontologically significant; it goes to who we are and have become. While all workers, paid or not, know that civilization rests on their shoulders, we are only now becoming aware that the forms of labor—or what scientists' euphemistically term human intervention—bear on the extent to which nature may be able to support life. Capital, which out of hubris imagines it creates the world, is indifferent to this fact because to question its domination is to question itself. Labor forms are not determined chiefly by the laborer but by those who hire labor; when extracting as much profit as possible, hirers are prone to ignore the ecological consequences of the choices they have made in shaping the labor process. But if capital's power can design the transformation of the material world, including the ordering of physical space and its forms, the rest of us must live with the results. At the same time, it is labor of all sorts that effects this transformation. The ecological question is a class question because the class power that configures the forms of labor bears on the fundamental well-being of the species, in the first place those charged with the tasks associated with execution. The struggles over class in the twenty-first century are likely to be about whether capital's logic can be thwarted and a new logic of democratic relations in society and nature put in its place.

While we experience ecological problems as effects, the basic issue is not whether the consequences of the attempts to dominate nature are deleterious; domination cannot succeed because the ecosystems of which we are a part will inevitably resist plunder. Yet the will to domination marks our relations with nature and the character of our social relations. Thus the struggle against class domination in its widest sense is the heart of the struggle to render our ecosystem safe for life, not merely for its survival but for its quality. The efforts to reform public policy to reduce the harmful effects of current configurations of industrial production, urbanism, and consumption are necessary, but the ecological crisis we face can be resolved only if we change our modes of labor and the concomitant social relations—at the workplace, in the cities, in the way we construe pleasure.

Ecological demands present the most compelling challenge to the capacity of global capitalism to solve its systemic problems without courting disasters that affect humans and other life-forms; but they also pose the question of the efficacy of rights, which marks many social movements today, particularly the latest human rights–based politics. Of the four great social movements of our time, ecological demands alone are not ostensibly based on identities that can be reduced to physical, biological, and cultural characteristics of specific social formations. On the contrary, the questions posed by the permutations of the ecosystems, indeed, the relations of humans to nature, expand biopolitics to include the issue of how to ensure the sustainability of life itself. The question has become whether, and how, the human species can reproduce itself under conditions in which its most developed forms of the production of knowledge and of material goods pose a threat to its own species and to many others as well.

On its face, the ecological interest may be regarded as transgressing the limitation of a politics that solely addresses the interests of particular social formations and, indeed, the human interest, by creating a politics that embraces all living things. Capitalists and workers, men and women, politicians and citizens all require action to remedy the serious deterioration of the environment. A growing number of bodies of water around the globe are polluted and kill or infect fish with harmful metals like mercury, rendering them inedible, and reduce the supply of potable water. Some studies claim that perhaps half the world's population will suffer severe water shortages by 2020. We are afflicted with unsafe air, especially in the urban centers, where asthma among children of all social classes is rampant and, together with contaminated foods, contributes to the cancer epidemic, one that seems to affect rich as well as poor, if not in equal proportions. And we are witnessing further relentless destruction of nature, not only of trees and animal forms but, through massive erosion, of the soil from which our physical sustenance ultimately derives. Droughts and their mirror images, floods, exacerbated by regressive industrial regimes such as single-crop economies and deforestation for mining and clean-cut lumber production, are depriving tens of millions of people of food.

Scientists have confirmed that global warming is no longer an unproven hypothesis. Since proof is equivalent to whether a consensus exists among those qualified to make judgments about scientific propositions, President Bush, upon the advice of a commission of scientists he appointed—including some leading climatologists—and after expressing skepticism, now admits that the emission of large quantities of carbon dioxide, so-called greenhouse gasses, endangers the environment and that means must be found to reduce them. But consistent with his nationalist predispositions, Bush has refused to sign the Kyoto Treaty limiting greenhouse gases on the grounds it would hurt U.S. economic growth and undermine the nation's sovereignty. Of course, the point of any international treaty is precisely to limit the ability of any signatory to act unilaterally. So we may assume that the president's acknowledgment of the danger is a rhetorical gesture made under conditions of embarrassment rather than conviction. The only problem is that, because the United States uses a third of the world's resources, what it does in relation to the environment is somewhat more consequential than what Sri Lanka or even a huge country like India does.[1]

The problems posed by the crisis of the ecosystems could counter the claims of this book that American as well as all modern societies are divided by classes. For is it not the case that regardless of our social station we all live in the same ecosystems? Can the wealthy find a sanctuary that would protect them from holes in the ozone layer or from the effects of global warming? Even a cursory reading of the obituary pages of the *New York Times* confirms that the relatively privileged—the almost invariable subjects of that newspaper's death notices—regularly die of cancer as well as of heart disease and other common afflictions. To the extent that cancer and heart illness are environmental diseases as much as of genetic predisposition linked to family histories, conditions of wealth go only so far in protecting the economically privileged from their ravages. Is it not in everyone's interest to find the path to restoring a healthy environment? It may be true that, as individuals, capitalists share the same fate as the rest of us, but as components of capital these individuals are embodiments of a system-logic they cannot oppose without contravening the system itself. That is why leading governments, multinational corporations, and transnational agencies of control resist the drastic measures advised by many scientists, environmentalist organizations, and some international agencies that would require them to significantly slow activities that produce greenhouse gas emissions, let alone reverse the prevailing regimes of industrial production and patterns of consumption that court disaster. Why do even the most enlightened among them rest content with palliatives like the Kyoto Treaty? Why have two of the most powerful countries, the United States and Italy, refused to sign on to even limited global environmental regulations? Are these social bodies merely blind or is there a systemic series of determinations that prevents them from taking the necessary steps to save themselves and the rest of us? Why are movements against the current global economic and political arrangements gaining ground and beginning to adopt an anticapitalist outlook?

The roots of capital's resistance lie in three of its major presuppositions:

1. The market is the only measure of social, cultural, and economic value; it supersedes traditional patriarchal and religious values and the propositions of bourgeois humanism (except during the Cold War, when secular Western powers made common cause with religious fundamentalists against the Soviet Union in, among other countries, Afghanistan);
2. Government regulation of private economic activity, except as it rationalizes unwanted competition between capitals, is inimical to the vital interests of the system. For this reason capital cannot recognize ecology as an imperative that supersedes the market. What accounts for its historical blindness is the fatal connection it makes between its Smithian definition of economic and social freedom and the imperatives for capital accumulation based on the exploitation of labor, which is coded as economic growth. In the latter context the devaluation of labor both in monetary and ideological terms is a symptom of the devaluation of nature. Capital encounters nature only as an obstacle that, armed with technology, it can overcome. Underlying this view is one of the historical legacies of the Enlightenment: that humans stand, somehow, outside nature, a situation mediated by transcendental Mind. In addition to freeing the market from the limitations imposed by the feudal system, capitalism triumphed through what Francis Bacon termed the conquest of nature, the leading edge of which was technology. As Max Horkheimer and Theodor Adorno have observed, the Enlightenment, which corresponds to the emergence of capitalism in the sixteenth century, viewed nature as fungible, subject to the will to power of scientific and technical knowledge. The domination of nature is intrinsic to the reliance of capital accumulation on technical development.
3. Finally, the compulsion to accumulate is innate. Thus regulation of the production of greenhouse gases can never go so far as to actually mandate growth limits. The imperatives of growth are intrinsic to the system-logic of capitalism. Despite the dubious claim that information technology is free of pollutants, the economies of advanced industrial nations still rely, in large measure, on the intermediate technology industries such as autos, lumber, and paper and the carbon-based industries of steel and electricity, which devour huge quantities of oil and coal.

Capitalist industrialization evoked dreams of a technologically wrought cornucopia in which nature would no longer rule humans. Until the 1960s many intellectuals and political and economic leaders in the major industrialized countries, both capitalist and state socialist, remained in the thrall of the technological sensorium that willfully ignored the ecological consequences of industrialization. In 1951, R. William Kapp made the obvious point that oil drilling, coal mining, nuclear energy, and other forms of industrial production left in their wake huge quantities of hazardous waste, the cleanup of which constituted a "social cost." When this was factored into the costs of production the actual price of commodities was much higher than their market value. If the government is charged with the cleanup and restoration of the waste by-products of the production process, these activities should be added to cost and are usually reflected in the tax bill, which is a deduction from profits and wages. To which must be added the social costs inherent in the ruined health of miners, chemical workers, and their families. Examples such as that of New York's Love Canal, a community near Niagara Falls, the site of large-scale chemical manufacturing until the late 1970s, illustrate the social costs of market-driven production. An appallingly high percentage of the local residents near Love Canal were afflicted with cancers that medical investigators determined were directly attributable to the water and air toxins spewed from the plants. Similar cancer and birth-defect epidemics afflicted people living at America's premier site of nuclear research and testing, New Mexico's Los Alamos installation and Yucca Flats, where the military detonated countless nuclear devices from the 1940s through the 1970s.[2]

Such calculations were ignored by industrial corporations and the United States government until, in reaction to mass protests initiated by environmentalists and subsequent legislative and juridical decisions, they were compelled to take some responsibility for cleaning up after themselves. But large corporations have enough political clout to evade some environmental regulations, or they have made deals by which they are awarded the privilege of self-regulation; as a result, many cleanups remain incomplete and in some cases thwarted. Many of these companies have refused, except under duress, to acknowledge their culpability and in an era of deregulation have benefited, to our collective harm, from slack enforcement and judgments by probusiness courts against holding them individually accountable.[3] The accumulated consequences of corporate decisions have left the natural and social ecologies of our planet in a precarious state. From their earliest period to the present, corporations in such industries as coal and metal mining, oil, steel, and chemicals arrogantly refused to take responsibility for their role in the despoliation of nature. Until the late 1970s travelers in New Jersey, Pennsylvania, eastern Kentucky, and West Virginia could not fail to observe the visible evidence of this dereliction: huge, gouged-out sides of mountains, abandoned mines that left untended holes in the earth, heaps of slag, and, in Delaware and New Jersey, among other states, chemical waste. And, especially in western Pennsylvania and West Virginia the sun and the stars were regularly hidden by a thick layer of smog.

Secure in their power to resist meaningful reform, the power blocs of these societies continue to operate under a consensus that nuclear energy, genetically modified organisms, and other artifices of technology will eventually liberate us from the brutal effects of nature, including sudden seismographic shifts that contribute to floods, droughts, and human and property destruction. They understand capital accumulation not only in terms of their own direct interest, but as a means to obviate material scarcity. Throughout history, the insufficiency of material goods has constituted a basis for class warfare that constantly threatened to disrupt social peace. The idea is that if scientifically wrought industrial production can abolish material scarcity, at least for the majority in the most industrially developed societies, even if the fruits are unequally distributed the economy will "raise all boats."

Since the inception of industrial capitalism, for some the price of future abundance was too steep. Early opponents, far from conflating market capitalism with freedom and democracy, saw industrial capitalism as a form of tyranny. Triumphant capitalism witnessed the birth of the so-called romantic rebellion against an industrial order that systematically killed or maimed its young and condemned large portions of the adult population to premature aging. The industrial system produced a virtual army of "misfits" who were unable to work because they were victims of industrial accidents or labor-induced diseases. Whole segments of the population were reduced to penury. William Blake, Percy Bysshe Shelley, and Thomas Hood railed against the debilitating effects of capitalist industrialization, which stunted the growth of children, sent men and women prematurely to their graves, and, equally egregiously, burdened the physical environment with vast quantities of pollution and industrial waste that turned large sections of cities and towns into cauldrons of disease and despair.[4]

In the nineteenth century, such figures as the naturalist Henry David Thoreau, the sociologist Lester Frank Ward, and the economist Henry George were among the few who were acutely aware of the dangers of unbridled industrialization and raised their voices on behalf of conservation of wilderness areas. Following the lead of the German zoologist and philosopher Ernst Haeckel, Ward insisted that humans and their civilizations "are attached [to the tree of evolution] by every organ and every function essential to the whole."[5] Calling for an appreciation of nature rather than adopting Bacon's position of conquest, Ward defined civilization as the "achievement of management and direction of the phylogenetic forces of nature."[6] Whereas Thoreau defended the natural environment for its own sake, even going so far as to engage in ecological sabotage to defend fish and other wildlife, many of his fellow environmentalists, such as George, framed their concerns in terms of the need to preserve nature as a resource for eventual human use.[7] Similarly, the group that formed the Society for the Prevention of Cruelty to Animals in the late nineteenth century and those who protested against child labor were not so much the conscience of capital as its rational side. The cry for protection of animals and children was directed at the system's own interest; these reforming groups urged legislation to inhibit the excesses of the capitalist labor market, which ruthlessly swept up any available labor regardless of the human cost. For if animals were wantonly sacrificed to sport—or to science—and children were used up before they attained adulthood, industrialists would produce labor and animal shortages that would eventually inhibit their own capacity for survival. If industrial capitalism was to prosper, they argued, it would be required to exercise restraint lest it destroy itself and the system it had built.

Ward and other conservationists conceded that industrial and urban development, suburbanization, and technological innovations such as labor-destroying machine applications within production, as well as cars, trucks, and airplanes were nearly identical to what they considered progress. The conservationists were an elite group of influentials, not a popular grassroots movement, and concentrated their energies on protecting discrete bodies of land and water from development. The New York lawyer Harold Ickes, later Franklin Roosevelt's secretary of the interior, was among some conservationists who rose to high governmental positions. In an era when the Democratic Party was tied to its urban and southern aristocratic agrarian base, whatever political support conservationism could muster originated in the Republican ranks. A progressive Republican in the tradition of Theodore Roosevelt, Ickes in the 1930s became the country's official champion of national parks, pressing for protection of wilderness areas through nationalization of huge tracts of vacant or abandoned land. But as was FDR's wont he did not hand over land policy entirely to a conservationist. He was acutely aware of the power of lumber and paper, oil, and gas interests and was not inclined to expose himself to their ire on this terrain even as he incurred their wrath on labor policy. Consequently, Ickes had to combat, and was partially neutralized by, other administration appointees. The struggles over oil prompted him to threaten to resign, but Roosevelt always moved far enough in Ickes's environmentalist direction to keep him on. When, in 1946 Roosevelt's successor, Harry Truman, appointed Ed Pauley, an oilman who was eager to keep tidelands oil reserves outside federal jurisdiction, as secretary of the navy Ickes offered the president his resignation, which Truman accepted, much to the chagrin of liberals.[8]

Environmental conservation was a crusade to save the economic system from devouring itself. From this followed the art and science of natural and human "resource planning": federal and state governments were urged to set aside some of their vast holdings from development by industry and housing interests. When reelected president in 1904, Theodore Roosevelt created a federal conservation policy and used his bully pulpit to urge the states to emulate it. This policy was the environmentalist equivalent of market regulation. The unregulated market had other enemies. The labor movement joined middle-class social reformers in opposing unsafe factory and living conditions and child labor. Before national legislation became politically feasible these alliances won support from state legislatures in industrial states and cities like New York and Chicago, which enacted health and safety regulations in factories and imposed new housing standards aimed at eliminating slum dwellings or at least making them safer and more healthy by requiring, for example, fire extinguishers, flush toilets, and safe stairwells. On the belief that uncontrolled capitalism was ruining its most precious resource, living labor, advocates for children proposed raising the mandatory age for school leaving and for employment. Because the proponents of natural conservation and those who fought against abuse of animals were often part of ruling formations, they did not generally overlap with children's groups. Although a few people from wealthy precincts saw the folly of child labor, it was the turn-of-the-century labor movement, muckraking journalists, and a small contingent of progressive middle-class reformers like Jane Addams who waged the fight.

Nearly two centuries after Blake railed against England's "satanic mills," which, he believed, had ruined its "green and pleasant land" as well as destroyed human labor, Rachel Carson's best-selling books called attention to the threat to our waters posed by industrial waste and especially by the leading technology designed to raise the productivity of agricultural labor, chemical pesticides. In 1962 Murray Bookchin's less disseminated but more analytic *Our Synthetic Environment* argued that the new mode of industrial production based on synthetic materials posed serious environmental and health hazards. Since World War II, which saw the invention of many new technologies that found their way into ordinary use, DDT and other industrial chemicals have become ubiquitous in everyday life. The use of these key substances informed the dream of those who sought to free capital from its dependence on nature for raw materials. To return now to prewar methods of production would entail a massive reorganization not only of our economy, but of our social world. We are simply so dependent, for example, on the hydrocarbon plastic that its ubiquity is all but invisible. Clothing, furniture, bottles, housewares, and appliances made exclusively or even mainly from cotton, wool, wood, glass, paper, and metals are now considered luxury items. The "raw" material employed in the mass production of these commodities is various forms of plastics, a hydrocarbon that, despite industry claims to the contrary, is not biodegradable and poses a toxic threat to the water table.[9]

The warnings of grave consequences are clear: we maintain energy policies that rely on nonrenewable and polluting fuels at our peril. We should be developing such virtually pollution-free energy technologies as wind, geothermal, and solar and seeking the reductions of greenhouse gas emissions to be derived from self-generating electrical engines in autos and other machines. Yet the alliance of governments and transnational energy companies has stayed the course. They were not impressed even by predictions that oil wells would soon run dry. In 1978, more than forty years after similar predictions by the critic Lewis Mumford, the environmental scientist Barry Commoner warned that, on the basis of significant annual increases in oil consumption, the supply of oil was near exhaustion and might last only fifty more years. But since the idea of planning is inimical to the neoliberal economic faith, energy corporations and government regulators have given only a passing nod to the development of alternatives. Although electrical engines for vehicles have passed the experimental stage and will be introduced commercially on a broad scale within the first decade of the twenty-first century, producing a viable electric car entails a relatively prolonged period of transition from service stations dispensing fuel and other oil products to sites where electrical engines may be replaced and recharged. In the absence of official and industry foresight, an omission that signifies that alternative energy sources are ideologically opposed by both, without powerful political pressure this technology will occupy a very small portion of the market in the near future.

A quarter century after President Jimmy Carter urged Congress to approve a large-scale research effort to find viable alternatives, oil- and coal-dependent electricity remain our main sources of energy, and nuclear reactors, which produce large quantities of hazardous waste, still account for a third of America's electricity output. Public skepticism about the motives of the oil giants was deepened by a series of ruinous oil spills, the most prominent of which was that of the tanker *Exxon Valdez* off the Alaska coast in 1989. During the 1980s and 1990s environmentalist organizations managed to mobilize sufficient political force to thwart many, but not all, plans for ecologically dangerous nuclear, coal, and oil production within the United States, prompting transnational oil corporations to relentlessly move offshore to Latin America and the Middle East in their quest for new sources. In 2001, a few months before the attack of September 11 at the World Trade Center in New York, President Bush's treasury secretary, Paul O'Neill, declared nuclear power to be perfectly safe and called for a new phase of expansion of the industry. Needless to say, he did not anticipate the effect that terrorist action could have on communities that host the more than one hundred nuclear reactors in the United States, including Indian Point in Westchester County, about thirty miles from the trade center.[10]

Since the oil and gas crises of the 1970s, the United States has become even more dependent on imported oil than before, and its consumption has more than doubled in twenty-five years. In addition to the effects of the world glut of crude oil in the 1960s and early 1970s, which made investment in new domestic sources of oil unprofitable, environmentalists had managed to limit production of crude oil within U.S. borders. But beyond legislation that mandated the elimination of lead in most gasoline they have been unsuccessful on the consumption side. Big Oil has been able to thwart legislation and administrative rules that would raise mileage standards for automobiles and trucks. On the contrary, in the midst of accelerated global warming in the 1990s, all of the world's leading car manufacturers, especially America's Big Three auto companies, introduced new gas-guzzling sports utility vehicles (SUVs), most of which far exceed the modest fuel efficiency standards established by the Environmental Protection Administration (EPA). Moreover, in an era of severe budget cuts for regulatory agencies and an increasingly conservative judiciary, the auto industry has been able to ignore even these inadequate levels. As long as gas prices remain relatively low, American drivers seem perfectly willing to drive heavy, fuel-inefficient vehicles regardless of the safety and environmental hazards they pose.

Thus the potential universalism of ecological issues is undermined by the recalcitrance of a resurgent fraction of capital whose wealth and power have succeeded, so far, in thwarting an aggressive public approach to ecological sanity. The profit imperative, it seems, overrules science as well as the new environmentalist common sense. For it was during the eight years of the Clinton administration that this fraction of southern- and southwestern-based energy corporations and the segment of the political directorate allied with them captured the preponderance of congressional seats and executive and legislative branches of state governments in the South, Southwest, and sizable sections of the industrial heartland, including Michigan, Ohio, Illinois, and Indiana. Having seized the White House in 2000, a new power bloc of ultra–right wing politicos and the fractions of capital associated with industrial and home energy production have insisted on ignoring or reversing environmental regulations: they have proposed modifications in the Clean Air and Water Act; and proposed rescinding prohibition of certain types of exploration like dredging oil from the sea and drilling for oil on the hundreds of thousands of protected wilderness and wildlife acres on the North Alaska coast. Under a new EPA, the Bush administration has relaxed pollution standards to permit coal corporations to expand mining activities and proposed reviving the dormant nuclear industry, which fell on bad times during the 1970s and early 1980s in the wake of the scare at Three Mile Island and the hugely destructive nuclear accident at Chernobyl in the Ukraine.

Sensing their vulnerability, the Bush administration has courted unions in the production and transportation sectors. The fraction of capital that envisions a new birth of American economic autarcky has made systematic efforts to reach out to the powerful teamsters' and carpenters' unions to support its energy policy by, among other inducements, making extravagant predictions about the job-creating effects of these programs. For example, at a time when industries engaged in material production and distribution have declined steadily in good times as well as bad, the media have routinely quoted the administration-floated figure of 780,000 construction and maintenance jobs resulting from opening Alaska drilling. And the otherwise progressive United Mineworkers' union, whose members are concentrated in politically crucial swing states like Kentucky, Tennessee, and West Virginia, has thrown in with Bush's program for coal expansion to fuel new power plants.

Yet in the aftermath of the tragic event at the World Trade Center on September 11, 2001, the mostly hidden face of class politics flashed on the screen. One of the most significant features of the disaster was the transformation of the environment, not only at the site of the twin towers but potentially in the entire region. Many, if not most, of the approximately three thousand people killed were unionized working people—restaurant workers, firefighters, police, and building service employees. The rubble produced by the crashes of two fully fueled commercial airliners left acres of toxic waste whose effects on the air are, at this writing, not fully known. Almost immediately after hundreds of firefighters and police perished in their efforts to save victims by entering the collapsing buildings, thousands of rescue workers filled the area in a mostly futile effort to save lives and then to recover comrades and friends who were buried in the tons of debris. Amid assurances from public officials that the area posed no health threats, they were exposed to dioxins and other toxic materials that later became the subject of investigations by scientists and public health officials. Like the postal workers in Washington and Trenton who, even as they were proclaimed heroes by politicians, the media, and the public, were exposed to anthrax but did not immediately receive treatment, firefighters and emergency health workers have taken the brunt of the risks. Just as union leaders who backed Bush's energy program chose, in past years, the ephemeral promise of jobs over the scourge of black lung and cancer, so the New York labor movement was slow to recognize the short- and long-term hazards to which their members were exposed by their heroism and the inequality of sacrifice it entailed.

Writing in the *Washington Post,* the columnist E. J. Dionne reminded his readers that, contrary to common belief, class was alive and well in America. The hierarchy of attention that placed Senate Majority Leader Tom Daschle's and other government officials' health above that of the people who handled the anthrax packages resulted in the deaths of two postal workers. And belatedly noting that airline companies were awarded $15 billion by Congress while tens of thousands of unemployed workers awaited an extension of benefits beyond the twenty-six-week limitation under existing federal law, AFL-CIO president John Sweeney suggested class interest when he issued a statement demanding that working people (coded in the communitarian buzzword working families) receive equal treatment in relation to the consequences of the terrorist attacks. He also suggested that corporations be required to undertake an equal measure of sacrifice if workers would be asked for concessions to fight the terrorists.[11]

URBAN ECOLOGY, SOCIAL ECOLOGY

In the founding of a distinctly American sociology the most influential contributor was Robert Park of the University of Chicago. Strongly influenced by environmental progressivism and by the ideas of the German sociologist and social philosopher Georg Simmel, the Chicago School, of which Park was a leading figure, understood urbanism as one of the great features of industrialization and its characteristic mode of life in terms of the concept of urban ecology. Social relations were intertwined with the interaction of humans and their physical and social environments, *physical* being understood as a built environment, the main outcome of human interaction with nature. So questions of social personality, education, and culture could not be separated from living conditions, especially housing, neighborhood life, ethnicity, and the presence or absence of public amenities such as parks and other recreational facilities. The sociologist must study forms of social interaction in the context of the ecosystem within which they occur. The neighborhood is seen as more than a series of dwellings and functional commercial establishments; it is an organic cultural site in which people build communities that are modes of life. Park fostered several generations of investigators, including Ernest Burgess, Lewis Wirth, and, a generation later, William Kornblum, whose ethnography *Blue Collar Community* chronicled the urban ecologies of Chicago's southside steel communities; Park's imprint can also be seen in such works as *The American Soldier,* a multivolume study by Morris Janowitz, and, perhaps most famously, in the immensely influential landmark community studies *Middletown* and *Middletown in Transition* by Robert S. Lynd and Helen M. Lynd.

Perhaps the most farsighted study of the pre–World War II era was *Technics and Civilization* (1934) by the writer and editor Lewis Mumford. The book, which made the connection between nature conservation and what Mumford called "social ecology," has been viewed by most readers as a critique of the twentieth-century view that machine technology is an unqualified boon to civilization.[12] But because the book appeared in the midst of labor upheaval and the Great Depression what was often missed was Mumford's unbridled attack on Bacon's call for the conquest of nature, his discussion of the relation between "carboniferous capitalism"—or what he calls the "paleotechnic phase in the development of civilization"—and "the destruction of the environment." "The first mark of paleotechnic industry was the pollution of the air," he writes. "Disregarding Benjamin Franklin's happy suggestion that coal smoke, being unburnt carbon, should be utilized a second time in the furnace, the new manufacturers erected steam engines and factory chimneys without any effort to conserve energy; nor did they at first utilize the by-products of coke-ovens or burn up the gases produced in the blast furnaces. In this paleotechnic world the realities were money, prices, capital shares; the environment, like all human existence, was treated as an abstraction."[13] More than fifteen years before Rachel Carson made the same observation but without the same analytic argument, Mumford carries the story of waste and pollution to the later emergence of the chemical industry: "If atmospheric sewage was the first mark of paleotechnic industry, stream pollution was the second. The dumping of industrial and chemical waste-products into the streams was a characteristic mark of the new order."[14]

Because "all human existence" was, like the physical environment, treated by capitalism as an abstraction, so was labor. Given that Kant's doctrine that "every human being should be treated as an end, not as a means was formulated precisely at the moment when mechanical industry had begun to treat the worker solely as a means, human beings were dealt with in the same spirit of brutality as the landscape."[15] Mumford notes the first requirement of the factory system must be to "castrate skill," second, to discipline the labor force through starvation, and, third, to "close up alternative occupations" through "land-monopoly and diseducation."[16] Just as science—relying on the authority of the nineteenth-century apologist for unbridled industrialization Andrew Ure, who proclaimed invention the key to securing labor "docility," and of Richard Awkwright, a capitalist entrepreneur whose most enduring "invention" was to promulgate in his factories a rigorous system of labor discipline—is recruited to subordinate the environment, so, Mumford claims, "technological improvement was the manufacturer's answer to labor insubordination."[17]

Mumford sees the degradation of the worker in the factory as part of a wider effect of capitalist industrialization, the "starvation of life," which has two principal elements: the adulteration of food and the "starvation of the senses" through physical and moral strictures against sexual pleasure, which affected the middle classes as well as the working classes. Thus for Mumford, the environment is not confined to its physical connotation but has a social content as well. Ten years before Horkheimer and Adorno were to argue in *The Dialectic of the Enlightenment* that the real process of abstraction that is an integral component of the commodity form and of the capitalist system of production and exchange leads to the domination of nature and of humans, Mumford draws the implications of its spread to all corners of the social world. From the perspective of capital the human has become simply another machine part.[18] Yet Mumford insists that humans are not merely the victims of their social and physical environment. Following his mentor, the biologist and town planner Patrick Geddes, Mumford finds that humans are both "creature and creator" of both the ends of the social environment and the means by which it is produced. And owing to their capacity to adapt to new conditions, they can negotiate the terms of their existence.

In the coming phase of civilization, "neotechnics," Mumford envisions the reduction of technology and its principal creation, the machine, to human scale. Humans' dependence on machine technologies to produce means of subsistence, to accumulate wealth, and to deal with disease and other bodily ailments will be loosened by the advance of the collective understanding of the physical universe and human physiology. Our advancing knowledge that human beings are part of nature and of natural history will help humanity achieve not conquest of, but "dynamic equilibrium" with the rest of nature. In turn, greater knowledge of the body may overcome our dependence on pharmaceuticals. And the social world, too, must become subject to ecological principles. For Mumford, the degradation of work and of the worker and the destruction of the environment is too high a price to pay for abundance. Sketching a program of urban ecology and of bioregionalism, Mumford suggests that the division of labor be radically restructured so that the separation of food production from manufacturing and single-industry and single-crop economies become extinct. In his proposal, regions themselves provide for many of the products they need. This concept has become the basis of a few experiments around the globe, notably Mondragón in Spain and the early kibbutz movement in Palestine.[19]

The concepts of urban ecology elaborated and extended by Mumford as social ecology spread beyond the academy to progressive policy makers. But progressives became caught up in what they considered an urgent need to rejuvenate the economic life of metropolitan regions, which had fallen into serious disrepair in the depression era. In the 1930s, conservation was advanced primarily as a jobs program: hundreds of thousands of unemployed youth were employed in a massive cleanup of America's forests and rural areas as well as in national parks and wilderness programs. After the war, many planners proposed to articulate development with conservation in terms of the general concept of urban renewal. From Los Angeles to the great and small cities of the East Coast, city and state governments employed progressive planners and administrators to undertake large-scale projects of social engineering. In alliance with business interests in Boston and New Haven, the planner Edward Logue changed the urban landscape of New England. By the 1950s, similar efforts were under way in Chicago, Newark, and St. Louis, where, with the financial and legal support of the federal government, major new roadways, airports, and housing developments were constructed.

In New York City, Robert Moses, in his pursuit of urban renewal—originally conceived as a land policy to overcome poverty and economic and social backwardness—led the effort not only to modernize the city, by subordinating its environment to the economic imperative, but also to preserve some of its crowded space for such aesthetic pleasures as recreation. Ignoring Mumford's warning, Moses derived his concept of modernity from the traditional progressives' faith in scientific and technical methods to solve human problems like poverty, unemployment, and poor living conditions. In the depression-ridden city Moses proposed to combine job creation with improvement of the human environment. With Roosevelt and Mayor Fiorello LaGuardia's enthusiastic support, he implemented policies to replace slum dwellings with new high-rise public housing and to soften the mean streets with playgrounds, public swimming pools, parks, and recreational centers—a conservationist favorite. His economic strategy was to update New York's transportation systems to facilitate the movement of goods through the city's tangled traffic. Moses organized the massive development of roads, port, rail, and airports. During the 1930s and the immediate postwar period, federal funds were allocated to construct the East River Drive (later renamed for FDR) and the West Side Highway. In the late 1940s and 1950s, Moses presided over the construction of a network of roads that all but surrounded the city: the Cross Bronx Expressway, the Major Deegan Expressway, the Brooklyn-Queens Expressway linking Manhattan, Brooklyn, and Queens to the Long Island Expressway, and the Grand Central Parkway among others; the roads fostered the development of LaGuardia Airport.[20]

Robert Caro's magisterial study *The Power Broker* registers Moses' contradictions in excruciating detail. It also reveals the limitations of a conservationism bereft of a critique of the idea of progress and of scientifically based technology. The book chronicles what happens when the fundamental discovery of urban ecology, that people create their own neighborhoods as places of sustenance, as ecologically sympathetic sites, is violated. For in the end, imprisoned by the logic of development (one that has gripped today's China, for example, with a vengeance), Moses became a veritable enemy of the people. In the pursuit of efficiency and economic viability for his beloved city and using the power of eminent domain by which for public purposes government may preempt property rights and compensate those displaced, Moses presided over the destruction of many of the city's most stable, culturally coherent neighborhoods. For example, construction of the Cross Bronx Expressway, which links New Jersey and Long Island, helped reduce several of the city's most closely knit neighborhoods to rubble. It bifurcated the Bronx on a north-south axis and destroyed tens of thousands of dwellings that in previous decades had housed some of the most viable working-class enclaves. The Cross Bronx project became one of the emblems of the ruthless urban renewal that spread throughout the city in the postwar period and became the core of federal and local urban policy.

Moses' passing did not signal a reversal of public policy. On the contrary, his program, embedded in the city's several master plans from the late 1920s to the present day, became the blueprint for development. These plans foreshadowed the virtual elimination of working-class neighborhoods below Manhattan's 125th Street. In 1952, under sponsorship of Columbia University, the city administration began a determined effort to clear and rebuild the Morningside Heights area by removing thousands of working-class families from the shadow of the university and replacing them with high-rise middle-income housing. Only an equally determined struggle by the Metropolitan Council on Housing, the successor to the tenant leagues and Workers' Alliances of the first forty years of the century, and its local affiliate in the neighborhood, led to a compromise that resulted in the construction of several hundred units of public housing alongside the middle-income buildings. A similar battle on the Lincoln Center site in late 1950s ended in the destruction of this largely West Side longshore workers' area and its reconstruction as a cultural center and living space for portions of the upper crust as well as professionals. A decade later the struggle was resumed, on a grander scale, in the proposed West Side Urban Renewal program involving the clearance of thousands of units of rent-controlled working-class private rental housing by subsidized middle-income cooperatives and rental housing. Again a coalition of tenant groups won some concessions; the city agreed to build public housing, but the area was permanently transformed as thousands of working-class households were forced to leave.[21]

In 1968, David Rockefeller, the leader of the constellation of banks, insurance companies, and industrial and real estate corporations that constitute one of New York's and Wall Street's major forces, proposed a Lower Manhattan Expressway. It was to have run along Delancey Street and would have necessitated the razing of most of the working-class housing in the surrounding area. The proposed expressway, planned as a transportation link parallel to the Cross Bronx between Long Island, New Jersey, and points west, would have utterly destroyed the extant urban ecology by forcing the emigration of at least twenty thousand residents and countless small businesses. But the proposal was opposed by one of the great neighborhood-based political alliances in recent urban history. Working-class Puerto Ricans from the Lower East Side united with residents of the traditional working-class Italian South

Village neighborhood and artists and intellectuals in the West Village to defeat Rockefeller's plan. A decade later, the New York Public Interest Research Group led a successful struggle to oppose a plan hatched by the same business interests and supported by the city administration of Mayor Edward I. Koch, to construct a beltway around Manhattan to alleviate traffic congestion and create a network linking the entire Metropolitan New York area.[22]

Underlying the contradictions of urban enlightenment was an implicit class politics. The bourgeois values of the planners and the corporate sponsors of renewal, their alienated conceptions of living space, exemplified in their proud sponsorship of high-rise public housing, were imposed on working-class urban ecosystems, many of which were populated by Jews and Italians, but also blacks and Puerto Ricans. Dr. Urban Development knew best how to administer its medicine to overcome urban "blight." Dismissed were the home remedies of neighborhood residents, remedies that might have preserved the essential character of the terrain by the building of low-rise cooperative housing and by rehabilitating and reconditioning existing housing stock rather than reducing it to rubble. In the Bronx, much of that stock was still structurally sound when Moses' bulldozers tore it down to make room for the Cross Bronx Expressway. In the name of better housing for the working poor and under the banner of creating jobs, jobs, jobs, a slogan near and dear to the hearts of the seasonal building trades, thousands of houses, often mislabeled slums, were demolished. Historical memory as well as the living neighborhoods, their streets, schools, stores, and childhood hiding places in old factories or icehouses, for example, were destroyed. In contrast, the first low-rise public housing buildings constructed in the 1930s on the Lower East Side and the union-sponsored cooperatives in the same neighborhood and in the northern Bronx were dedicated to providing rich cultural and recreational amenities. But subsequent projects in Chicago, St. Louis, and New York were built vertically and strung out over vast parcels of land, more or less isolated from the rest of the city. Fifty years later, decimated by crime, poverty, and municipal neglect, many of these projects were torn down, and those left standing became subject to screening procedures that required residents to work off their subsidized rents.

Ironically, it was not the programs of the seriously misguided progressive proponents of urban development that ultimately devastated the economically and socially diverse lower Manhattan communities, but rather the coalition of banks and real estate companies intent on capturing some of the most valuable tracts in the nation. For even though the city's master plan envisioned a radically gentrified Manhattan, housing organizations and other institutions of social activism—and the relative decline of the city's economy brought about by deindustrialization—had postponed implementation of this vision. New York's fiscal crisis of 1974–77, however, itself a consequence of industrial emigration and the accompanying white working-class flight, provided the political space for a business offensive in behalf of development. In Mayor Koch, a traditional liberal elected on a populist platform of supporting municipal unions, especially teachers, protecting tenants, and addressing the city's growing population of the working and unemployed poor, Wall Street found a welcome, if unexpected, ally. Following Koch's belated acknowledgment that, in the wake of deindustrialization, New York City's economy was tied hand and foot to the financial services industry, which was not only the largest private sector employer but the richest, Koch became a corporate-booster. The twelve years of his administration were marked by open subservience to business interests, a loyalty carried on by his successors. Koch abruptly shifted ground and became a determined champion of conversion of a portion of the city's 1½ million rent-regulated apartments to high-priced cooperatives and condominiums; a firm supporter of the conversion of industrial lofts sweetened by accompanying tax abatements for developers; and, in contrast to his immediate predecessors, who despite their harsh rhetoric presided over the phenomenal growth of public employees' unionism, a hard-line foe of further labor union advances.

For thorough gentrification to be imposed, the rent laws had to be changed to permit massive conversions so that the upper middle class could be brought back to the city. But even many lawyers, physicians, and other professionals found that by the time Koch left office in January 1990 rents and cooperative housing prices had become prohibitive in most of Manhattan and nearby Brooklyn. The three mayors who occupied City Hall in the late 1970s, 1980s, and 1990s—Koch, David Dinkins, and Rudolph Giuliani—sponsored measures to weaken rent control and denied rent regulation to commercial buildings, the effect of which was to drive hundreds of small manufacturers and wholesale firms from lower Manhattan lofts, thereby reducing the industrial workforce by tens of thousands. Commercial capital's hunger for new sources of investment and profits met with resistance from neither Democrat nor Republican, neither black nor white politicians. Imploding the city's population to expel its least economically desirable fractions from the lower half of Manhattan became the guiding principle of city government. Even before the Welfare Reform Law of 1996, Giuliani had begun his own war on the poor: mass incarceration of black and Latino men and relentless enforcement of federal and state drug laws bulked the prisons;

a war on sin led to the cleanup of the Times Square area, which helped raise property values in midtown so that small merchants as well as the working class were all but banned from the area as businesspeople or residents. Like his predecessors, the mayor wholesaled tax abatements for conversions and "condemnations"—a prelude to urban renewal—for new luxury housing in Manhattan.

Closely synchronized with real estate interests, Giuliani was an equal opportunity warrior. His dedication to the upper crust was unwavering. He clamped down on low- and middle-income housing with equanimity. The most egregious ruling by his appointees to the city's Rent Stabilization Board, made in 1999, classified as luxury all apartments with rents over two thousand dollars a month and thereby deregulated them. By the late 1980s Manhattan below 125th Street, except for Harlem, had become too expensive for middle-income people, let alone the poor, to rent or buy apartments. By the late 1990s most New Yorkers were priced out of housing in the majority of Brooklyn neighborhoods from Brooklyn Heights on the west to Park Slope on the east. Bank-backed developers and real estate corporations made deep incursions into Harlem, some traditional black middle-class neighborhoods like Brooklyn's Clinton Hill and Fort Greene, and traditional working-class neigborhoods like Astoria, Queens. And the steamroller of gentrification had already spread to nearby Jersey City, a long-time working-class city of a quarter million residents that had likewise suffered deep losses of manufacturing jobs and commercial exodus in the last three decades of the twentieth century.

Boston, Chicago, Los Angeles, and San Francisco experienced the same sea change as New York in their social ecologies. Lacking rent regulations, some of these cities, notably San Francisco—whose Mission District had long been the principal Latino community of the city—witnessed large-scale evictions of residents from desirable neighborhoods to make way for the growing number of computer and financial services professionals and managers. In Chicago's Hyde Park neighborhood, a traditional dwelling place of academics, rents and condo prices had risen so steeply that the University of Chicago found itself unable to recruit new faculty, and those that came anyway experienced difficulty finding affordable housing. Driven by the technological revolution, Boston, once a city of preponderantly working-class residential housing, was transformed into a bedroom community for the burgeoning computer software industries in Cambridge and on Route 128.

By 2000 a confluence of circumstances—capital flight that deprived millions in cities and towns of their livelihoods, gentrification in many large cities, the ceaseless migration from the farms, and immigration from and to postindustrial America—conspired to deprive urban Americans of a sense of place. Since affordable housing became elusive for many who grew up and worked in the city, a second exodus since World War II occurred, but not to suburbs because these, too, had become financially prohibitive. The new frontier was the rural exurbs far from the sites of employment. In California it was not uncommon for eight-dollar-an-hour Hewlett-Packard assembly plant workers to travel the same fifty or sixty miles one way that better-paid programmers did. Although the programmers were better able to afford the commute, both suffered from freeway madness. Their working time, including travel, exceeded their time for rest and recreation by a factor of two. And when the 2000–01 recession hit the computer hardware and software industries with heavy blows and corporations scrambled to solve their profit slump by mass layoffs, even willingness to make the fifty-mile commute wasn't enough to secure another job. Seeking work, many were forced to leave the rent-inflated region.

WHAT IS NATURE?

The debate about how to address the problems arising from increased human intervention in and altering of the ecosystems that sustain life—its condition of homeostasis—rests on differing conceptions of what nature is. On the one hand, the spearhead of the scientific Enlightenment, the Copernican revolution, repudiated the Aristotelean/Ptolemaic worldview according to which the Earth was the center of the universe and cast a radically new perspective that placed earth in a much-reduced position. On the other hand, Enlightenment philosophy, the hegemonic ideology of the bourgeois epoch, constructed nature, including all lower living beings, as other and at the same time declared the primacy of human thought and its presumed seat, mind, over nature. For Descartes, the seventeenth- and eighteenth-century English philosophers, and Kant, mind was ontologically separate from the material world and thus could not be equated with the brain; the human mind could reveal nature's secrets by means of its unique possession, reason. In turn, philosophical idealism tended to put mind at the center of the universe, relegating both natural history and the environment—the necessary condition for human life—to the status of servant, slave, worker. Just as in bourgeois civilization the elites take and the people pay, Nature yields its fruits, and those in power enjoy the power to harvest them at will.[23]

But others challenged the notion that nature was extrinsic to either reason or social practice. Following Spinoza, historical materialism disputes the idea of nature as other, and Marx argued that "the first premise of all human history is the existence of living human individuals. Thus the first fact to be established is the physical organization of these individuals and their consequent relation to the rest of nature." In short, in concert with the theory of evolution developed by Charles Lyell, Charles Darwin, and other nineteenth-century geologists and biologists, our species is simply the latest moment of natural history, and its characteristics are presupposed by previous physical, chemical, geological, and biological development.[24] The physical organization of humans—that we require shelter and clothing to protect us from the elements and that, except in tropical climates, we must produce our food—drives the imperative for production. Marx wrote, "The way in which men produce their means of subsistence depends first of all on the actual means of subsistence they find and have to reproduce."[25] This is the natural context: conditions of climate, the availability of water, the geographic terrain. But production is an activity involving interactivity and, indeed, mutual determination between humans and their environment. Production is not merely reproductive of physical being but a "definite mode of life . . . as individuals express their life, so they are."[26]

Even in the earliest human communities the production of material life involved both the transformation of what is taken as external conditions and of humans as nature—the unalloyed other of physical and biological scientific and industrial practice—and the creation of a built environment suffused with the products of labor. Modes of reason, especially systematic theories of nature's laws, are as constitutive as are the material conditions for production. While it may be argued that the so-called physical building blocks of the universe have remained constant throughout the evolution of life, the organization of the earth's space, both physical and social, has constantly changed. From the advent of soil cultivation and animal husbandry, which has often entailed cross-breeding in the creation of new organisms, to industrial production, which alters the givens of the social world, human societies have utterly transformed not only the forms of earth and its physical and chemical components, but also themselves. Human evolution in the genetic sense may not have changed for millions of years. But the social and psychological predispositions of humans, our sense of time and space, our perception of the world, and our forms of intervention in it make us a different animal from our ancestors, sociobiological reductionism notwithstanding. We code the results of our observations of trees and grass, hills and mountains—as opposed to the bricks and mortar of cities—as nature. But rural as much as urban space is incessantly transformed by labor: by landscape architecture as much as by farmwork and by the ways new roads, housing subdivisions, industrial parks, mines, and malls drive fauna as well as flora further back from development sites. As development accelerates, some species of life disappear or thin out.

Does development inevitably change nature's balance? For example, are floods caused by one of the results of the relentless commercialization of agriculture, soil erosion? Even the weather, which most of us on the everyday level believe is caused by purely natural forces, is conditioned by greenhouse gases that over time change the climate by elevating environmental temperatures. If unchecked, global warming will inevitably reduce or eliminate the prospects for growing food in certain regions and even make some residential areas unlivable. And acid rain, the result of the pollution largely produced by urbanization and industrialization, may render water undrinkable, reduce the quantity of fish in streams, rivers, and oceans, and make soil unfertile. Even a particularly beautiful sunrise or sunset is often produced by chemical emissions emanating from human activity. In sum, what we take as nature always already incorporates social labor and social activity. The material forms of capital's expansion ingress and fuse with the other. Nature in itself has more than ever become nature by and for us.

There are important differences between the marxist focus on social labor as world-builder and the work of writers like Jean Baudrillard and Michel Foucault, who, while refusing a conception of nature as independent of language and power, reject the centrality of labor in the process of the construction of the natural environment. Foucault speaks as if the natural world is discursively constituted. When, in an interview, he was asked why he had no provision for the role of biology or of nature in his theory of power, Foucault replied that discourse has all but driven the biological level underground; it cannot be known on its own terms. We cannot consider it apart from the language of power. Consequently, the biological or the natural is overdetermined; they must be understood, in practical terms, as signifiers without a concrete referent. What unites marxism and those who follow the linguistic turn in historical and social theory is the conception that despite its status as "lived experience"—defined not as emotion but scientifically, what the eye can see—in science as well as everyday life nature is a reified external reality. Thus they agree that the legacy of history has been that nature has been incorporated into human dominion.

But can nature be understood entirely in terms of capitalization and other forms of development that alter the environment? Do the ecosystems that preserve life set limits to growth? or is capitalism sustainable (where *sustainability* signifies that nature itself has unlimited resources to facilitate capital accumulation in the forms of industrial and commercial expansion)? Since the 1960s a chorus of voices has been raised against this eighteenth- and nineteenth-century taken-for-granted assumption of nature's fungibility. Each dissenting voice in its own way asserts that, despite the ineluctable imprint of social practice, nature exists autonomously. Put philosophically, all life-forms are as much modalities of natural history as nature has been subjected to the (flawed) practices that seek to consolidate human dominion over all forms of being. If ecological thought and environmental movements share a single underlying concept, it is the irreducible being of nature. But here the agreement ends. Ecology, the science and social practice of respecting nature's autonomy, divides by three key positions:

1. Liberal environmentalism presupposes that economic growth is necessary but must be regulated by government in order to protect the natural environment or by changing individual and collective behavior through curbs on the consumption of waste. The conservationist wing has fought to protect wilderness, forest, and other areas from development; the regulators are concerned that air and water be protected by limiting development and setting pollution and solid waste standards for private enterprise. Reformers have gone further to argue for the development of renewable energy resources and the gradual phasing out of nonrenewable energy, such as oil and coal. In recent years their advocacy of alternative energy sources has been pressed in the context of dangers posed by global warming. Liberal environmentalists have backed international agreements such as the Kyoto Treaty, which calls for policies to reduce greenhouse gas emissions, for example, by limiting development of rain forests and wilderness areas.
2. A broad spectrum of thought has framed the solution to the ecological crisis in terms of an extension of liberal political theory. Just as markets and states, especially in advanced industrial democracies, recognize that individuals have inalienable rights (except, of course, in times of war and other military and police emergencies, when these rights are often constricted, some say by necessity), so these rights should be extended to nature and to other life-forms on the utilitarian ground that social policy should seek the greatest good for the greatest number (the definition of *number* here including all life-forms). Some, like the ethical philosopher Peter Singer, would transform human food appetites so that, in consideration of animal rights, vegetarianism

becomes a norm. In any case, animal rights advocates argue that we dehumanize ourselves when we treat other life-forms as fungible and subject to arbitrary cruelty. They oppose the scientific vivisection of primates, rodents, and other animals for research purposes. Moreover, from a utilitarian perspective, Singer claims that protecting animals from witting and unwitting human cruelty is, on balance, in the human interest. And the most celebrated view within this perspective, so-called deep ecology, would emulate, on ethical grounds, Albert Schweitzer's reverence for all life-forms, including insects, trees, and shrubbery. In the interest of saving life itself, we must oppose any form of development, for example, the clear-cutting of trees, that potentially or actually threatens the planet. Here we encounter the slogan Earth First, signifying that earth is the source of life and humans only derivative of its beneficence. Hence by placing the protection of nature above immediate human interests we are insuring the survival of life itself.[27]

3. The third position includes ecological marxism and ecoanarchism—or social ecology—and argues that the domination of nature is implicated in processes of human domination. Although they differ philosophically on whether the domination of nature gives rise to the domination of humans (Marx and Horkheimer and Adorno) or whether the domination of humans is at the origin of nature's domination (anthropological evidence purportedly shows the latter) (Bookchin), each concludes that the logic of domination—in its political-economic form, capital, and in patriarchal relations—is at the heart of the ecological crisis. In both instances the largely moral basis of liberal and deep ecological thinking is rejected in favor of a social-theoretical argument that relies on a critical historical assessment of the contradictory character of liberal political theory and practice.

Written in 1944 as a reflection on the relation between, on the one hand, the triumph of fascism in most of Western Europe and the spread of authoritarianism in most of the rest of the world and, on the other, the Enlightenment's worship of science and technology, Horkheimer and Adorno's *Dialectic of the Enlightenment* was perhaps the most compelling immanent critique of capital's sovereignty over nature and humans. The first text of what later became known as ecomarxism, its core argument is that in the interest of freeing humanity from the thrall of church-imposed ignorance of the laws of nature and of feudal tradition, which acted as a fetter on progress, the bourgeois Enlightenment substituted another fetter: it bridled nature in the service of the advance of technical mastery, a domination that became the model for human domination. The main tendency of social relations—in the family as much as in the workplace and civil society—is to regard humans as fungible, subject to an administration that parallels that in which nature is regarded as subject to the will to power.

Having this common understanding of the symbiosis of patriarchy and the domination of nature, both tendencies acknowledge that the achieving of an ecological society is a question of political power, not of abstracted morality. Granting that capitalism bears principal responsibility for the crisis, Bookchin rejects the conventional marxist designation of the working class as the engine of change because of its excess historical baggage and alternatively proposes the concept of the people as the historical agent of change. Bookchin's ecoanarchism and ecomarxism—whose leading American proponents are the group around the journal *Capitalism, Nature, Socialism* and its editor, the economist James O'Connor—agree that addressing the current ecological crisis is perhaps the overriding contemporary task in the struggle for freedom. Their arguments are grounded not in survivalist ideology but in the proposition that what thwarts a solution to the ecological crisis is to be found in the economic, political, and cultural contradictions of the prevailing capitalist system.

O'Connor understands the ecological crisis by revising a fundamental precept of historical materialism: that social transformation is driven by the contradiction between the development of the forces of production—machine technologies and the skills of human labor but also scientific knowledge that has become the basis of technology—and the relations of production, that is, relations of ownership and control of the means of production. Relying on Marx's argument that a major premise of human history is that production presupposes natural conditions—climate, availability of water, and other natural resources—as much as labor, O'Connor declares a "second contradiction," the antagonism between capital's drive to accumulate by its conquest of nature and subordination of labor and the "reproduction of the conditions of production." Following William Kapp's observation, O'Connor argues that the reproduction of the conditions are a largely hidden—and ignored—cost for society as well as for the individual employer. For example, despite its deleterious ecological consequences, the industrial system remains joined at the hip to nonrenewable fossil fuels like oil, iron and aluminum ore, and coal. Capital's expansion entails not only the costs associated with the production and distribution of the commodity, but also the costs of reproducing the conditions of production. Replenishing trees, finding new energy sources as old ones are depleted, cleaning up sites to remove hazardous waste, sending boats further out at sea to harvest fish as waters close to shore become polluted, and restoring soil-eroded agricultural land all constitute a limit on capital formation by driving up the costs of production and restricting profits. In a word, natural conditions are incorporated as a silent social cost in accounting as well as in public policy. Owing to the rising costs associated with reproducing production conditions, capital may reach a limit to its expansion.

The second contradiction is perhaps capitalism's new crisis. As it exhausts its own conditions of reproduction, it is driven to seek exemption from environmental restrictions by forcing the state to sanction the opening of previously restricted areas; it also spends billions of dollars for exploration and development, money that must be charged in the form of higher prices and diminished public funds for cleanup and restoration of devastated areas. Capital's expansion therefore affects the use values available for production.[28] The implication is not that capitalism is destined imminently to break down, any more than a traditional economic crisis leads to the end of the system. But the ecological imperative has substantial effects on the economic system and forces a new set of problems. For example, because forests are a major pollution absorbent, the illegal clearing of the Brazilian rain forest for agriculture and for the extraction of raw materials to be supplied to the housing, paper, and furniture industries has already reduced the prospect of reducing greenhouse gases on a global scale.

In the battle to contain global warming, we may observe the degree to which the logic of capital, in its quest for profit, especially its tendency to colonize all social and physical space, has become a threat to life itself. Whereas early capitalism successfully presented itself as a means by which humans could achieve freedom, its chief strategy, namely, the domination of nature, now threatens to recast natural and social space so that within decades only some regions of the world may remain viable for agriculture and even human habitation. Capital's logic—that is, accumulation is the condition of its existence—has, in the sixth century of its global dominion, turned into a danger to life as we have known it for ages. As Hegel remarked, the struggle between master and slave, lord and bondsperson is a fight to the death: the current struggle against the power of capital to construe the natural and the built environment in its shortsighted interest may be the true apotheosis of that ancient combat.

8
UTOPIA ON HOLD

Nothing that has ever happened should be regarded as lost for history.

—Walter Benjamin

HISTORY AND MEMORY

History is written by the victors. They define what counts as history, what is remembered and what is forgotten, what is important and what is not, and, most crucially, what is usable for informing the relation of present to the future. As Walter Benjamin has noted, an important element of the class struggle is to reclaim history for the excluded by capturing historical memory from the rulers. Worth remembering, in the first place, are the "crude struggles" for material things:

> The class struggle . . . is a fight for the crude and material things without which no refined and spiritual things could exist. Nevertheless it is not in the form of spoils which fall to the victor that the latter make their presence felt in the class struggle. They manifest themselves in this struggle, as courage, honor, cunning and fortitude. They have retroactive force and will constantly call in question every victory, past and present, of the rulers. As flowers turn toward the sun, by dint of a secret heliotropism, the past strives to turn toward the sun which is rising in the sky of history.[1]

From the perspective of the rulers, framing the past by focusing on events and personalities removes movements from below from consideration. Thus we conveniently talk of the Framers as the great men of the American Constitution and virtually identical with the rise of the American nation. Playwrights and historians tell the story of the French Revolution in terms of the conflict between the crown and the third estate, an unspecific conglomeration of commoners, but speak of the days of the first Republic as an internal conflict of two great revolutionary leaders, Robespierre and Danton; in turn, the postrevolutionary decades in France are called the Napoleonic era, and our image of the period is intimately bound up with the personality of its main protagonist. Most historians capture the essence of the American Civil War by referring to Lincoln's heroic act of freeing the slaves, and, as we have already seen, Roosevelt's New Deal is grasped as the context for Depression-era reform. Ronald Reagan's rise to the presidency helps explain the Reagan Revolution of the last two decades of the twentieth century, during which the doctrine of minimum federal government disguised the fact that his administration was one of the most profligate spenders in recent American history. Thus, as Hans Zinsser noted, biography not only replaces social commentary—in fact, it is the preferred form of all political discourse—but also displaces the novel as the main literary genre that illuminates the social and historical roots of our time. Of course, the rulers rarely speak for themselves; their perspective is filtered through the political directorate and the intellectuals who rewrite history. The relation between rulers and intellectuals is one not of command but of elective affinity. For it is intellectuals who elaborate the "imagined community" of the nation-state, and history is among their main weapons.[2]

The elite universities are the incubators of the organic intellectuals of ruling classes as well as of the opposition. The intellectual opposition contests the main narrative on several planes: for one, it proposes a past different from that promulgated by the leading institutions of collective memory, chiefly, the book, the school, and popular media. For another, it elaborates a cultural and social imagination that contradicts prevailing common sense. Thus in the last half of the twentieth century radical democrats, through meticulous archival investigation, attempted to demonstrate that history was made from below and hence made a large difference in the way we live now. The degree to which their effort succeeds depends less on the talent of the historian or the validity of the uncovered facts than on whether the subordinate classes are contesting power. For example, that we have a treasure of African American and feminist historical writing in the past thirty years is a testament to the force of social movements, just as the new labor and social history bore a strong affinity to the emergence of the new radicalism of the 1960s and 1970s that found expression in, among other domains, rank-and-file trade union insurgencies.

Flushed with victory over ideological as well as economic and military opponents, rulers and their ideologists are prone to declare that their regime stands at the end of the evolution of human societies. Voltaire's Panglois declared prerevolutionary France the "best of all possible worlds." Just so Francis Fukuyama, on the heels of the collapse of the Soviet Union and its client states, declared "the end of history," surely one of the most momentous intellectual events of the 1990s. Even before the collapse his celebrated article of 1989 provided economic liberals and political conservatives with a Grand Narrative that, despite its conservative worldview, refuses to succumb to ordinary left-bashing. On the contrary, as Jacques Derrida observed, his account of the demise of "actually existing socialism" of the Soviet variety is a form of mourning insofar as, under the sign of liberal democratic capitalism, the future is bound to have the characteristics of everyday banality.[3]

For Fukuyama, Communism was more than an "evil empire," in Reagan's simplistic term. Although a force of evil, it endowed humankind with the gift of undergoing an epochal struggle worthy of Hegel's fight to the death between dominator and dominated. Fukuyama's essay set the terms of the debate: What we may be witnessing is not just the end of the Cold War or the passing of a period of postwar history, but the end of history as such; that is, the end point of mankind's ideological evolution and the universalization of Western Liberal Democracy as the culminating form of human government.[4]

In place of theories that separate capitalism from liberal democracy, Fukuyama substitutes the notion of their indissolubility: the traditional distinction between economics and politics—the inside/outside separation that often propels social change—is denied. In the conjunction of capitalism and democracy, the others of the now-eclipsed revolutionary epoch, including the radical left, the third world, the permanent wretched of the earth, have disappeared before the ideological cum economic hegemony of the capitalist market. For Fukuyama, hegemony justifies erasure. History need not record the persistence of the mass unemployment, widespread poverty, and spreading diseases that afflict billions of people. Although still striving for the Good Life, those who were in full-throated rebellion against colonialism and capitalism just thirty years ago now vie for favors from the institutions of world capitalism and are rewarded to the extent they agree to open their nations to private investment and trade and impose austerity on their citizens so long as their country is in debt to Western banks.[5] But Fukuyama's blithe assumption that liberal democracy is an entailment of markets grates against the stark reality that the planet is littered with nations that have adopted capitalist economic relations but are supported by repressive states. The new world order does not require that states agree to evolve into liberal democracies and espouse one of its traditional entailments, human rights—witness the admission of China into the WTO.

In a tone of exhilaration Fukuyama judged the twentieth century's communist revolutions as well as their ideological inspiration, marxism, massive failures. In concert with earlier prophets of endings—notably Daniel Bell, whose influential *End of Ideology* (1960) announces the eclipse of class and ideological politics—Fukuyama acknowledges that there are still conflicts but no contradictions; present and future battles have no historicity.[6] Social formations will fight for greater shares of the expanding pie, and cultural differences will endure. Some societies will remain mired in backwardness owing to the strength of their premodern cultural traditions, for instance, religious fundamentalism, and the patriarchies that sustain them; these are doomed to dwell outside the modern world. Gone forever are the epochal revolutionary struggles of the twentieth century that vowed to abolish capitalist social relations and establish collective or, more accurately, state ownership of the means of industrial and agricultural production.

But even before the Berlin Wall came down it was evident to many that the foretold communist utopia had given way to dystopia: as the Soviet system entered its long descent, many who had been inspired by its early triumphs recognized that the present did not forecast a different future for humanity. Instead of holding out hope for a better world, it seemed we were condemned to go through life without impossible dreams. By the dawn of the twenty-first century, even as some parties calling themselves Communist remained in power, the so-called experiment in the abolition of private property, state-owned means of production, and largely nonmarket modes of exchange had in large measure given way to old ideals of private property and the capitalist market. The dream of radical democracy, in which the major institutions of society would be controlled by committees elected by workers and other citizens in the workplace and in the neighborhoods, enjoyed a flicker of life in the Paris Commune of 1871, reinforced by the formation of workers councils in the 1905 Russian revolution, and was the benchmark of many general strikes from Seattle in 1919 to the May events in France almost a half century later, but now seems to belong to a bygone era. No organized force, except the growing battalions of anarchist, antiglobalization activists, maintains even the aspiration of a radical democratic future.

China's embrace of capitalist market modernity, initiated in 1978, a few years after the death of Mao, has been partial: it entered global markets, opening its doors to foreign private investment, downsized its state-owned industrial and agricultural enterprises, and created a huge private capitalist sector. As recently as 2001 the Communist Party considered admitting private employers into its ranks, a proposal that was finally thwarted by the whisper of a dying tradition that only workers, peasants, and intellectuals can belong in the party. But in China liberal democracy, let alone radical democracy, remains a distant shore. One-party rule, the policy of large-scale enclosures in the countryside that have driven more than one hundred million peasants from their ancestral lands, state-imposed human rights violations such as the suppression of student protest at Tiananmen Square, continued imprisonment of vocal dissenters, and severe press and media restrictions attest to the persistence of authoritarian rule.

From the point of view of capital, which has never truly embraced political freedom, China is a stunning success. Conditions in Poland, the Czech Republic, Slovenia, and Hungary have improved for many since 1991. But Vietnam has struggled to attract foreign capital; and in the former Communist countries of Eastern Europe, all of which have adopted the main institutions of liberal democracy, life for most ordinary citizens is nothing short of disaster. Even in Poland, often held up by American economists as a model of successful transition to market capitalism, all is not well: responding to economic and social deterioration in 2001, voters returned former Communists to government and soundly defeated the neoliberal parties, including Solidarity, which had been among the most vocal critics of the former regime. Wherever such neoliberal policies as privatization have been implemented, economic growth has been purchased at the price of lower living standards for the majority of people. Even as wages have lagged, prices have skyrocketed as many of these countries become dependent on imports. Most former Communist nations not only suffer higher unemployment rates than Western Europe, but also lack a safety net because, in their haste to qualify for Western financial aid, they have reduced pensions and other benefits such as income security for unemployed workers.

Russia, by far the largest nation in the former Soviet orbit, has experienced a precipitous decline in living standards. Under the influence of Harvard and Chicago neoliberal economists, its first post-Soviet president, former Moscow Communist leader Boris Yeltsin, swiftly dismantled many state enterprises and handed them over to ex-Communist managers who have, characteristically, milked their assets for private gain. Meanwhile, plagued by poverty, rampant alcoholism, and heavy pollution—the legacy of Soviet-era industrialization distortions—the country has seen its infant and adult mortality rates skyrocket. Russia's infant mortality is the highest in Europe. An average Russian man can expect to live to fifty-five, a drop by ten years since the Soviet collapse. Income inequality between the new capitalist class created with government support and the impoverished working class approaches that of the United States, but without the lure of consumer society to allay popular anger. As a result, the Communist Party, discredited in the immediate aftermath of the breakup of the Soviet Union, regained considerable ground in the last half of the 1990s. Today it is the largest party in the Duma, although its program dare not speak the name of socialist revolution. In effect the party has, at least for the time being, accepted the political framework of liberal democracy, as have the leading socialist and communist parties of Europe, Japan, and Latin America.

The core of Fukuyama's theory is his appropriation of Hegel's philosophy of history. For Fukuyama, no less than for Hegel, the end of history is an imaginary resolution of the dialectic of labor, for it posits what remains to be shown: that in liberal democratic societies, at the workplace as much as in civil society, employer and worker, citizen and ruler are placed on a sufficiently equal footing to assure mutual recognition. Marx criticizes Hegel for bringing history to an end: on the one hand, Hegel correctly describes the dialectic of labor, which brings the worker to the point of consciousness, but refuses to remain faithful to his own dialectical logic, which demands the overcoming of the contradiction between lord and bondsman. On the other hand, Marx's critique extends to Hegel's conception of the state. Fourteen years after the *Phenomenology* Hegel published his second version of the end of history, *The Philosophy of Right.* The main thesis is that the contradictions in the family and civil society—between men, women, and children and between owners of commodities (including capitalists and workers)—are incapable of resolution within their respective spheres. The state arises to resolve their contradictions on the basis of the self-recognition by citizens that they cannot bring harmony to human affairs without the negation of their sovereignty by a higher power.

Even as he celebrates the end of utopia—that is, of creative history in which the idea of a revolutionary future informs the present and inspires people to take action against hierarchy and domination—Fukuyama exhibits not a little nostalgia for the years when capitalism trembled at the prospect of socialist revolution and, during the Cold War, devoted most of its economic, political, and ideological energy to containment of the perceived Soviet threat to Western capitalism. Now that Communism has been defeated, what remains is to clean up the debris left by premodern and antediluvian regimes. Accordingly, the cleanup includes the arduous tasks associated with bringing liberal democracy to totalitarian and authoritarian third world societies like those strewn throughout Africa and the Middle East. Fukuyama interprets the Gulf War and the post–September 11 U.S. antiterrorist campaign that began with the overthrow of the Taliban government in Afghanistan not as a repudiation of the end of history thesis, but as a vindication—but only if these states evolve out of their recent totalitarian past into capitalist democracies, an eventuality that, even for the most devout conservatives, is highly dubious. Answering critics who assert that the terrorist attacks on the World Trade Center on September 11, 2001, refute his claim, Fukuyama insists that "modernity is a very powerful freight train that will not be derailed by recent events, however painful. We remain at the end of history because there is only one system that will dominate world politics, that of the liberal democratic west."[7]

Judging from post-Communist and postcolonial experience, the burden of proof is on those who celebrate the triumph of the West and hold that capitalism is an entailment of liberal democracy. Certainly any concept of economic democracy is missing from most capitalist countries. And capitalism without democracy seems just as prevalent as capitalism with democracy, notwithstanding the conservative affirmation of their mutual dependence. The easy refutation is to adduce evidence that gross inequality remains in much of the world. Reliable statistics show that a third of the global working population is unemployed or underemployed.[8] Billions suffer poverty and hunger, and this condition is especially widespread among children. In dozens of countries in Africa, Asia, and Latin America the mortality rate among children of all ages in far higher than in Russia, and the gap between life expectancy in North and South is large. Workplaces in most of what are termed developing countries are often marked by physical coercion of workers, long working hours, unsafe environments, and abysmally low wages. Workers subjected to these conditions have responded by staging mass strikes in Korea, Mexico, Brazil, China, and many other countries. Some strike leaders have been murdered or imprisoned for attempting to withhold their labor.

But factual refutations have failed to penetrate public discourse, for Fukuyama, who is often invited to address such global financial organizations as the WB and IMF, has crafted an ideology that has become the new common sense. Lacking the weight of political resistance, ideological hegemony trumps facts. If those who control the means of information and public communication have determined that resistance to global neoliberalism and its practical consequences is only residual, rearguard action by desperate people destined to be brought into the liberal capitalist camp, even when reported as news, is rarely given the significance accorded to a genuine opposition.

It does not matter that few in the general population know who Fukuyama is. What counts as political truth is in the embrace of his concepts. He is an organic intellectual of the new world order; his constituency is, in the first place, the managers of the global ruling bloc, and then his fellow intellectuals of whatever persuasion. And the measure of the dissemination of his ideas is the degree to which those who would oppose his motives have nevertheless adopted the line of endings. Left intellectuals like Russell Jacoby confirm this common sense when they write, ruefully, of the end of utopia.[9] Other erstwhile intellectual radicals, notably Sean Wilentz, Paul Berman, Michael Kazin, Todd Gitlin, and many others who are resigned to the prevailing framework, would vehemently deny their complicity in the end of ideology or of history but spare few occasions to bash those who refuse to recognize the ineluctability of the liberal consensus and the populist faith in electoral or statistical majorities. Thus, some of these writers condemned intellectuals who supported the anticorporate presidential campaign of Ralph Nader in 2000 on the grounds that, in Florida and a few other states, his votes had defeated the Democrat and, in effect, elected George Bush. This is not the place to rehearse the issues in that event. I invoke the controversy to indicate the degree to which the conception of antiutopian liberal democracy frames the political strategies of a growing number of left intellectuals whose oppositional fire has been tamped by political pessimism.[10]

Has the distinction between inside and outside been overrun by modernity? Put another way, has the other of modern societies upon which a possible radical future is always based disappeared? Fukuyama assumes, as did all modernity theorists of the Cold War era, that actually existing socialist countries could not withstand the "freight train" of an economically and politically superior liberal capitalism. That is, once having embarked on the road to industrialization, which entails technological innovation, mass consumer society, and broad educational opportunities that enable a substantial portion of the population to attain class mobility, these societies could not long resist the inevitability of the capitalist market and of liberal democracy. The events of the past fifteen years appear to confirm this judgment. The fabled popularity of Calvin Klein jeans, television, email, and other ornaments of American culture in the most economically starved third world nations seems to attest to the inevitability of capitalist culture, if not of freedom. If consumer culture is present, can the economic and political relations that sustain and follow from it be far behind?

Or does the new global context portend new forms of struggle that may lead to new institutions and social arrangements? While it is typical of modernity boosters to dub terrorism premodern, it is more plausible to view its rise as a symptom of the incompleteness of modernity or even as a sign of its failure. Perhaps we should understand terrorism, which is always the strategy of the weak in the face of a global system that ratifies economic and political domination, as a wake-up call. Surely there is no justification for acts of terrorism that punish innocent civilians for the calumnies perpetrated by transnational ruling classes in alliance with local and regional despots. But it is unlikely that military reprisals, however legitimate they may be in the eyes of an aggrieved nation, will solve more than superficially the issues that produced terrorism in the first place. A mighty military machine may be able to smoke Osama bin Laden and his associates from their holes or crush thousands of Palestinians into the dust. The more urgent question is whether Western powers and their allies in the developing world have the capacity to take measures to overcome the blatant inequalities that mark the world system and that have fomented forms of resistance, including terrorism. Often emanating from religious fundamentalism, such resistance is felt throughout the developing world as well as in the metropoles, the leading nations and corporations that rule the empire.

There is mounting evidence that new challenges face a triumphant West, not only from the southern and eastern world, where development problems and economic and social inequality have become nearly intractable, but also from semiperipheral societies. In the latter, economic crisis born in part of their own relatively successful but distorted development can be attributed to the effects of the countries' subordination to globalization. In many of these semiperipheral societies, for example, Argentina and Brazil, the economic and political crisis is already tearing at the social fabric and threatening political stability. The late 1990s were marked by a resurgence of both left and right movements, a development that emphatically denied the ideology of endings. As we saw in chapters 6 and 7, the emergence of new social movements, including those arrayed against globalism—really resistance to the attempt to establish the new world order—is grounded in the widespread perception as well as in scientific evidence that the planet's ecosystems are in serious trouble, that capitalist globalization has sharpened inequality, not only in economic and political systems but in the everyday lives of masses of people, and that the predominant Western style of tinkering is simply failing to adequately address the the apocalyptic implications of the situation.

The movement proposes to make history once again by holding liberal capitalism to nature's standard that economic growth be halted or severely limited, that the wide economic gap between North and South be narrowed, and that the everyday life of advanced industrial societies be fundamentally changed. Anti-sweatshop agitation, protests against the economic and social exploitation of women and children, and labor struggles against the propensity of transnational corporations to migrate when workers organize into unions may all be a refusal of the end of history thesis, a rejection of the proposition that any struggles within the global capitalist context are subject to technical adjustment. Thus the euphemism "structural adjustment" is used to characterize the mandatory austerity program of the leading international neoliberal institutions. Their loan and grant programs are portrayed as rational solutions to the problem of debt. If client countries wish to embark on the road to economic development they simply must renounce decent living standards for the overwhelming majority—the class of the opposition and excluded. Even though it bowed to structural adjustment policies, Argentina's moderate government fell at the end of 2001, and its Peronist successors declared default on their huge debt to the WB. As a result of the subsequent turmoil for months no party was able to form a stable government. Still, officials at the WB and the IMF defended their policies as economically sound and have obdurately refused demands to cancel or substantially reduce the debt in order to save cooperative regimes. Their solution is to lend Argentina more money, but in the wake of near political and social chaos, this time without conditions.

In power at least temporarily, the Right in the United States has responded to the interlocking economic and social crises of the system by testing the limits of liberal democracy. Congress lost no time after September 11 in passing the Patriot Act, which severely restricts immigrant rights and extends these restrictions to citizens who may criticize the war policies of the government. After two months of investigation that sought to tie them to Islamic terrorism or to Saddam Hussein, the villain of the Gulf War, American security agencies concluded that the anthrax attacks of post–September 11 had been conducted not by central Asian terrorists but probably by elements of the American Right. Bombings and harassment of legal abortion clinics, anti-Semitic defacements, and intimidation of native and immigrant residents of Middle Eastern and Central Asian citizens and residents signaled that despite early White House pleadings anti-immigrant sentiment was rising. But the rightist threat emanated not only from small groups. The White House itself used the war against the Taliban as an occasion for advancing its own anti–civil liberties agenda. As the war proceeded, the White House itself became an agent of immigrant persecution. In fall 2001 more than eleven hundred foreign nationals from Middle Eastern countries were detained under special powers granted by a submissive U.S. Congress to the attorney general and government security agencies. These powers included expanded surveillance of suspected terrorists and the right of security agencies to detain suspects without proffering charges for more than the conventional forty-eight hours allowed by previous law. No sooner had the ultraright attorney general, John Ashcroft, procured his initial legislative victory than he proposed relaxing thirty-year restrictions on the scope of FBI investigative powers to permit the agency to spy on domestic political groups, a throwback that portends the revival of repression characteristic of the infamous McCarthy era. At the same time, fearing that he could not win congressional approval, President George W. Bush issued an executive order establishing special military courts to try suspected terrorists. Presumably, secrecy in these courts would safeguard secure information and obviate the obligation, well established in civilian courts, of the government to produce genuine evidence of wrongdoing.

The Bush administration had reason to want to bypass civilian jurisprudence and the legislative process. Executive orders are often means of avoiding the messiness of democracy. In times of war Congress has repeatedly shown its propensity for obsequious consent, but there are conservative as well as center-liberal objections to proposals to bring the war home to the political opposition. Despite its full-throated support for the war, the labor movement can't be constrained from protesting against such austerity measures as drastic cuts in social spending in the service of bolstering the war expenditures proposed by the administration. And unless they can discern, in the words of Justice Oliver Wendell Holmes, a "clear and present danger" to domestic tranquility federal courts are leery of setting aside constitutional protections. This is the same court system that, earlier in the year, ultimately prevented the Clinton administration, no friend of civil liberties, from persisting in its flimsy espionage case against the Los Alamos physicist Wen Ho

Lee and reversed months of house arrest by a South Carolina government of five black Charleston trade unionists who conducted a demonstration at the statehouse. It can be argued that if the assault by the Bush administration on democratic rights succeeds, history will be born again. Or, to be more exact, unless one accepts the idea of progress unconditionally, a new regressive authoritarian history may emerge from the events of September 11.

THE IDEOLOGY OF ENDINGS

The fundamental defect of the ideology of endings—whose explicit assumption is that class and class struggle are relics of a bygone era—lies not only in the action-critique posed by social movements to this mode of reasoning, but also in the view that history has a fixed definition that precedes its making. Like the preponderance of marxist thinkers, Fukuyama agrees that history consists exclusively in epochal change. And epochal change means a transformation in ownership of productive property and the political and juridical relations that emanate from the economic infrastructure. Given the sweep of Fukuyama's concept of history and its finality, anything short of revolution that seizes and holds state power in the image of great evolutionary transformation from one stage to another is consigned to modernity's housekeeping. There will always be "hotspots," and military action to discipline or topple rogue regimes will continue to be part of the new world order's police keeping function, but capitalism, according to this thinking, has overcome all threats to its existence.

For socialists of all persuasions the relation of reform and revolution has always been ambiguous. Throughout the twentieth century parties committed to the socialist transformation of society have fought in parliaments and on the streets for social reforms that ameliorate the living and working conditions of workers. Rejecting arguments made by ultralefts throughout socialism's history that reforms acted to buttress the illusion that workers can solve their problems without taking on the system as such, socialist parties have gone so far as to enter bourgeois governments; they have cooperated with liberal and conservative parties to enact and administer social programs and upon occasion to join national capital in wars against systemic opponents. For example, the British Labour government pursued policies of empire from the 1940s through the 1970s, when they were frequently in power; similarly, French Socialist governments conducted wars against anticolonial national independence movements in Algeria and Southeast Asia. Although some argue that reforms within the prevailing capitalist system are necessary but not sufficient to achieve human emancipation and point out that in history revolutions are almost invariably preceded by unfulfilled mass reform demands, the preponderance of practical socialists and left-liberals—that is, those who engage in struggles within the liberal democratic framework of Western, including American, politics—are so deeply sunk in the sewer of reform that in the words of the turn-of-the-century German Socialist Eduard Bernstein, "The struggle is everything, the goal nothing."[11]

Here I advance the idea that "history" is constantly being made by humans through their practices, and not necessarily in terms that can be identified with the idea of progress. I argued in chapter 2 that history is made when through self-constitution the subordinate classes succeed in changing the mode of life in significant ways. That these changes rarely involve transformations in the ownership of productive property does not disqualify them from being historic. Moreover, rulers make history when they are able to abrogate previous gains made by insurgent social formations and return to some previous time. In this sense Nietzsche's comment that nothing disappears but, instead, returns to bite us is entirely vindicated by current events. The form of the return is never identical to its previous incarnation, but it is recognizable as the past. Whether lurking or not, it is not ordained that history proceeds in cycles, as Arnold Toynbee and Arthur Schlesinger, Jr., have claimed. For the making of history is a creative act, but one constrained in part by conditions already in existence. Because change is self-generated by social formations it is always different in many respects, always new.[12]

At issue is what counts as history. Are the innumerable changes that occur in everyday life—the changes wrought by the actions of people creating their own environments and struggling to preserve their self-created forms of association, which are frequently disrupted by political decisions over which they have little control, by war and war preparations, and by changes in economic conditions—are these historical? Thus when feminist and black freedom movements lay claim to have made history by changing the terms of political, social, and cultural relations, especially in law and everyday life, are these changes viewed by theorists of modernity—Left as well as Right—as reforms that correct certain inequalities but fail to change things in any fundamental way? Do the vast changes that have occurred in the technologies of information and communications and that have transformed much of industrial production, business administration, and, equally striking, the everyday lives of hundreds of millions of people over the last half of the twentieth century amount to real history? I will not invoke the term *revolution,* which has been used to describe these phenomena, because its appropriation by the advertising industry and by the media has drained it of its original meaning. The question is whether the way we live has been decomposed and recomposed by air, auto, and truck travel, the characteristic methods of getting from here to there; indeed, where is here and where is there? And has history been changed by the introduction of word processors attached to an electronic device known as a computer into our workplaces and our homes, let alone the regulatory function of computerization in every business and public enterprise from industrial production to the retail sector to public services of all sorts? What about the changes in modes of communications induced by electronic mail and the Internet? are they generating new forms of social relations and new opportunities for the global opposition to coordinate its activities? and are these aspects of a new history? To restrict history to its eighteenth- and nineteenth-century meanings, even to retain the traditional notion of revolution, as a measure of historicity is as arcane as is the claim that with liberal democracy we have attained the pinnacle of human evolution.

Scientifically based technological innovations such as the computer, laser technologies, and genetic engineering—and the new modes of organization linked to them—constitute nothing less than a historical break with the past.[13] Many Americans have discovered that nothing is nailed down, that disruption has become as ordinary as breakfast. The kinds of jobs that are available and whether we will have paid employment, new educational requirements, what we eat and, perhaps most important, our sense of time and place have all been altered beyond the recognition of an observer of the nineteenth and early twentieth centuries. For example, as the technologies spread and penetrate business organization and the capitalist market we may no longer anticipate working for a single employer or even practicing a single craft or profession for the whole of our working lives. In 2001, thousands of workers in the computer software and hardware industries in the Pacific Northwest were laid off. Bewildered, a thirty-six-year-old computer professional found himself unemployed for the first time in fourteen years. "I didn't think it could happen to me," he said. Beyond their imagination, managers in such correlative occupations as food service, which are ordinarily inured from market fluctuations, were lining up for unemployment benefits.[14]

Geographic vertigo has become a way of life for many among us. The idea that we are born, raised, live, and work in the same city or town or even region is rapidly becoming an expectation for fewer people. For it is not only rural China and peasant regions of Mexico and Brazil that are in upheaval: the whole of humanity, including the population of the United States, is frequently obliged to leave their dwellings and consequently is experiencing a loss of the sense of place. This is not to devalue the opportunities that might be available in areas far from home. For professionals and managers, students, many skilled manual workers, and, of course, retirees, the pull of California, Florida, New York, and the Northwest was one of the most important mobility stories of the twentieth century. Indeed, the growth of these regions attests to the persistence of the metaphor of the frontier as diffusing discontent. In 1940, Los Angeles was a medium-sized city, San Diego a smallish navy town, Fort Lauderdale little more than a place in the road, and Seattle a small city that shipped and processed lumber and fish. California was utterly transformed by World War II when the federal government made its southern region into a major aircraft and ship production center and the San Francisco and Oakland ports major sites of troop and matériel embarkation for the Pacific war theater. In the postwar era these cities became the hubs of some of the fastest growing regions in the country.

But the story that is so easily forgotten is the push of prolonged joblessness, agricultural and small business failure, and, on a domestic as well as a global plane, poverty and hunger. The idea that capital is mobile but that labor is rooted in the land or in specific cities has lost some of its salience. The twenty-first century may resemble the sixteenth and seventeenth centuries more than it does the twentieth. Hundreds of millions of people around the globe are on the move. Many are likely to occupy different geographic space four, five, even ten times during their lives. As children many attend schools in different regions, even different countries, throughout elementary and secondary education as well as during college years. It is no longer only the military and the diplomatic corps that require their employees to take assignments throughout the nation and on foreign shores. The transnationalization of corporations means that skilled workers as well as executives are typically required to change places for extended periods. As old industries disappear or relocate, so do many industrial and service workers, either following the company or, more often, rendered unemployed by the move, of necessity seeking work far from their homes. Once believed to be properties of a bygone era, the migration images of the *Grapes of Wrath* have returned with a vengeance, albeit the cars and the clothes are in better condition. Even if the plant or office stays open, it will draw many workers whose homes are fifty or sixty miles away. From the turn of the century to the 1950s, millions of Americans, black and white, migrated from rural areas of the South and Midwest to the burgeoning industrial cities. This migration has been repeated at the turn of the twenty-first century. To the second great immigrant wave, now originating in Latin America, Asia, and Russia, we may add a third wave: the internal migration of first- and second-generation Americans of African, Caribbean, and European origin who have lost their purchase on place, some after only a few generations of relative stability. How moderns experience and define such concepts as home, neighborhood, family, and friendship is only partially commensurate with how people at other historical moments did so.[15]

Social and biographical time is different as well. In contrast to a half century ago, when, typically, most children spent eleven to thirteen years in school and only a small fraction attended college, more than half of children in the United States undergo schooling for as long as twenty years. We enter the full-time paid labor force as adults later than in the past and, for this reason, remain unmarried and often without children longer. While many of our predecessors became parents before age twenty—and many still do—nowadays parenthood occurs at a later age than at any time in history. It is not uncommon for women to have their first child in their late thirties or early forties, a phenomenon that reduces the chances they will be able to retire from paid labor before reaching seventy. Perhaps equally important, because people can't earn a living by performing only one job or by working eight hours a day, more and more take on two jobs; industrial workers accept all the overtime they can get just to pay the bills, so that life is experienced as work without end; and many professionals and managers take their work home and spend the time once reserved for rest working into the night. We have become a nation of pill poppers because many of us suffer from severe stress owing to overwork born of mounting bills amid job insecurity.

Of course, this brief catalogue of temporal and spatial anxiety still requires explanation. The optimism of modernity theory is belied by its performance on the ground. From the rise of religious fundamentalism, at home as well as abroad, to the events of September 11, 2001, modernism's rejection by some societies and cultures has revealed how profound is the discontent fomented by modernity's new form, globality. Americans can no longer remain indifferent to what is happening thousands of miles beyond the water's edge. Some will interpret this imperative to mean that Americans must reconcile themselves to permanent war, to long-term sacrifice in public goods and living standards, to indefinite surrender of liberty. Others, notably the leader of the AFL-CIO, are not convinced that workers should surrender their living standards in the corporate interest. Speaking at the

AFL-CIO convention in December 2001, its president, John Sweeney, condemned these assumptions. While praising U.S. foreign policy in regard to the war in Afghanistan, he said, "In the months ahead, we must take the offensive in a war here at home. President Bush and his administration are doing an excellent job of waging war on the terrorists, and we commend them for that. But at the same time, he and his corporate backers are waging a vicious war on working families . . . and we condemn them for that."[16] Sweeney called on organized labor to resist the administration's austerity policies, including severe cuts in education and health care. But if the past is any guide, these sentiments will be expressed mainly in electoral rather than direct action.

Are populations destined to live in a state of permanent migration? Is a life without genuine and enduring social ties to be endured as the inevitable price of capitalism's economic viability? There are still parts of the world in which the whole population treasures long periods of social time away from paid labor. For example, large sections of the nations of southern Europe and North Africa have held fast to cultural traditions that provide for two- or three-hour lunch periods and strictly prohibit most Sunday store and factory labor; and they have enacted laws that mandate five- or six-week annual vacations for the whole working population. That this culture of self-controlled time is under assault from global capitalism testifies to one of its fundamental aims: to break social practices that resist accumulation, that safeguard workers' health, that preserve the elements of conviviality, and that maintain a measure of horizontal social relationships; for these practices are independent of capital's logic and sometimes constitute the glue of collective action against capital investment that results in the destruction of cities and towns and of the ties of community life. The idea of progress is supplemented by that of cost-containment. Those whose admiration for modernity is unconditional may snort that sentiment must not be permitted to stand in the way of progress; these people assert that the old ways tend to perpetuate material deprivation. But it must be pointed out that, predictions to the contrary notwithstanding, capital has not succeeded in melting "all that is solid . . . into air."[17]

The United States is, perhaps, among leading societies, the one most deeply and most thoroughly organized according to capital's logic. Not the least of its accomplishments is to have turned work from a necessity of life into a way of life. Capital's once severely contested historic doctrine of boundless work time has overtaken the efforts of the labor movement and of workers themselves to institute a different ethic. Begun in the 1880s, the fifty-year struggle for shorter hours—exemplified in the American labor movement's pioneering fight for the eight-hour day—was once a beacon to labor throughout the world. Through mass strikes, demonstrations, and public statements labor urgently called upon Congress and employers to accede to its demand. Finally, after rejecting the Black Bill, which mandated a six-hour day, Congress enacted the wages and hours law in 1938, which embodied a severely modified version. It provided for time and a half pay after forty hours but did not extend this regulation to the working day. It was left to collective bargaining to improve on this framework.

Still, the concept of limits on working time had been established. By the 1980s this stricture was in ruins. The labor movement was no longer the bastion of shorter hours, as a combination of coercion and cultural shifts prompted many to climb aboard the nonstop workhorse. Indeed, we are in the throes of 24/7—the sign of work without end—where everyone is always on call. Many people walk around all day, every day with beepers and cell phones. This is the era of the twenty-four-hour supermarket, of Sunday store openings. If the law provides for six national holidays, they are honored in the breach as much as in the observance, and nobody protests.

Labor's acquiescence was not necessarily secured by persuasion. After the onset of world economic instability in the 1970s, capital launched an offensive that still reverberates today. With the coming of the Reagan Revolution, when workers struck or otherwise protested against capital's demands for "flexibility," a key precept of neoliberal economics, capital openly threatened them with joblessness in the form of capital flight to greener domestic as well as foreign venues. Flexibility entailed wage and benefit cuts, enforced overtime, and relaxation or repeal of hard-won work rules to facilitate the reorganization of the labor process by piling more tasks on workers. To these setbacks must be added the efforts by conservatives to roll back the once-formidable welfare state or social wage. After nearly two decades of retreat, at the turn of the twenty-first century, despite indications that some in organized labor, in movements of the aging, and in the black freedom movement were gearing up for battle, it was plain that a new culture of subordination had taken root.

The culture was grounded more in fear than in the so-called work ethic. For the love of labor has never been prevalent among working people; the idea of work as a redemptive activity is the imposition of a quasi-religious morality by the state and its ideological apparatuses, especially schools and the media and their intellectuals. The heavy hand of neoliberal economics was felt widely after Reagan fired eleven thousand striking air traffic controllers in August 1981. This bold stroke was followed by a series of employer demands for concessions from union and nonunion workers. At first, many locals resisted: in the mid-1980s Decatur, Illinois Stacey, Caterpillar, and American Home Products workers struck to preserve their gains. In Austin, Minnesota, Hormel's meatpackers struck when the company demanded wage reductions, a measure that was supported by their international union. Continental Airlines management took a long strike by unionized workers but succeeded in breaking the union for fifteen years. In nearly all instances in which they stood up against concession bargaining, union militants were defeated—in part because their national unions were unprepared for the intensity of the employer offensive and intimidated by the conservative political climate. For these reasons national unions became habituated to granting concessions to the employers.

Working people, including educated professional and technical employees, had, by the mid-1980s, become victim to ontological insecurity, which tempered their will to fight. By the mid-1970s the forward march of the public employees' unions had been halted and in some respects reversed when, strapped by fiscal crisis, local governments demanded benefit and salary reductions and embarked on policies of mass layoffs, a concomitant of reductions in services. In the 1980s many urban areas with substantial black and Latino populations were on their knees, even as they regularly voted black politicians into municipal office. When they assumed office, newly elected black public officials discovered that the treasury was bare and that capital flight and widespread poverty deprived them of resources with which to rebuild their cities. Under the banner "If you can't beat 'em, join 'em," many allied with the corporations and became managers of austerity. Eventually, some found themselves turned out of office by those who elected them.

As a consequence of years of the less-than-benign neglect of working conditions and city services, especially education, the labor and progressive revival of the late 1990s was constrained by its essential defensive character. The coalition of trade unions and organizations that had survived the social upsurge of the 1960s and early 1970s fought to preserve past gains, disdaining new ideas and new strategies for achieving power as a distant shore not worth even contemplating. Instead, they became fiercely electoral, placing much of their political capital in the effort to elect a moderate president and Congress that, above all, would "do no harm." But expectations had been significantly lowered. Hence, having expected next to nothing, they received little from a two-term Democratic president, Bill Clinton, who without the assistance of organized labor would have surely lost his first bid to be elected.

Meanwhile, the class struggle raged unabated: employers fiercely opposed union organization, and capital flight left many communities bereft and hopeless. Nor did the boom deter neoliberals from dismantling the welfare state. They forced Clinton to repeal income supports for the long-term unemployed when he signed the Welfare Reform Act in the face of the 1996 election. And for the overwhelming majority, with concession bargaining and betrayal still fresh in their memory, risk taking was not on their agenda. Wages stagnated as the long economic boom of the 1990s passed unaccompanied by a concomitant rise in real wages. Month by month, year after year, the conservative chairman of the Federal Reserve Bank, Alan Greenspan, gloated that wage restraints acted to moderate inflation and keep interest rates lower than would have been necessary if workers had done what they nearly always did before—initiate a wave of mass strikes to take advantage of the boom. Stricken by fear, many raised their incomes by putting in fifty-, sixty-, even seventy-hour workweeks; at least in industries that produced durable goods like auto, steel, and electrical supplies, workers' gross pay often approached eighty to a hundred thousand dollars a year.

During the 1980s and 1990s, America was at work. Women entered the paid labor force in record numbers; by the end of the nineties, more than two-thirds of adult women were holding part- or full-time jobs or were looking for paid work. Some men said they were happy to be making enough money to pay bills and send their kids to college, and a few preferred the comradeship of the shop floor to the tensions they felt at home. But the unpaid labor of homemaking and child rearing did not abate. What Arlie Hochschild termed the "double shift" became a new source of discontent among women. Of course, noting the burden that women have been obliged to assume does not speak to the conservative call to return women to the home. Women entered the paid labor force not only out of economic necessity, but also in quest of financial independence and the opportunity to acquire technical and professional credentials. Women who have the means to support themselves and their children are less likely to submit to the unreasonable demands of their husbands because they have freed themselves from dependency. Moreover, the fact that more than half of American women hold jobs strengthens their argument that household tasks should be shared by their partners. It has also resulted in a rising divorce rate and placed women in a better position to resist male violence in the household because they have the option to exit.[18]

The conjunction of recession and war in fall 2001 accelerated the attack against workers' rights and hard-won gains. When a thousand teachers struck for pay and to preserve their health benefits in Middletown, New Jersey, parents sided with the courts, which quickly jailed more than one hundred teachers for violating a state law prohibiting strikes by public employees. The teachers and their union were severely criticized for conducting militant action in a time of national emergency, a refrain often heard under these circumstances in American history. The strike was broken. In Hartford, Connecticut, the huge Pratt and Whitney corporation, one of America's leading producers of aircraft engines and spare parts, announced it would reduce health benefits for its workers in order to save money. Workers and their union prepared for a strike and succeeded in holding the line. In the wake of the World Trade Center disaster, New York's outgoing mayor, Rudolph Giuliani—after reconciling himself to the Bush administration's broken promise to provide aid to the city and to Congress's dawdling—announced a 15 percent budget cut for all city agencies except police, fire, and board of education, a reduction that would inevitably lead to significant layoffs and cutbacks in services. The order was issued at a time when the city was facing a major health crisis, as the mayor and his Health Department were forced, after initial denials, to admit that the trade center rubble posed serious environmental problems over a far-flung area. Meanwhile, there were no real plans by federal and state governments to address the hardships suffered on two fronts: by nearly eighty thousand employees whose jobs disappeared with the destruction of the towers and by seventy thousand workers who made their living from the decimated tourism industry and were now reduced to three- and four-day weeks.[19] By spring 2002, the official national jobless rate rose to 6 percent, and workers braced for new assaults on wages and benefits as employers sought to transfer the burden of the recession onto their backs.

Since the early 1970s, when conservative economic doctrine ruled politics and policy, Western nations have experienced little economic and social reform. They have slowed the pace of cultural transformation, signified principally by the advances of women, immigrants, and blacks against flagrant discriminatory practices in employment, personal security, and everyday relationships. The inability of weak social movements, including the trade unions, to maintain the tempo of social reform that marked the 1960s resulted in a thirty-year hiatus; even the ecological movements could not sustain the protection of safeguards to air and water that they had won against the ravages of industrial development. The 1990s witnessed a desperate struggle, not to extend ecological law, but to prevent the neoliberals from rolling back regulation in the name of the free market. Combined with the collapse of Communist societies and their transformation into neoliberal poster children, the stalling of reform has given rise to a new surge of radicalism that has, for the first time since the mid-1960s, raised the question of whether capitalism itself is subject to substantive reform. But a new generation of social activists—chiefly students and younger trade unionists—have framed their protests in distinctly anticapitalist terms. While rhetoric still exceeds genuine strategies of change, even after September 11 conferences as well as militant demonstrations at sites of world economic institutions have resumed and taken on new urgency.

TESTING THE LIMITS OF LIBERAL DEMOCRACY

Long working hours, the breakup of long-term personal associations, and, most important, the disappearance of women from neighborhoods during the day have accelerated the decline of civil society, the stuff of which the amenities of everyday life are made. In the 1980s and 1990s membership in voluntary organizations such as the Parent-Teachers' Association, veterans' groups, and social clubs declined but, perhaps more to the point, many of them lost activists, the people who kept the organizations together. Labor unions, whose membership erosion was as severe as it was disempowering, became more dependent on full-time employees to conduct organizing, political action, and other affairs as rank-and-file leaders disappeared into the recesses of the nonstop workplace. The cumulative effect of this transformation is the hollowing out of participation and democracy where it really counts, at the grass roots. For the democratic polity cannot alone be defined and measured by the percentage of eligible citizens who exercise their vote; indeed, fewer than half of eligible voters turn out for state and local elections and only half participate in presidential polls. The United States has chronically lagged behind other capitalist democracies in this respect. As Benjamin Barber, Robert Putnam, and others have argued, the measure of democracy is the degree of participation by ordinary citizens in the social and cultural as well as the political institutions of society. A vital liberal democracy is one in which representatives are selected in an electoral process that is the outcome of a series of intense discussions and debates over issues that affect the polity at every level of social rule. This would apply to the workplace, to school boards, and to the leadership of voluntary organizations as well as national and international institutions that control or otherwise regulate economic and political life.[20]

The democracy of the twentieth and twenty-first centuries bears little resemblance to that of the previous two centuries. In the 1920s, John Dewey's rueful meditations on the decline of the public still held out hope for its revival. Reflecting on his own late nineteenth-century Vermont upbringing, Dewey recalled the tradition of direct democracy and argued that American social arrangements and political jurisdictions needed to be scaled down in order to implement democratic aspirations. But eighty years after his book *The Public and Its Problems* (1925) appeared in the era of mass democracy, such concepts as direct participation in the decisions affecting the collective life are no longer in the political vocabulary. The town meeting, in which all members of the local polity make the decisions affecting the community, survives in some New England villages and small towns, but at best participation in cities and suburbs is confined to testimony at public hearings conducted by elected councils and boards—of education, of energy, and of other locally based utilities. Although a small fraction of the population takes part in various institutions of local government and a larger group participates mostly through membership in voluntary organizations like parent associations, the social programs of churches and other charitable agencies, chambers of commerce, and unions, tens of millions of Americans regard democracy as consisting almost exclusively in the ritual of voting; only opinion polls mitigate, to an extent, our sense of distance from the process of political decision making.

Yet however weak liberal democracy is, the United States has by no means tested its institutional limits. In fact, of the political systems of the leading capitalist societies, that of the United States is perhaps the least democratic. Undoubtedly because of religious objections, for example, Tuesday rather than Sunday is the conventional voting day, which discourages turnout, especially by working people. The president is elected by an electoral college whose members are selected on the basis of who wins the popular vote in a given state; this system thus gives disproportional weight to states with smaller populations and has occasioned outcomes in which the victor has received a minority of the popular vote. (One need look back no further than George Bush's win in 2000 for an example of this virtual paradox.) And unlike some countries whose constitution and practices are designed to ensure representation by minority parties in legislative bodies, the United States is dedicated to a winner-take-all system of representation that, for most intents and purposes, excludes minor parties. In some states and localities these parties receive as much as 15–20 percent of the vote, a showing not uncommon in recent elections. State and federal election laws provide that the party winning a majority or plurality of the votes has been elected to office, and the other parties are excluded from governance.

As we saw in chapter 3, the same system has informed the development of a self-perpetuating bureaucracy in the unions as well, one that only a system of term limits can hope to remedy. But term limits restrict the prerogatives only of individuals, not of self-perpetuating ruling parties. Even where majorities are required to elect an office seeker, most statutes mandate a runoff between the two top vote getters. A substantial minority of citizens are thus routinely deprived of representation, a situation that militates against pluralism in the electoral and legislative processes. The mantra of electoralism is that voters should not "throw away their vote" by selecting the candidate(s) of parties having no chance to win. As a result, Americans are saddled with the politics of the lesser evil. Faced with the prospect that our vote for someone who holds political views close to or identical to our own might, in close races, elect a candidate whose views are entirely unacceptable, we tend to hold our noses and vote for the least objectionable candidate.

Imagine an electoral system based on proportional representation. Like many other countries, among them Italy, Israel, and Germany, the United States under such a system could elect a Congress and state legislatures that would be more broadly representative, and the major parties would be obliged to form coalitions in order to rule. While some argue that European systems introduce instability into politics—this is especially the case in Italy—a little uncertainty would make social reform if not inevitable, at least more likely. In any case, proportional representation, a system that ensures representation for minorities who achieve a minimum percentage of the popular vote, might energize those who have decided that the narrow differences between the two major parties do not warrant exercising their franchise, let alone participating in the political process in other ways.

It is fairly rare to hear calls for radical democracy in this era in which power seems ever more concentrated at the top of the economic and political systems. By radical democracy political theorists connote a system of governance in which power is widely shared among the citizenry and institutions are controlled in direct ways from below. Put another way, radical democracy would change relations of power, allowing entrance to those who are partially or entirely excluded from participation in civil society under representative forms and are unable to influence, let alone share, power over key decisions affecting their lives. Many political observers have noted the passivity of Americans in the wake of the enormous changes that have swept through the institutions of the economy and government, especially those that have transformed everyday life in such a way as to conspire to widen the economic and political inequalities of power. I would deny that the word *passivity* or, in another vocabulary, *consent,* let alone *consensus,* adequately describes the current situation. But we cannot discern the signs of discontent in the usual places and among the traditional radicals.

As Jean Baudrillard has perceptively argued, abstinence from the shriveled institutions of politics and governance may signify neither apathy nor consent but a form of resistance. The silent majorities who fail to go to the polls or to participate in a rigged civil society are neither left nor right in their sentiments but have determined, often tacitly to be sure, that the institutions of liberal democracy—including unions and many voluntary organizations which, in the end, are extensions of the state—are irrelevant to their lives or, worse, impediments to their interests. If it can be shown that the fabled deadlock of democratic institutions has produced very little to advance the general welfare in the past thirty years, if Congress and European parliaments are subsumed under a centralized executive authority that in turn is deeply beholden to the network of transnational corporations and international bureaucratic economic institutions, then the act of voting simply legitimates the swindle that so-called representatives are accountable to their constituents, at least on matters that affect their modes of life. While Baudrillard may have overstated the case for abstinence as a form of resistance, many young people and a considerable fraction of the poor share the assessment that, given the alternatives offered by the electoral system, their participation simply legitimates a process that does not serve them. These views may be mistaken. But unless we accept the theory according to which legislative bodies are generally responsive to active constituents—a theory that is unable to explain the disparity between a high level of trade union and middle-class liberal voting and the gross indifference of Congress and most state legislatures to these sectors' needs and views—the abstainers act not only out of indifference but also out of skepticism.[21]

During times of emergency many Americans seem prepared to concede more authority than usual to the executive, which hastens to suspend the autonomy of representative institutions and, as Eric Foner has shown, tends to "shred the Constitution." The Bush administration is not alone in this regard: the Alien and Sedition Laws enacted during John Adams's presidency, the federal government's jailing of war opponents during World War I, its internment of Japanese-American citizens during World War II, and the McCarthy period's attack against labor and radical movements, which received the approbation of the Truman and Eisenhower administrations, all circumvented the constitutional rights of individuals and organizations in the name of national security. We may learn from Benjamin's remark: "The tradition of the oppressed teaches us that the 'state of emergency' in which we live is not the exception, but the rule. We must attain a conception of history that is in keeping with this insight."[22]

The new movements directed against capitalist globality, but also the new libertarian Right, have adopted elements of the analysis that liberty under liberal capitalist democracy is fragile and that democracy itself, although frequently protected by courts, is chimerical. There are signs that a new wave of activists is changing the political landscape. While the traditional Left is generally programmatic, the new opposition is issue-oriented and not content to use the familiar tactics of petition and lobby to achieve its aims. The new activism is discontinuous with the social reformism of the social democratic and liberal organizations, whose typical form of participation entailed working for legislative remedies. Instead, it has a distinct direct action orientation that it recovered from the feminist, gay and lesbian, and black freedom movements and, in the mid-1990s, from the anti-AIDS movement ACT UP. Reflecting their suspicion and even disdain of the tools of liberal democracy, direct action rather than petition and legislation has been the hallmark of the antiglobalization movement as well, and this strategic shift is evident in campus-based anti-sweatshop groups who have used the labor and civil rights tactic of the sit-in in college presidents' offices to replace entreaties to academic authorities to change their procurement policies.

These differences may be dismissed on the ground that the resistance has not advanced to alternative; the opposition rarely proposes new arrangements that depart substantially from reform. In fact, as we saw in chapter 7, many environmental protesters who engage in direct action still hope that nations will come to their senses and enact a series of treaties to remedy global warming and other ecological hazards. Furthermore, the discrediting of Socialism and Communism has left a huge vacuum in alternative, let alone utopian, thinking. If there is a crisis of the intellect, it resides in the bereft imagination. Collectively we are still unable to imagine a qualitatively different future. Indeed, radical democracy itself lacks contemporary specification. The Soviet constitution, which promised a new form of social rule, was betrayed by its own authors, and, contemporaneous with those events, John Dewey could offer only a rural miasma of democratic participation. Since the New Left's notion of participatory democracy achieved a degree of influence, especially in the black freedom movement, radical democracy has been largely an intellectual discourse.

Put simply, utopia is on hold. A partial exception is the imaginative thinking of social ecologists who have proposed bioregionalism, in which agriculture and manufacturing would be integrated within a restricted geographic space and radical democratic municipalism would replace the prevailing centralist, business-oriented metropolitan governments, whose development policies are destructive of natural and urban environments. Social ecology has gone beyond the slogans of libertarian marxism to propose alternatives, but thought is not equal to its practical challenges. In the near future we are likely to see concepts of decentralization, economies of "human scale," demands to ban vehicular traffic except buses, taxis, and trucks, for limited hours at least, from large cities, and varieties of neighborhood governance jurisdictions to encourage broader participation. Given the American way, we are not likely to see these proposals attain practical urgency until another disaster befalls us, and even then, given our penchant for denial and forgetting, there is no assurance that the climate will be favorable to changing our poisonous environmental practices.

Yet what is entirely new is a perception which, curiously, the Gulf and Afghanistan wars reinforced, namely, that even though they are worth preserving, appeal to the institutions of liberal democracy within the nation-state is no longer the exclusive context for politics and class struggle. One of the effects of the protests at Seattle, Washington, Quebec, and Genoa was to "smoke out," or open up, international economic organizations that affect the global population. Monetary and economic policy in general is no longer the sovereign function of nation-states, especially not in the South and East, but not in the West either. For this reason what happens to labor in, say, Mexico or Korea is the concern of workers in the United States. That the American labor movement has not yet fully grasped this development detracts neither from the salience of the fact of interdependence nor from what seems the likelihood that eventually labor and other movements will recognize the multinational context of their struggles. If North American labor is still mired in the necessary, but incomplete step of trying to limit imports in order to protect its dwindling jobs, surely the next step is to adopt the only viable strategy left, that is, movement toward global equality in living standards, including wages and social protections. Upon this platform we can expect instances of coordinated direct action on a global scale, action based on the recognition that living standards in all countries will continue to deteriorate as long as the bulk of humanity is held in economic and political abjection.[23]

An equally urgent task is to reflect on the forms of power itself. How can the opposition address the subordination of the vast multitudes of humankind? the hollowing out of the state's social functions and its reduction to a fortress of national security? Certainly individual liberties worth protecting for the ability to speak without fear, to act without police intimidation, to assemble without incarceration, and to think beyond the prisonhouse of the politics of the possible, are the necessary condition of forming a democratic society. But the sufficient condition is to establish the basis for freedom. Beyond ensuring liberty, how can the elusive goal of freedom be pursued? At the outset it must be recognized that the libertarians on the Right more than the statist Left have been concerned with this question. Libertarians have distinguished themselves from conservatives by defending abortion rights, opposing draconian drug laws, and sometimes advocating legalization of controlled substances; in addition, during the recent war they were vocal in their opposition to the Bush administration's attempt to restrict the civil liberties of domestic as well as immigrant groups. Their defense of liberty has, on the whole, been more forthright than that of any other ideological tendency.

But the major flaw in the doctrines of right-wing libertarians is that they insist, with Adam Smith, that only a market unfettered by state regulation can guarantee freedom. Like Fukuyama and other neoliberals, they accept the oxymoron free market. The market for commodities and ideas is never really free but is lopsided in favor of those who own and control the preponderance of productive property. One thinks of Anatole France's bitter quip that the law in its majesty forbids, equally, the rich and the poor from sleeping under bridges; or, to paraphrase A. J. Liebling, the free market, like the press, is free only for those who own one. When the economy is in recession and many small businesses face ruin because of declining demand, their alternative is often to choose bankruptcy. But when the airline and auto corporations face declining profits, they can and do seek partial protection from the market's vicissitudes by securing subsidies from the federal government. When the small independent farmers are plagued by lower prices imposed by processors or wholesale corporations, they sell the farm to a real estate developer. When an agricultural corporation is faced with rising costs and stable prices, it appeals to the government for subsidies or invests in technology to reduce its labor costs. Competition among equals is generally confined to property owners, but small businesses confronting large corporations and those whose only property is their skills and credentials only occasionally enjoy an advantage over the buyer. For the most part the small proprietor is either forced out of business or, if the holder of a patent, is obliged to allow the business to be absorbed by the larger competitor. As for the worker, even in so-called good times only collective organization is capable of giving her or him some edge, and, as we have seen, even this weapon is not always sufficient.

But freedom is not identical to liberty or to the exercise of such human rights as speech and assembly. As an individual I cannot achieve freedom, if by that concept we mean the ability to control the conditions of life by making those decisions that affect it. Freedom cannot be legislated, and liberal democratic institutions are hostile to its precepts because they rest on formal representation by organized political parties that are beholden to economic and other powers. Freedom is the outcome of the direct exercise of autonomy by individuals and groups in the self-constitution of institutions and practices that form social arrangements. Freedom is therefore an effect of collective self-creation and presupposes a break from the social and historical context of its institution. To be sure, nothing is forever. Since the context within which labor and other social movements operate is generally hostile to direct, radical democracy, and because the political environment can, in a relatively short term, turn 180 degrees, in order to save themselves movements tend to become institutions controlled from above. These organizations often adopt systems of representative governance and hire staffs who effectively control their programs; the leadership becomes more or less completely severed from the activist base. Whence, as often as not, rumblings from below explode in either of two forms: internal revolt against the leadership, as in the rank-and-file union caucuses; or breakaways such as the Student Nonviolent Coordinating Committee, which, in the early 1960s, rejected the legalistic, go-slow policies of organizations like the NAACP.

There are many instances of such creativity, whereby people generate alternative institutions, usually on a relatively small scale, but these innovations are often not in the public eye. For example, dissatisfied with the local school or available day care options, a group of Brooklyn parents and teachers start their own institution, adopt a somewhat different curriculum, and hire teachers who care about pedagogy. Moreover, for a substantial time the school is jointly run by parents and teachers who, on the basis of criteria they have a voice in establishing, select the director. In most instances schools run by parents and teachers must address the constraints of law and of established practices. Before they are able to operate they must procure licenses from Health, Buildings, and Education departments. Securing these documents entails undergoing inspections and, in the case of education, credentials and curricular reviews, processes that usually involve a prolonged series of meetings, sometimes confrontations, with the authorities, including unions, who are prone to protect their turf. If they win approval, it is often at the expense of their autonomy, although the extent of victory depends on the extant political and cultural environment. Nevertheless, more often than not something new is created, something that does not depend on the initiative of the bureaucracy.

Dissatisfied with their union's bureaucratic, top-down practices, workers may form a caucus that seeks to replace the existing national or local leadership in favor of a more democratic union that attempts to share power broadly among the rank and file. Rather than remaining an organization dominated by full-time officials, it decentralizes functions and power in order to make decisions. Like their educational counterparts, the victorious candidates invariably face the problem of reconciling their intentions with the hidebound rules and practices of the established international union leadership and staff; but, perhaps more urgently, they must deal with the constraints of law that have turned unions from autonomous movements into apparatuses, ideological and political, of the state. The extent to which they are able to pursue their own star depends on a variety of factors, the most important of which is how far they are willing to go to defend their principles. Risk is the rock against which innovation shatters. But all over America there are local unions and even some national unions for which rank-and-file participation is both an end and a means. We have the rich experiences of the feminist, ecology, and black freedom movements of the late twentieth century. These movements were largely self-created, advanced their own leaders, and, at least until they were integrated into mainstream politics in the 1980s, were much more democratic than traditional voluntary organizations. It is important to continue to reach into the deep recesses of repressed memory and be prepared to conduct the class struggle on the terrain of historiography.

While the moment of September 11 seems to have temporarily foreclosed the possibility of a new class politics, we have seen these traditions live in movements which recreate them, sometimes consciously drawing from the experiences of earlier generations. The impulse to freedom, however feeble in some historical moments, is inextinguishable. For centuries this impulse has driven the struggles of the insurgent classes against entrenched power. Because it consists in imposing constraints, enforcing established rules, and punishing those who insist on challenging authority, power is always inimical to freedom. And there are no guarantees that, having been subordinated for generations, the powerless in power will not reproduce the conditions of domination, both of their own and of their adversaries. The failsafe, whether the making of history issues from a new institution or political insurgency, is that the unconscious, which has a welter of historically induced scars, is made an object of reflection by the insurgencies and that the past and present are subjected to ruthless critique. This would entail adopting a notion of education, not as the transmission of ideologies and other received truths, but as a process of constant examination of social practice, in the first place in the institutions of governance and of everyday life.

What are the prospects for the formation of a class alliance that can contend for social and political power? By "class alliance" I refer to social formations which, because of their economic, political, and cultural exclusion from power, organize into movements that seek to change the conditions of life. That social formations and the movements emanating from them have historicity signifies that in every space of social time some will be more crucial for challenging prevailing authority than others. In this respect there is always the possibility that one or more insurgent movements of the past will be made part of the hegemonic power bloc while others will remain on the outside and form an opposition. Within the vast multitudes of those whose interests coincide with social and political transformation only a specific constellation of social forces is likely to put these tasks on the historical agenda. But the agents of a new alliance must be identified in a global rather than a national context. The uneven development of an alliance between some fractions of the labor movement and the movements of women, blacks, youth, and ecologists will remain an enduring feature of the coming period. That is to say, we are not on the verge of a new, stable Grand Coalition on a global level. To ask the question of prospects is to assess the possibility that the opposition will at any time soon go on the offensive, an eventuality that presupposes a fairly long period of refusal and resistance to prevailing power and debate about alternative futures not only among intellectuals but among activists as well. We live in a time when the traditional Left is exhausted, intimidated by the rightist surge; or it has joined the antiutopian consensus. The new activist legions are still in the midst of defining resistance as the farthest horizon of politics. For the time being it is likely that the alliance will continue to take the form of global combinations of trade unionists, sometimes supported by official labor federations, students, the growing number of activists who gave life to social movements and remain committed to direct intervention, and radical intellectuals.

So this is a time for analysis and speculation as much as organization and protest, a time when people have a chance to theorize the new situations, to identify the coming agents of change without entertaining the illusion that they can predict with any certainty either what will occur or who the actors will be. It is a time to speak out about a future that is not yet probable, although eminently possible. The new venues for discussion will be found online, complemented by print journals, magazines, and newspapers. Moreover, the complexity of issues and the novelty of the situation demands new ideas that traditional Lefts seem incapable of providing. But some parties of opposition will become tribunes of new thought. Their ideas will be labeled utopian by those who have determined that power is too overwhelming to rethink their options and, for this reason, have decided either to abstain or to become loyal supplicants of liberal democratic regimes in the hopes of reducing their venality. And it is surely a moment for political organization, stretching the limits of electoralism without relying on liberal democratic institutions to provide the vehicles for change. The events in Seattle in December 1999 and in Genoa in 2001 as well as the struggles inevitably to come attest to the fact that people have a way of creating history without much preparation and setting new conditions for political struggle. As the opposition matures it will find new paths not only of resistance but of alternative.

NOTES

INTRODUCTION

1 Barbara and John Ehrenreich, "The Professional-Managerial Class," in Pat Walker, ed., *Between Labor and Capital* (Boston: South End Press, 1979); Stanley Aronowitz, "New Middle Class or Middle Strata?" in Walker, ed., *Between Labor and Capital.*

2 Top managers continue to make many corporate decisions regarding product lines, mergers and acquisitions, and capital investment; boards of directors, which are usually composed of representatives of major stockholders, rubber stamp many of these. But since the 1970s boards increasingly hold managers accountable for corporate performance, especially profits and stock values. After quarterly earnings are reported we are accustomed to announcements of sudden CEO or CFO (Chief Financial Officer) departures or "early retirements."

3 Lawrence Goodwyn, *Democratic Promise: The Populist Moment in America* (New York: Oxford University Press, 1976); James Weinstein, *The Decline of Socialism in America, 1912–1925* (New York: Monthly Review Press, 1967).

4 Robert Dahl, *Who Governs? Democracy and Power in an American City* (New Haven: Yale University Press, 1961).

5 William Appleman Williams, *The Contours of American History* (Cleveland: World, 1961); Gabriel Kolko, *Railroads and Regulation* (Westport, Conn.: Greenwood Press, 1977).

6 W. E. B. Du Bois, *The Souls of Black Folk* (1903; New York: Vintage Books/Library of America, 1990).

7 Benedict Anderson, *Imagined Communities: Reflections on the Origin and Spread of Nationalism* (London: Verso, 1983).

8 Adam Przeworski, "Proletariat into Class: The Process of Class Formation from Karl

Kautsky to Recent Controversies," *Politics and Society* 7, no. 4 (1977). Although I agree that struggles are about class, I disagree with Przeworski's view that liberal democracy is the farthest horizon of political possibility.

1. CLASS MATTERS

1 Karl Marx, preface, *A Contribution to the Critique of Political Economy,* trans. N. I. Stone (Chicago: C. H. Kerr, 1904).

2 Thomas Hobbes, *Leviathan,* ed. C. B. Macpherson (Harmondsworth: Penguin Books, 1968); Adam Smith, *An Inquiry into the Nature and Causes of the Wealth of Nations,* ed. Edwin Cannan (Chicago: University of Chicago Press, 1976); John Locke, *Two Treatises of Government,* ed. Peter Laslett (Cambridge: Cambridge University Press, 1960).

3 Lawrence Goodwyn, *Democratic Promise* (New York, 1976).

4 Frederick Jackson Turner, *The Frontier in American History* (New York: Dover Editions, 1996); Werner Sombart, *Why Is There No Socialism in the United States?,* trans. Patricia M. Hocking and C. T. Husbands (London: Macmillan, 1976).

5 Gordon S. Wood, *The Creation of the American Republic, 1776–1787* (Chapel Hill: University of North Carolina Press, 1969); Gordon S. Wood, *The Radicalism of the American Revolution* (New York: Alfred A. Knopf, 1991).

6 Eric Foner, *Free Soil, Free Labor, Free Men: The Ideology of the Republican Party Before the Civil War* (New York: Oxford University Press, 1970); David Montgomery, *Beyond Equality: Labor and the Radical Republicans, 1862–1872* (Urbana: University of Illinois Press, 1982); Herbert Gutman, *Work, Culture and Society in Industrializing America* (New York: Random House, 1977).

7 Arthur M. Schlesinger Jr., *The Age of Jackson* (Boston: Little, Brown, 1945); Lee Benson, *The Concept of Jacksonian Democracy: New York as a Test Case* (New York: Atheneum, 1964); Sean Wilentz, *Chants Democratic: New York City and the Rise of the American Working Class* (New York: Oxford University Press, 1984). For a critique of Wilentz and civic republican interpretations of working-class adherence to Jacksonian democracy, see Anthony Gronowicz, *Race and Class Politics in New York City Before the Civil War* (Boston: Northeast University Press, 1999).

8 Stanley Aronowitz, *The Knowledge Factory: Dismantling the Corporate University and Creating True Higher Learning* (Boston: Beacon Press, 2000); Sheila Slaughter and Larry L. Leslie, *Academic Capitalism: Politics, Policies, and the Entrepreneurial University* (Baltimore: Johns Hopkins University Press, 1997).

9 Paul Attewell, *Radical Political Economy since the Sixties* (New Brunswick: Rutgers University Press, 1984).

10 Stanley Aronowitz and William DiFazio, *The Jobless Future: Sci-Tech and the Dogma of Work* (Minneapolis: University of Minnesota Press, 1994); Jeremy Rifkin, *The End of Work* (New York: G. P. Putnam's Sons, 1995).

11 Thorstein Veblen, *The Theory of the Leisure Class* (New York: Penguin Books, 1979); John Kenneth Galbraith, *The New Industrial State* (Boston: Houghton Mifflin, 1985); C. Wright Mills, *The Power Elite* (New York: Oxford University Press, 1956).

12 See Dahl, *Who Governs?* for the classic statement of this position.

13 Robert Reich, *The Work of Nations* (New York: Vintage, 1992).

14 Milton Friedman, *Capitalism and Freedom* (Chicago: University of Chicago Press, 1962); Samuel Brittan, *A Restatement of Economic Liberalism* (Atlantic Highlands, N.J.: Humanities Press International, 1988); Francis Fukuyama, *The End of History and the Last Man* (New York: Free Press, 1992).

15 Przeworski, "Proletariat into Class."

16 I give a more elaborated account of this event in *Working Class Hero* (New York: Pilgrim Press, 1983).

17 Aronowitz and DiFazio, *Jobless Future.*

18 The literature on globalization is proliferating rapidly. For a solid account, see Robert J. S. Ross and Kent C. Trachte, *Global Capitalism: The New Leviathan* (Albany: State University of New York Press, 1990); also valuable is William Greider, *One World, Ready or Not: The Manic Logic of Global Capitalism* (New York: W. W. Norton, 2000).

19 International Labor Organization, *Report on World Employment and Underemployment* (Geneva, 2000).

20 United Nations Food and Agriculture Organization, *The State of Food Insecurity, 2001,* United Nations Reports (New York: 2001).

21 Norman Podhoretz, *My Love Affair with America* (New York: Free Press, 2000).

22 Ron Lembo, *Thinking Through Television* (Cambridge: Cambridge University Press, 2000).

23 In this neoliberal era we are witnessing a revival of Keynesian economic action even as conservative American presidents declare plans to shrink the federal government. The Reagan administration presided over the largest military spending program since World War II, and certainly the biggest so-called peacetime military budget in American history. As soon as he was sworn into office President George W. Bush, with lightning speed, introduced one of the more sumptuous tax cut proposals since the Reagan tax cut of 1983. With the stroke of a pen he awarded America's rich and corporate elite with most of a $1.5 trillion cut, a reduction that was resisted by the Democratic minority in Congress to no avail. In the Reagan and Bush presidencies working people bore even more of the tax burden while those with the largest incomes saw their taxes sharply reduced.

2. TIME AND SPACE IN CLASS THEORY

1 C. Wright Mills, *The Power Elite* (New York: Oxford University Press, 1956).

2 I reserve a fuller treatment of the ruling class for chapters 4 and 5.

3 The group of theorists who have been termed representatives of "Western" marxism—those who tried to comprehend the changes that advanced industrial capitalism has wrought—may be characterized by the attention they give to the con cepts of ideology and culture. This tendency spans an otherwise diverse, even contentious group: from Georg Lukács and Karl Korsch in the 1920s, to the Frank furt School and Antonio Gramsci, to Henri Lefebvre's series the *Critique of Everyday Life,* begun in 1947 and culminating almost thirty years later in his classic *The Production of Space* (trans. Donald Nicholson-Smith) (Oxford: Blackwell, 1991) and Louis Althusser's further development of Gramsci's thought, especially in his seminal article "Ideology and Ideological State Apparatuses," in Louis Althusser, *Lenin and Philosophy,* trans. Ben Brewster (New York: Monthly Review Press, 1971).

4 The sad, almost tragic story of the failure of American unions to organize southern workers has been told in terms of specific case histories by several labor historians, but there is still no general treatment of the saga. Janet Irons's exhaustive account of the National Textile Workers' strike of 1934 illustrates some of the major problems (Janet Christine Irons, "Testing the New Deal: The General Strike of 1934" [Ph.D. diss., Duke University, 1988]). See also Barbara Griffith, *The Crisis of American Labor* (Philadelphia: Temple University Press, 1988) for the CIO's post–World War II unsuccessful effort to organize the South. For the role of the Communists in southern organizing, see Karl Korstad, "Black and White Together: Organizing in the South with the Food, Tobacco, Agricultural and Allied Workers Union (FTA-CIO)," in Steve Rosswurm, ed., *The CIO's Left-Led Unions* (New Brunswick, N.J.: Rutgers University Press, 1992). For the role of black Communists, see Robin D. G. Kelley, *Hammer and Hoe: Alabama Communists during the Great Depression* (Chapel Hill: University of North Carolina Press, 1990). Michael Honey (*Southern Labor and Black Civil Rights: Organizing Memphis Workers* [Urbana: University of Illinois Press, 1993]) goes a considerable distance in articulating the role of racism within the movement and as an employer weapon in thwarting organized labor in the South.

5 The most ambitious attempt to theorize the women's movement in terms of class liberation is in Shulamith Firestone, *The Dialectic of Sex: The Case for Feminist Revolution* (New York: William Morrow, 1970). Her effort to suggest a feminist historical materialism is pioneering and singular in the literature of feminism in its intensity and consistent argument. More recently, continuing in this vein, Nancy Hartsock has made a valuable contribution (Nancy Hartsock, *Money, Sex and Power: Toward a Feminist Historical Materialism* [New York: Longman, 1983]).

6 Michael Hardt and Antonio Negri, *Empire* (Cambridge: Harvard University Press, 2000). I shall discuss this important contribution to the debate in chapter 5.

7 The slogan "All power to the Soviets" was advanced in 1917 by the Bolsheviks. It was part of their strategic maneuver to undermine the authority of the Central Liberal Republican government of Alexander Kerensky by making the workers' councils both administrative and legislative bodies. It recalled the 1905 revolution's great innovation. However, during the period of "War" Communism which followed the Bolsheviks' seizure of state power, they "temporarily" dissolved the councils and established an even more centralized state. The councils were restored but never enjoyed much authority. They became a fig leaf for the regime's party-led state.

8 Alain Touraine, *The May Movement,* trans. Leonard F. X. Mayhew (New York: Random House, 1971); Fredy Perlman, *Worker and Student Committees* (Detroit: Black and Red, 1969).

9 Georg Lukács, *History and Class Consciousness,* trans. Rodney Livingstone (Cambridge: MIT Press, 1971). The question of revolutionary class consciousness has plagued marxism throughout the twentieth century. In his essay "Reification and the Consciousness of the Proletariat," Lukács offers a powerful explanation for the collapse of the revolutionary upsurge in post–World War I Europe: the universalization and reification of the commodity-form had become a property of actual proletarian consciousness. This theme ran through the body of Western marxist social theory in the twentieth century like a red thread which neither the so-called linguistic turn of structuralism nor the allegorical efforts of Lukács himself could pull out. For the fact was that fascism was able to excite the imagination of a substantial fraction of the underlying population, and consumerism and the welfare state were able to accommodate desire, an accommodation that was challenged on several occasions but never overcome.

10 Firestone, *Dialectic of Sex.*

11 Wood, *Radicalism of the American Revolution.*

12 Clyde Barrow, *More than a Historian: The Political and Economic Thought of Charles A. Beard* (New Brunswick, N.J.: Transaction Publishers, 2000); Richard Hofstadter, *The Progressive Historians: Turner, Beard, Parrington* (Chicago: University of Chicago Press, 1979). In contrast to Hofstadter's claim that "Beard's reputation as a radical 'is not sustained by his writings,'" Barrow supplies convincing evidence not only of Beard's radicalism in general, but of his working-class perspective throughout his career and not just in his earlier socialist years. Needless to say, as he is perhaps America's preeminent proponent of the view that consensus rather than struggle marks American politics and culture, Hofstadter's judgments, even his misstatements, have become common sense among American intellectual historians.

13 Charles A. Beard and Mary R. Beard, *The Rise of American Civilization,* 2 vols. (New York: Macmillan, 1927).

14 *America Past and Present,* ed. Robert A. Divine (New York: Longman, 2001).

15 Talcott Parsons, "An Analytic Approach to the Theory of Social Stratification," in *Essays in Sociological Theory,* rev. ed. (Glencoe, Ill., Free Press, 1954).

16 G. William Domhoff, *Who Rules America?* (Englewood Cliffs: Prentice- Hall, 1967); G. William Domhoff, *The Higher Circles: The Governing Class in America* (New York: Random House, 1970).

17 Erik Olin Wright, "A General Framework for the Analysis of Class Structure," in *The Debate on Classes* (London: Verso, 1989). The term "analysis" in the title refers not to the commonsense usage but to the precepts of the school known as analytic Marxism, whose other major figures are John Roemer and Adam Przeworski. In an attempt to purge marxism of its speculative and utopian problems, the fundamental project of this tendency is to subject the propositions that constitute the body of historical materialism to a realist criterion—that is, the general correspondence between its concepts and "reality." Further, they wish to test all theoretical claims according to the rules of empirical evidence, especially claims of falsification. Hence history is compressed into categories, class struggles into class maps.

18 Pierre Bourdieu, "What Makes a Social Class?" *Berkeley Journal of Sociology* (1998): 4.

19 Ibid.

20 Pierre Bourdieu, *Distinction: A Social Critique of the Judgment of Taste,* trans. Richard Nice (Cambridge: Harvard University Press, 1984), 245.

21 Ibid., 315–16 (emphasis added); Pierre Bourdieu and Jean-Claude Passeron, *Reproduction in Education, Society and Culture,* trans. Richard Nice (Beverly Hills: Sage Publications, 1977).

22 Lefebvre, *Production of Space.*

23 Bourdieu, *Distinction; Reproduction in Education, Society and Culture.*

24 Bourdieu, "What Makes a Social Class?" 10.

25 Daniel Foss and Ralph Larkin, *Beyond Revolution: A New Theory of Social Movements* (South Hadley, Mass.: Bergin and Garvey, 1986).

26 J. Craig Jenkins and Kevin Licht, "Class Analysis and Social Movements: A Critique and Reformulation," in John R. Hall, ed., *Reworking Class* (Ithaca: Cornell University Press, 1997).

27 Ronald Lawson, ed., with the assistance of Mark Naison, *The Tenant Movement in New York City, 1904–1984* (New Brunswick, N.J.: Rutgers University Press, 1986).

28 Margaret R. Somers, "Deconstructing and Reconstructing Class Formation Theory: Narrativity, Relational Analysis, and Social Theory," in Hall, ed., *Reworking Class.*

29 The concept of the political unconscious was suggested by Fredric Jameson in *The Political Unconscious* (Ithaca: Cornell University Press, 1981); I take the concept of the cultural unconscious from Ellen Willis. Both suggest that history, politics, and culture owe as much or more to the unconscious as they do to rational choices. But the unconscious can be understood as irrational only if we take that in our actions of which we are aware as normative.

30 C. Wright Mills, *White Collar: The American Middle Classes* (New York: Oxford University Press, 1951); Magali Sarfatti Larson, *The Rise of Professionalism: A Sociological Analysis* (Berkeley and Los Angeles: University of California Press, 1977).

31 Erik Olin Wright, "Rethinking, Once Again, the Concept of Class Structure," in Hall, ed., *Reworking Class.* The concept was originally developed in Erik Olin Wright, *Class, Crisis and the State* (London: New Left Books, 1978).

32 Parsons, *Essays in Sociological Theory,* 325.

33 The major works having bearing on this debate are André Gorz, *Strategy for Labor,* trans. Martin A. Nicolaus and Victoria Ortiz (Boston: Beacon Press, 1967); Serge Mallet, *The New Working Class,* trans. André Shepherd and Bob Shepherd (Nottingham: Spokesman Books, 1975); Nicos Poulantzas, *Political Power and Social Classes,* trans. Timothy O'Hagan (London: New Left Books, 1973).

34 Antonio Negri, *The Politics of Subversion* (London: Polity Press, 1989).

35 Karl Marx, "The 18th Brumaire of Louis Napoleon," in *Selected Works,* vol. 2 (New York: International Publishers, 1964), 414–15.

36 Ibid., 415.

37 Ibid., 318.

38 Walter Benjamin, "Theses on the Philosophy of History," in *Illuminations,* ed. Hannah Arendt, trans. Harry Zohn (New York: Schocken Books, 1969), 255.

39 Many of the movements against capitalist globalization today and in the 1960s have been sustained by unwaged or marginally waged workers. In the late 1990s, demographic factors such as an aging population and the fact that more than half of people between ages eighteen and twenty-five were enrolled in institutions of higher education constituted some of the material conditions for the growth of political and social protest. At the same time, in a period of relatively full employment, pressures to enter the paid labor force thwarted many neighborhood-based movements, and the two- and three-job phenomenon acted as a counterforce to labor activism, especially trade union organizing. Many workers simply lacked the time to participate as rank-and-file leaders of organizing campaigns.

40 For a further elaboration of these developments, see chapter 6 below.

41 Raymond Williams, *The Country and the City* (New York: Oxford University Press, 1973).

3. HISTORY AND CLASS THEORY

1 Benedict Anderson, *Imagined Communities: Reflections on the Origin and Spread of Nationalism* (London: Verso, 1983).

2 Edward Hallett Carr, *The Bolshevik Revolution, 1917–1923,* 3 vols. (London: Macmillan, 1950–53).

3 Philip S. Foner, *History of the Labor Movement in the United States,* vol. 10 (1947; New York: International Publishers, 1994).

4 Harry Braverman, *Labor and Monopoly Capital: The Degradation of Work in the Twentieth Century* (New York: Monthly Review Press, 1974); Stephen Meyer, *The Five Dollar Day: Labor Management and Social Control in the Ford Motor Company, 1908–1921* (Albany: State University of New York Press, 1981).

5 Frederick Winslow Taylor, *Principles of Scientific Management* (New York: Harper and Brothers, 1911); Meyer, *Five Dollar Day.*

6 Siegfried Kracauer, *Die Angestellten* [Office Workers] Shriften 1 Die Sociologie als Wissenshaft; Emil Lederer and Jacob Marshak, *The New Middle Class,* trans. S. Ellison (New York: Works Progress Administration, 1937). Of course the most comprehensive theoretical work on various white-collar categories remains C. Wright Mills's *White Collar: The American Middle Classes* (New York: Oxford University Press, 1951).

7 Theodor Adorno et al., *The Authoritarian Personality* (New York: Harper, 1950). This work, perhaps the largest empirical study of the authoritarian character ever conducted in the American context, was, according to its authors, "strongly influenced" by Wilhelm Reich's *The Mass Psychology of Fascism* and Erich Fromm's *Escape From Freedom,* among others (Adorno, 31). One of the more significant findings of the work is the correlation between conservative ideology and ethnocentrism and its corollaries: anti-Semitism, racism, and opposition to trade unions (131).

8 Georges Sorel, *Reflections on Violence,* trans. T. E. Hulme (New York: P. Smith, 1941); Oswald Spengler, *The Decline of the West* (New York: Knopf, 1932). Sorel's later elective affinity to fascism should not detract from his concept of revolutionary myth, which he advanced within the framework of a left-wing political strategy. But Spengler had no affinity to fascism. His work was intended to point out the dogmatism of Enlightenment thought, not to argue for a new, repressive social and political order.

9 Georgi Dimitrov, *The United Front Against Fascism and War* (New York: Workers Library, 1935).

10 Max Horkheimer, "The Authoritarian State," in Andrew Arato and Eike Gebhardt, eds., *The Essential Frankfurt School Reader* (New York: Urizen Books, 1978).

11 Max Horkheimer, *Critical Theory: Selected Essays,* trans. Matthew J. O'Connell et al. (New York: Continuum, 1982), 54.

12 Wilhelm Reich, *Mass Psychology of Fascism,* trans. Theodore P. Wolfe (New York: Orgone Institute Press, 1946).

13 Herbert Marcuse, *Technology, War and Fascism* (New York: Routledge, 1998), 220.

14 Herbert Marcuse, *One Dimensional Man* (Boston: Beacon Press, 1964), 3:4. "Total administration" signifies the reduction of all social problems to technical problems, the instrumentalization of thought, and the reduction of language to its operational modes. According to Marcuse, the language of one-dimensionality, which is the condition for total administration, is marked by the obliteration of distinctions, particularly that between thought and reality.

15 Philip S. Foner, *History of the Labor Movement in the United States,* vol. 10 (New York: International Publishers, 1994); Janet Christine Irons, "Testing the New Deal: The General Strike of 1934" (Ph.D. diss., Duke University, 1988).

16 Robert McElvaine, chapter 7 of *The Great Depression: America, 1929–1941* (New York: Times Books, 1984). McElvaine demonstrates how conservative Roosevelt's first proposals for dealing with the crisis were: "In the light both of what has been said here about the changing values of the American people and of the New Deal actions that subsequently won public approval, it may seem incongruous that a program so conservative that it would have pleased Calvin Coolidge and Ronald Reagan should have lifted the nation's spirits." McElvaine's explanation was, in part, based on Roosevelt's personality. This indeed may have been a significant factor, especially as compared to the personality of his predecessor, Herbert Clark Hoover, who, to be generous, was not among the presidency's great communicators.

17 Art Preis, *Labor's Giant Step: Twenty Years of the CIO* (New York: Pioneer Publishers, 1964).

18 As Roosevelt took office in March 1933, trade unions were at or close to their lowest level, organizationally and politically, since the 1890s. AFL affiliates organized barely 3 percent of the labor force and, in many cases, union membership signified no real power at the workplace. Without collective bargaining agreements with employers, many unions managed to keep the institution alive but barely afloat. This was true not only of mass production industries such as steel and auto, but also of the once-powerful building trades unions. Only the mineworkers, clothing, and ladies' garment workers in production industries and some crafts, for example, truck drivers and plumbers, still had any semblance of union organization. Although for symbolic and historical considerations Roosevelt felt obliged to nod at workers' rights, there was no real pressure yet to do more than that.

19 Preis, *Labor's Giant Step.*

20 The best account of the Minneapolis Teamsters' strike provides an urban and political context for the struggle: Charles R. Walker, *American City: A Rank-and-File History* (New York: Farrar and Rinehart, 1937). For the Toledo Auto-Lite strike, see Preis, *Labor's Giant Step.* For the San Francisco longshore workers and general strikes, see Irving Bernstein, *The Turbulent Years: A History of the American Worker, 1933–1941* (Boston: Houghton Mifflin, 1970). A contemporary chronicle of the auto workers' struggles during the depression decade by a firsthand observer is Henry Kraus, *The Many and the Few,* 2d ed. (Urbana: University of Illinois Press, 1985). Perhaps the premier account of the events of this period as they affected a major American city is Lizabeth Cohen, *Making a New Deal: Industrial Workers in Chicago, 1919–1939* (Cambridge: Cambridge University Press, 1990). Not confining her scope to the industrial struggles, especially in the city's leading industries—steel, packing, and agricultural implements—Cohen addresses such issues as ethnicity, "mass culture," and radicalism in order to understand how labor's upsurge was played out and ultimately resolved. Most important, she provides powerful narratives and other forms of evidence in support of the view that the New Deal was made by the workers themselves as well as by the Roosevelt administration.

21 Irons, *Testing the New Deal.*

22 Karl Klare, "Judicial Deradicalization of the Wagner Act and the Origins of Modern Legal Consciousness," *Minnesota Law Review* 62 (1978): 265–339; Karl Klare, "Labor Law as Ideology: Toward a New Historiography of Collective Bargaining Law," *Industrial Relations Law Journal* 4:450–82; Katherine Van Wezel Stone, "The Post-War Paradigm in American Labor Law," *Yale Law Journal* 90, no. 7 (1981): 1509–80. Klare and Stone both claim that the creation of the NLRA, combined with the subsequent record of judicial decisions, was part of a long historical effort by the government to regulate labor, while tilting the law heavily toward the side of employers. In "Judicial Deradicalization," Klare goes further to argue that the courts reinterpreted the law, violating its original radical intent to redress the balance between workers and their employers. The authors have adduced impressive evidence for the proposition that judicial decisions have acted to restrict the purview of collective bargaining, thereby awarding employers greater freedom to disregard the bid of workers and their unions for a stronger voice in industrial decision making.

23 Arthur M. Schlesinger Jr., *The Coming of the New Deal* (Boston: Houghton Mifflin, 1988).

24 Steve Fraser, *Labor Will Rule: Sidney Hillman and the Rise of American Labor* (New York: Free Press, 1991). On the strength of Fraser's account, it can plausibly be argued that in the 1920s, the Amalgamated Clothing Workers' union's pioneering innovations in labor-management relations paved the way for the New Deal's labor policy and played an important role in providing an alternative ideology to that of the marxist left and to the subsequent politics of class formation and class struggle.

25 Melvin Dubofsky and Warren Van Tine, *John L. Lewis: A Biography,* abridged ed. (Urbana: University of Illinois Press, 1986), 152.

26 At the end of the era of tumultuous but exhilarating years of mass strikes begun in 1938, the CIO settled down to institution building. There were some unfinished organizing tasks such as Ford Motor Co., some smaller steel corporations, and, of course, the huge textile industry in the South. But wartime collaboration with the government and the atmosphere of the Cold War tempered the leadership's will to fight—except, with the assistance of federal security agencies, to rid themselves of the Communists. After that there was nothing left to do but merge with the AFL.

27 Histories of the American Communist Party reflect the contentiousness that has surrounded its existence from the party's founding in 1919 to its virtual demise after Khruschev's report at the Twentieth Congress of the Soviet Communist Party in 1956. Critical treatments include Irving Howe and Lewis Coser, *The American Communist Party: A Critical History* (New York: Praeger Publishers, 1962); and Harvey Klehr, *The Heyday of American Communism: The Depression Decade* (New York: Basic Books, 1984). Among the sympathetic treatments is Otanelli M. Fraser, *The Communist Party of the United States: From the Depression to World War II* (New Brunswick, N.J.: Rutgers University Press, 1991). Edward Johanningsmeier, *Forging American Communism: The Life of William Z. Foster* (Princeton: Princeton University Press, 1994), is much more than a biography. Its trenchant account of the strategic debates within the party are unique in the literature. A defense of the party's role in the labor movement can be found in Roger Keeran, *The Communist Party and the Auto Workers Unions* (Bloomington: Indiana University Press, 1980). For a critical but balanced treatment, see Bert Cochran, *Labor and Communism: The Conflict that Shaped American Unions* (Princeton: Princeton University Press, 1977).

28 Klare, "Judicial Deradicalization of the Wagner Act."

29 Martin Glaberman, *Wartime Strikes: The Struggle Against the No-Strike Pledge in the UAW during World War II* (Detroit: Bewick Editions, 1980); Nelson Lichtenstein, *Labor's War at Home: The CIO in World War II* (Cambridge: Cambridge University Press, 1982); Jeremy Brecher, *Strike!* (Boston: South End Press, 2000).

30 Brecher, *Strike!*

31 Labor's ability to forge a viable strategy to arrest, let alone reverse, its loss of political power and public prestige was undoubtedly hurt by the onset of the Cold War. When they agreed to abide by the government's agenda of placing the fight against Communism ahead of all other concerns, including their own members' economic and social needs, unions became relatively helpless to resist the right's relentless attacks. Unions also faced other obstacles, equally of their own making. The tasks of institutionalization made necessary by the demands of the labor relations laws and the collective bargaining agreements meant that unions had to create a bureaucracy to run their day-to-day affairs. This took precedence over organizing and even political interventions. Taken together, post–World War II American unions had become ideological state apparatuses, drained of their capacity for resistance and for independent political action.

32 Vincent Bugliosi, *The Betrayal of America: How the Supreme Court Undermined the Constitution and Chose Our President* (New York: Thunder's Mouth Press/Nation Books, 2001).

4. DOES THE UNITED STATES HAVE A RULING CLASS?

1 Karl Marx, *Political and Social Writings,* ed. Lewis Feuer (New York: Doubleday, 1963), 8.

2 Frederick Engels, preface, in Feuer, ed., *Political and Social Writings*.

3 Marx, ibid., 328.

4 The decline of the family farm as well as the sharp reduction in the number of corporate farms has weakened the national legislative and political power of major farm organizations such as the Farm Bureau, the Grange, and the National Farmers' Union. The latter has been reduced to a few local groups, especially in Iowa. But their social weight has not suffered a commensurate decline. These organizations are still important in perhaps fifteen states with a large number of electoral votes and, since the distribution of Senate and House seats continues to hurt states with much larger populations and farm products comprise a substantial portion of commodity exports, corporate farms are still a major factor in national politics.

5 Kirkpatrick Sale, *Power Shift: The Rise of the Southern Rim and Its Challenge to the Eastern Establishment* (New York: Random House, 1974).

6 C. Wright Mills, *The Power Elite* (New York: Oxford University Press, 1956).

7 Robert Dahl, *Who Governs?* (New Haven: Yale University Press, 1961).

8 Neither the federal government nor local governments have ever permitted the so-called free market to function without their assistance. And in fact, business interests have always demanded public support. It is only the form of support that varies. For example, since 1938 the military budget has been a major factor in the reproduction of the U.S. economy. With the exception of nuclear weapons, the government fulfills its military needs by means of contracts with privately held corporations. In 2001, military expenditures accounted for about 20 percent of the federal budget, and for more than six decades, military spending has been the largest category in the budget and the most important aspect of fiscal economic policy, although as a proportion of the gross domestic product it has declined since the collapse of the Soviet Union. But the public sector provides other major subsidies to the private sector: money for roads and other public building; farm subsidies; and contracts for innumerable federal, state, and local services, many of which were once performed by public employees. In this respect the call from market libertarians to shrink the government must be understood to refer chiefly to social welfare expenditures. Few have proposed to seriously reduce military spending or the tens of billions of dollars appropriated by Congress every year to build and repair roads.

9 Ernesto Laclau and Chantal Mouffe, *Hegemony and Socialist Strategy,* trans. Winston Moore and Paul Commack (London: Verso, 1985).

10 Stephen Steinberg, *The Ethnic Myth: Race, Ethnicity and Class in America* (Boston: Beacon Press, 1989); Michael Omi and Howard Winant, *Racial Formation in the United States: From the 1960s to the 1990s* (New York: Routledge, 1994).

11 For an empirical study of class segregation in suburbs, see Ralph Larkin, *Suburban Youth in a Time of Cultural Crisis* (New York: Oxford University Press, 1979).

12 William Dobriner, *Class in Suburbia* (Englewood Cliffs: Prentice-Hall, 1963).

13 Michael Goldfield, *The Color of Politics: Race and the Mainsprings of American Politics* (New York: New Press, 1997).

14 Stanley Aronowitz, *From the Ashes of the Old: American Labor and America's Future* (Boston: Houghton Mifflin, 1998).

15 Stanley Aronowitz, *The Knowledge Factory* (Boston: Beacon Press, 2000); Sheila Slaughter and Larry L. Leslie, *Academic Capitalism: Politics, Policies, and the Entrepreneurial University* (Baltimore: Johns Hopkins University Press, 1997).

16 Richard Berke, "Examining the Vote: Lieberman Puts Democrats in Retreat on Military Vote," *New York Times,* 15 July 2001.

17 Matthew Josephson, *The Robber Barons: The Great American Capitalists, 1861–1901* (New York: Harcourt, Brace, and World, 1962); Matthew Josephson, *The President Makers* (New York: Harcourt, Brace, 1940).

18 Adolph A. Berle and Gardner C. Means, *The Modern Corporation and Private Property* (New York: Macmillan, 1939); James Burnham, *The Managerial Revolution* (New York: John Day, 1941).

19 Ida Tarbell, *History of the Standard Oil Company;* Henry Demarest Lloyd, *Wealth Against Commonwealth;* Gustavus Myers, *The History of Great American Fortunes* (New York: Modern Library, 1936).

20 Lincoln Steffens, *The Shame of the Cities.*

21 Karl Polanyi, *The Great Transformation* (New York: Farrar and Rinehart, 1944).

22 Richard Drinnon, *Facing West: The Metaphysics of Indian-Hating and Empire-Building* (New York: New American Library, 1980).

23 Kenneth Stampp, *The Peculiar Institution: Slavery in the Ante-Bellum South* (New York: Knopf, 1968); Eugene D. Genovese, *The World the Slaveholders Made* (New York: Vintage Books, 1971).

24 Charles A. Beard and Mary R. Beard, *The Rise of American Civilization*, 2 vols. (New York: Macmillan, 1927).

25 Eugene D. Genovese, *Roll, Jordan, Roll: The World the Slaves Made* (New York: Pantheon Books, 1974); Eric Foner, *Reconstruction: America's Unfinished Revolution, 1863–1877* (New York: Harper and Row, 1988); W. E. B. Du Bois, *Black Reconstruction in America* (New York: Atheneum, 1962).

26 Gabriel Kolko, *Railroads and Regulation, 1877–1916* (Princeton: Princeton University Press, 1965); William Appleman Williams, *The Contours of American History* (Cleveland: World, 1961).

27 Lawrence Goodwyn, *Democratic Promise: The Populist Moment in America* (New York: Oxford University Press, 1976); Scott G. McNall, *The Road to Rebellion: Class Formation and Kansas Populism, 1865–1900* (Chicago: University of Chicago Press, 1988).

28 Lloyd C. Gardner, *Economic Aspects of New Deal Diplomacy* (Madison: University of Wisconsin Press, 1964).

29 Trevor Williams and T. K. Derry, *A Short History of Twentieth-Century Technology* (Oxford: Clarendon Press, 1982).

30 For most of the 1930s and the wartime years, the government had built airports under the rubric of national defense. Needless to say, after the New Deal, not only did the state finance public works, but it also managed and oversaw their construction. During this period the federal government directly hired hundreds of thousands of workers to build roads, post offices, libraries, and other public buildings, and to clean and refurbish national parks. When the two emergencies were declared over in the late 1940s, the state reverted to supporting private builders.

5. NATIONAL AND INTERNATIONAL BLOCS

1 C. Wright Mills, *The Power Elite* (New York: Oxford University Press, 1956).

2 Martin Shaw, *Theory of the Global State: Globality as an Unfinished Revolution* (New York: Cambridge University Press, 2000); Sol Yurick, *The Global Metastate* (New York: Autonomedia, 1993); Michael Hardt and Antonio Negri, *Empire* (Cambridge: Harvard University Press, 2000).

3 Stanley Aronowitz, *False Promises: The Shaping of American Working-Class Consciousness* (Durham: Duke University Press, 1992).

4 Nelson Lichtenstein, *The Most Dangerous Man in Detroit: Walter Reuther and the Fate of American Labor* (New York: Basic Books, 1995). Within a sympathetic account of Reuther's career, Lichtenstein nevertheless notes that despite his liberalism Reuther "never strayed far from the consensus that shaped American foreign policy in those years" (the early fifties) (334). Reuther's fealty led him, in 1950, to negotiate an unprecedented five-year agreement with General Motors which, among other provisions, made the wartime no-strike pledge an article of faith in the new collaborative labor relations environment he sought to establish. Within a few years, auto workers were engaged in a plethora of unauthorized strikes that, by the next agreement, forced the union leadership to modify the no-strike provision by permitting strikes over health and safety and work rule issues.

5 Hardt and Negri, *Empire.*

6 Antonio Negri, *The Politics of Subversion,* trans. James Newell (Cambridge, Mass.: B. Blackwell, 1989), chap. 3.

7 It may be difficult for some to remember the impact of the events of 1968 on the structure of political power, not only in France but in the United States and Mexico as well. The anti–Vietnam War movement may not have been solely responsible for President Lyndon Johnson's decision not to seek a second full term, but it did play an enormous role in forcing his departure. When the progressive Mexican president Luis Echeverría ordered troops to fire on protesting students in the nation's largest university (UNAM), the seeds were planted for what Vicente Fox later reaped in 2000: the removal from power of the PRI, which had ruled Mexico for more than sixty years.

8 Robert B. Reich, secretary of labor for most of the Clinton administration, delivered many speeches that argued for the advent of the "symbolic analyst" as the characteristic worker of the New Economy. His perspective was consonant with that of many who were absolutely convinced that knowledge had displaced manual labor. Needless to say, he was only partially correct.

9 *New York Times,* 23 July 2001.

10 William Greider, "A Dangerous Crank," *The Nation,* 16 July 2001.

11 United Nations Environment Programme, "Global Issues", chap. 2 in *Global Environment Outlook 2000* (New York, 2000).

6. THE NEW SOCIAL MOVEMENTS AND CLASS

1 Stuart Hall, "Cultural Studies: Theoretical Legacies," in Cary Nelson, Lawrence Grossberg, and Paul Treichler, eds., *Cultural Studies* (New York: Routledge, 1992).

2 Christopher Hill, *Society and Puritanism in Pre-Revolutionary England* (New York: Schocken Books, 1964); Christopher Hill, *Puritanism and Revolution: Studies in Interpretation of the English Revolution of the 17th Century* (New York: Schocken Books, 1964).

3 John Locke, *Two Treatises of Government,* ed. Peter Laslett (Cambridge: Cambridge University Press, 1960).

4 E. P. Thompson, *The Making of the English Working Class* (New York: Pantheon Books, 1963).

5 Dorothy Thompson, *The Chartists: Popular Politics in the Industrial Revolution* (New York: Pantheon Books, 1984).

6 Aileen S. Kraditor, *The Ideas of the Woman Suffrage Movement, 1890–1920* (New York: Columbia University Press, 1965); for the relation of the socialists to women's suffrage, see chap. 6 in Mari Jo Buhle, *Women and American Socialism, 1780–1920* (Urbana: University of Illinois Press, 1981).

7 Before the 1960s, women's participation in the labor movement was, in the main, confined to the needle and retail trades, where women predominated in the labor force. While hundreds of thousands of women entered industrial plants during World War II, as soon as the war ended they were displaced by returning veterans and sexist practices. But with the unionization of the expanded public service workforce, especially teachers, postal workers, and clerical and other administrative workers in state, county, and municipal governments, in addition to the growth of unionism in supermarkets, hotels, and other retail services, women became a significant presence in some of the largest unions in the AFL-CIO. The contemporary history of the relation of blacks to unionism begins with their recruitment by employers as strikebreakers during the first two decades of the twentieth century. But in the 1920s and 1930s, they constituted a solid and permanent formation in the industrial workforce, especially in packing, auto, and steel. This period witnessed the emergence of the Brotherhood of Sleeping Car Porters, a small but influential union under the leadership of A. Phillip Randolph, Benjamin Caruthers, and others. After World War II, blacks became the core and the most militant fraction of many urban branches of the U.S. Postal Service and of the rapidly growing American Federation of State, County, and Municipal Employees, which is today the largest affiliate of the AFL-CIO and second among unions in size only to the National Education Association, the leading teachers' union.

8 Eric Foner, *Free Soil, Free Labor, Free Men: The Ideology of the Republican Party Before the Civil War* (New York: Oxford University Press, 1970); Foner, *Reconstruction: America's Unfinished Revolution: 1863–1877* (New York: Harper and Row, 1988).

9 Mark Naison, "The Communist Party in Harlem, 1926–1936" (Ph.D. diss., Columbia University, 1975); A. J. Muste, *The Essays of A. J. Muste,* ed. Nat Hentoff (Indianapolis and New York: Bobbs Merrill, Co., 1967); Bayard Rustin, *Down the Line: The Collected Writings* (Chicago: Quadrangle Books, 1971); see especially sections 1 and 2 for the pacifist contribution to the early civil rights movement.

10 Harvard Sitkoff, *A New Deal for Blacks* (New York: Oxford University Press, 1978); Harvard Sitkoff, *The Struggle for Black Equality* (New York: Oxford University Press, 1980).

11 Aldon Morris, *The Origins of the Civil Rights Movement* (New York: Free Press, 1984); Charles Payne, *I've Got the Light of Freedom: The Organizing Tradition and the Mississippi Freedom Struggle* (Berkeley and Los Angeles: University of California Press, 1995); Jervis Anderson, *A. Phillip Randolph: A Biography* (Berkeley and Los Angeles: University of California Press, 1987).

12 Roberto Unger and Cornel West, *Progressivism and the Future of American Politics* (Boston: Beacon Press, 1999).

13 William Burroughs, *The Air-Conditioned Nightmare* (New York: Grover Press, 1978).

14 Isaiah Berlin, "Two Concepts of Liberty," in Michael Sandel, ed., *Liberalism and Its Critics* (New York: New York University Press, 1984).

15 Alice Echols, *Daring To Be Bad: Radical Feminism in America* (Minneapolis: University of Minnesota Press, 1990), is a convincing account of the crucial role of radical women in the origins and development of the "second wave" feminist movement of the 1960s and 1970s.

16 Murray Bookchin, *The Ecology of Freedom* (Bay City, Wash.: Cheshire Books, 1983); Andrew Light, ed., *Social Ecology Beyond Bookchin* (New York: Guilford Press, 1997), is a series of critical articles, from widely divergent viewpoints, of Bookchin's concept of social ecology. Some criticize the concept itself; others, although sympathetic, try to extend Bookchin's thought into territory he himself has not visited.

17 C. Wright Mills, "Letter to the New Left," in Irving Louis Horowitz, ed., *Power, Politics and People: The Collected Essays of C. Wright Mills* (New York: Oxford University Press, 1963); Students for a Democratic Society, *The Port Huron Statement* (1962).

18 Shulamith Firestone, *The Dialectic of Sex: Toward Feminist Revolution* (New York: William Morrow, 1970).

19 Lucien Truscott IV, "Gay Power Comes to Sheridan Square," *Village Voice,* 3 July 1969. This article is the best of contemporary accounts of the event. The *New York Times* and the *New York Post* gave only perfunctory reports. For the sexual freedom movement of gays and lesbians, Stonewall enjoys the same status of turning point that the Montgomery bus boycott did for the Black Freedom Movement.

20 Todd Gitlin, *The Sixties: Years of Hope, Days of Rage* (New York: Bantam Books, 1993).

21 By the term "center-right", I mean to evoke the tendency of the Democratic Party, since the 1980s, to adopt the program of the Democratic Leadership Council, founded by Bill Clinton, Al Gore, and others, who argued that the party's fall from the White House since 1968—Jimmy Carter's single term excepted—was due to its old-fashioned adherence to New Deal-Fair Deal Keynesian policies. These attempted to address economic and social problems through deficit spending; in fact, they were the core of the liberals' doctrine that the market was not capable of self-adjustment and that therefore fiscal policies were the key to prosperity. While the Democrats under Clinton retained the social liberal policies foisted upon them by the civil rights, environmental, disabled, and women's movements, they became converts to neoliberalism, a dogma that entailed primary reliance on supply-side public economics: fiscal austerity, tax relief for investors, balanced budgets, and the like.

22 Warren Belasco, *Appetite for Change: How the Counterculture Took on the Food Industry, 1966–1988* (New York: Pantheon Books, 1989).

23 The bureaucratization of social movements, including the unions, has provoked heated debate among their supporters. To the charge that the growth of a permanent class of executive staff in many of these organizations stifles membership initiative and autonomy, rather than viewing bureaucracy as an evil, some have argued that bureaucracy is a natural consequence of the efforts of organizations to stabilize after periods of organizing and protests. The debate was rehearsed in Stanley Aronowitz, "On Union Democracy," in *The Last Good Job in America: Work and Education in the New Global Technoculture* (Lanham, Md.: Rowman and Littlefield, 2001); also in Steve Fraser, "Is Democracy Good for Unions?" *Dissent,* Summer 1998.

24 Gustav Le Bon, *The Crowd: A Study of the Popular Mind* (New York: Ballantine Books, 1969); Sigmund Freud, *Group Psychology and the Analysis of the Ego* (New York: Liveright, 1951).

25 The theory of social movements derives originally from the historical writings of Karl Marx. In its sociological incarnation, particularly in the United States, under the influence of Talcott Parsons and functionist theory, social movements have come to designate precisely those manifestations of group action that are not linked to the labor movement and to the workplace. "Collective action" therefore is presumed to require that which the labor movement presupposes: resources with which to mobilize constituents and to secure political influence, if not power. Thus much of the literature is dedicated to delineating the degree to which movements can succeed in the wake of their relative resource deprivation. For a representative sampling: Sidney Tarrow, *Power in Movement: Social Movements, Collective Action, and Politics* (Cambridge: Cambridge University Press, 1994); William Gamson, *The Strategy of Social Protest,* 2d ed. (Belmont, Calif.: Wadsworth, 1990); Charles Tilly, *From Mobilization to Revolution* (Reading, Mass.: Addison Wesley, 1978); Mayer N. Zald and John D. McCarthy, *Social Movements in an Organizational Society* (New Brunswick: Transaction Books, 1987).

26 Antonio Gramsci, *Selections from the Prison Notebooks,* trans. and ed. Quintin Hoare and Geoffrey Newell (New York: International Publishers, 1971).

27 Judith Butler, *Gender Trouble* (New York: Routledge, 1995).

28 Aronowitz, "On Union Democracy."

29 The best summary of Foucault's intellectual position, including his perspective on history, may be Michel Foucault, *The History of Sexuality,* vol. 1: *An Introduction,* part four (New York: Vintage Books, 1980); also Michel Foucault, "Two Lectures," in *Power/Knowledge: Selected Interviews and Other Writings 1972–1977,* ed. Colin Gordon (New York: Pantheon Books, 1980).

30 Isaiah Berlin, "Two Concepts of Liberty," in Michael Sandel, ed., *Liberalism and Its Critics*. This immensely influential essay has advanced the notion that only "negative" liberty is plausible because it refers to the right of individuals to privacy, speech, and the like. The concept of "positive" liberty, which presupposes that the collective has common interests to create and sustain a series of values that may ground social conduct and social institutions, Berlin disdains because it leads almost inevitably to totalitarian or authoritarian results. Thus the concept of freedom is conflated with liberty. For a view that criticizes Berlin for antisociological concepts and defends a positive concept, see Orlando Patterson, *Freedom in the Making of Western Culture* (New York: Basic Books, 1991).

31 Robert Gottlieb, Gerry Tenney, and David Gilbert, "Toward a Theory of Social Change in America," *New Left Notes,* 22 May 1967.

32 Orlando Patterson, *Slavery and Social Death* (Cambridge: Harvard University Press, 1983). Patterson's powerful argument is that oppression of a social formation presupposes the deracination of its members by the rulers. For this reason, as we shall see in chapter 8, collective memory is not merely an important cultural posit but a weapon of the struggle for collective freedom.

33 Georges Canguilhem, *The Normal and the Pathological,* trans. Carolyn R. Fawcett (New York: Zone Books, 1989).

34 William Julius Wilson, *When Work Disappears* (Chicago: University of Chicago Press, 1995).

35 The United Way Report on Regional Living Standards.

7. ECOLOGY AND CLASS

1 Stephen M. Schneider, *Global Warming: Are We Entering the Greenhouse Century?* (New York: Vintage Books, 1990): "Human vulnerability to changes in climate depends as much on how our societies are organized as on the nature of the climate change itself" (65). Schneider writes as the head of Interdisciplinary Climate Systems at the National Center for Atmospheric Research.

2 William Kapp, *Social Costs, Economic Development and Environmental Disruption* (Lanham, Md.: University Press of America, 1951).

3 In 2001, Christine Todd Whitman, head of the federal Environmental Protection Agency, ordered the Hudson River cleanup after incontrovertible evidence was adduced to show that the presence of PCPs and other pollutants resulted from decades of dumping by General Electric. The corporation fought for years to prevent the decision, right up until the final hour. It waged a campaign in upstate New York communities to claim that the river would be damaged by the cleanup. Some residents were fearful but most favored the cleanup.

4 English poets at the turn of the nineteenth century were suffused with anger and sorrow as they prowled what Blake called "each dirty street" of London "near where the dirty Thames does flow / And mark in every face I meet / Marks of Weakness, marks of woe." William Blake, "London," *Complete Writings,* ed. Geoffrey Keynes (London: Oxford University Press, 1969). The writings of Percy Bysshe Shelley and Thomas Hood express similar sentiments.

5 Lester Frank Ward, *Pure Sociology.*

6 Ibid.

7 Henry George, *Progress and Poverty* (New York: Robert Schalkenbach Foundation, 1949).

8 Alonzo Hamby, *Beyond the New Deal: Harry S. Truman and American Liberalism* (New York: Columbia University Press, 1973), 71–74.

9 Rachel Carson, *Silent Spring* (Boston: Houghton Mifflin, 1962); Murray Bookchin, *Our Synthetic Environment,* rev. ed. (New York: Harper Colophon Books, 1974). This book was first published in 1962 under the pseudonym of Lewis Herbers. Bookchin's prescience in this work extends to his insistence that cancer is not an individual disease but the outcome of a multiplicity of influences, not the least of which is environmental pollution, including chemical additives in food and carcinogens in water and air.

10 Secretary Paul O'Neill's claim that nuclear energy plants were perfectly safe came before the events of September 11. After the World Trade Center disaster, residents of Westchester County insisted on a public hearing to determine whether conditions were unsafe at the nearby Indian Point Reactor. At public hearings held in October the outcry was sufficient to cast doubt that the plant would reopen. Meanwhile, *The New Republic*—whose evolution into a neoconservative journal of opinion over the past three decades has been as steady as it has been stunning—editorialized favorably about a proposal to open federal lands in North Alaska to oil development. "Go Ahead, Drill," *The New Republic,* 20 August 2001. The editorial's main argument is that since the protected area is relatively small and underutilized for recreation, why not undertake exploration?

11 John Sweeney's remarks were made several times, notably in his keynote speech at the Las Vegas AFL-CIO convention in December 2001.

12 Lewis Mumford, *Technics and Civilization* (1934; New York: Harcourt Brace and Company, 1963).

13 Ibid., 168.

14 Ibid., 170.

15 Ibid., 172.

16 Ibid., 173.

17 Capital's answer to complaints deriving from labor's subordination has focused on two claims: technological improvements will expand the social surplus enough to provide a rising living standard for nearly all; and wars, which until recently were times of nearly full employment in part because many able-bodied men were subject to conscription. These arguments have lost their force in an era of small wars and volunteer armed forces and at a time when technology seems, over the long run, to destroy more jobs than it creates.

18 Mumford, *Technics and Civilization,* 179–81.

19 Spain has been the site of several important experiments in workers' and peasants' cooperatives, among them Mondragón, which may be the most vertically integrated. Mondragón is not only a producers' cooperative; it also owns a bank and controls its own distribution and marketing. It has prospered even as others have failed or, to be more exact, have mutated into enterprises owned by collective capitalists that, in turn, exploit wage labor. This mutation seems to have affected the Israeli kibbutz movement, which embraced enterprises from diverse ideological perspectives, ranging from religious, labor Zionists to left-wing socialists who tried to install soviets on the arid desert land of Palestine in the 1920s. By the 1950s many of them became vertically integrated but hired substantial numbers of Arab Palestinians to perform wage labor, workers who, in nearly all instances, were excluded from the institutions of kibbutz governance.

20 Robert A. Caro, *The Power Broker* (New York: Knopf, 1974). Caro estimates that

Moses' prodigious development programs, especially highways, "threw 250,000 people out of their homes" throughout the country (19).

21 In the 1950s and 1960s, I was involved in community-based movements and coalitions that battled urban renewal in Moses' model (although not all of them directly supervised by Moses himself). As a resident of West Harlem in the early 1950s, I was a member of the tenants' association that fought the Morningside Gardens plan. When I was active in Newark's Clinton Hill Neighborhood Council, we defeated the city administration's proposal to build a light industrial park in the middle of the neighborhood because it would have thrown out about fifteen hundred families. In the mid-1960s, while a resident of the Upper West Side, I joined others to support a plan that would have built low- and moderate-income housing; this was offered as an alternative to the city administration's idea of replacing the existing housing stock with housing for the upper middle class. The leader of the movement, Father Henry Brown, pastor of St. Gregory's Catholic Church, supported urban renewal but agreed with the militants that low-income housing should be included in the mix. Later, disillusioned by what he perceived to be the city's duplicitous shenanigans, he became an opponent of the final plan. For his forthrightness he got into trouble with the archdiocese and was exiled to Paterson, New Jersey. In 1968, while associate director of Mobilization for Youth, a social agency on the Lower East Side, I became an organizer for the Coalition for Human Housing, one of the partners in the opposition movement to the Lower Manhattan Expressway.

22 The collapse of the lower half of the West Side Highway in the early 1970s became the occasion for a proposal to rebuild and extend the highway so that it became a feeder, not only of cars but also of commercial vehicles into Long Island on the north and east and New Jersey on the south and west. The plan was developed after the demise of the Moses dynasty but bore the mark of ambition characteristic of the Master Builder. It fell to Steve Max, a staff member of the New York Public Interest Research Group, to organize the long fight against the project. After years of struggle, the city and state administrations abandoned it and made the sensible decision to build a street-level highway below the 57th Street exit.

23 René Descartes, "Discourse on Method," *Philosophical Works of Descartes,* vol. 1, trans. Elizabeth R. Haldane and G. R. T. Ross (New York: Dover, 1955); Immanuel Kant, *Critique of Pure Reason,* trans. Norman Kemp Smith (New York: St. Martin's Press, 1965).

24 Karl Marx and Friedrich Engels, *German Ideology,* part 1 (Moscow: Foreign Languages Publishing House, 1964).

25 Ibid., 42.

26 Ibid.

27 Roderick Frazier Nash, *The Rights of Nature: A History of Environmental Ethics* (Madison: University of Wisconsin Press, 1989); Peter Singer, *Animal Liberation: A New Ethics for Our Treatment of Animals* (New York, 1975); for a concise summary of the position of deep ecology, see Nash, "The Greening of Philosophy," esp. 146–52. In Nash's account, one of the roots of this tendency is the process philosophy of

Alfred North Whitehead, according to which the individual, nature, and the cosmos are indissoluble. Thus in this interpretation posing the interests of individuals or, indeed, of *Homo sapiens* above those of the rest of nature is both unfeasible and unethical.

28 James O'Connor, "Capitalism, Nature, Socialism: A Theoretical Introduction," *Capitalism, Nature, Socialism,* vol. 1, no 1. (1985).

8. UTOPIA ON HOLD

1 Walter Benjamin, "Theses on the Philosophy of History," in *Illuminations,* ed. Hannah Arendt (New York: Schocken Books, 1969), 254.

2 Hans Zinsser, *Rats, Lice, and History* (Boston: Atlantic Monthly Press, 1935), 3–6.

3 Francis Fukuyama, *The End of History and the Last Man* (New York: Free Press, 1989).

4 Francis Fukuyama, "The End of History," *The National Interest,* no. 16 (Summer 1989).

5 Argentina is perhaps the poster child for the claims of the anticorporate globalization movement. Beleaguered by debt, austerity, and eroding living standards, the country has experienced political and economic turmoil that has all but overcome the liberal capitalist processes that have sustained the New World Order.

6 Daniel Bell, *The End of Ideology* (New York: Collier Books, 1960).

7 Francis Fukuyama, "The West Has Won," *The Guardian,* 11 October 2001.

8 *World Unemployment and Underemployment* (Geneva: International Labour Organization, 1999).

9 Russell Jacoby, *The End of Utopia* (New York: Basic Books, 2000).

10 Todd Gitlin and Sean Wilentz, "To Those Who Supported the Nader Campaign," *Dissent,* Spring 2000. In the same issue Ellen Willis replies.

11 Eduard Bernstein, *Evolutionary Socialism* (Ann Arbor: University of Michigan Press, 1969).

12 Cornelius Castoriadis, *The Imaginary Institution of Society,* trans. Kathryn Blamey (Cambridge: MIT Press, 1987).

13 Stanley Aronowitz and William DiFazio, *The Jobless Future* (Minneapolis: University of Minnesota Press, 1994).

14 Sam Howe Verhoven, "Northwest Goes from High-Tech to High Jobless," *New York Times,* 14 December 2001.

15 Perhaps the rise of communitarianism can be explained as a symptom of the loss of a sense of place in American everyday culture. The communitarian impulse is a form of nostagia for a bygone era when most lives revolved around family and neighborhood. In today's climate, it functions as a legitimating ideology that succeeds to the extent that it expresses a yearning for human ties in the wake of the ravages of late capitalist globalization.

16 John Sweeney, address to AFL-CIO Convention, Las Vegas, Nevada, December 8, 2001.

17 Karl Marx and Friedrich Engels, "The Communist Manifesto," in Karl Marx, *Selected Works,* vol. 1 (New York: International Publishers, n.d.).

18 Arlie Hochschild, *The Second Shift* (New York: Avon Books, 1999).

19 Steven Greenhouse.

20 Benjamin Barber, *Jihad vs. McWorld* (New York: Times Books, 1995); Robert Putnam, *Making Democracy Work: Civic Traditions in Modern Italy* (Princeton: Princeton University Press, 1993).

21 Jean Baudrillard, *In the Shadow of Silent Majorities* (New York: Autonomedia, 1986).

22 Eric Foner, Interview, "All Things Considered," National Public Radio, 15 December 2001.

23 Benjamin, "Theses on the Philosophy of History," 257.

INDEX